THROUGH A GREEN LENS

Books *by* ROBERT MICHAEL PYLE

PROSE

Wintergreen: Rambles in a Ravaged Land
The Thunder Tree: Lessons from an Urban Wildland
Where Bigfoot Walks: Crossing the Dark Divide
Nabokov's Butterflies (Editor, with Brian Boyd & Dmitri Nabokov)
Chasing Monarchs: Migrating with the Butterflies of Passage
Walking the High Ridge: Life as Field Trip
Sky Time in Gray's River: Living for Keeps in a Forgotten Place
Mariposa Road: The First Butterfly Big Year
The Tangled Bank: Essays from Orion
Through a Green Lens: Fifty Years of Writing for Nature

POETRY

Letting the Flies Out (chapbook)
Evolution of the Genus Iris
Chinook and Chanterelle

ON ENTOMOLOGY

Watching Washington Butterflies
The Audubon Society Field Guide to North American Butterflies
The IUCN Invertebrate Red Data Book (with S. M. Wells & N. M. Collins)
Handbook for Butterfly Watchers
Butterflies: A Peterson Field Guide Coloring Book (with Roger Tory Peterson
& Sarah Anne Hughes)
Insects: A Peterson Field Guide Coloring Book (with Kristin Kest)
The Butterflies of Cascadia

Through a Green Lens

Fifty Years of Writing for Nature

R O B E R T   M I C H A E L   P Y L E

Oregon State University Press   Corvallis

Library of Congress Cataloging-in-Publication Data

Names: Pyle, Robert Michael, author.
Title: Through a green lens : fifty years of writing for nature / Robert Michael Pyle.
Description: Corvallis : Oregon State University Press, 2016.
Identifiers: LCCN 2016032782 (print) | LCCN 2016036920 (ebook) | ISBN 9780870718816 (original trade pbk. : alk. paper) | ISBN 9780870718823
Subjects: LCSH: Natural history.
Classification: LCC QH81 .P965 2016 (print) | LCC QH81 (ebook) | DDC 508—dc23
LC record available at https://lccn.loc.gov/2016032782

∞ This paper meets the requirements of ANSI/NISO Z39.48-1992 (Permanence of Paper).

Oregon State University Press
121 The Valley Library
Corvallis OR 97331-4501
541-737-3166 • fax 541-737-3170
www.osupress.oregonstate.edu

To my grandchildren,
David, Francis, Cristina, & Edward
and my grandnephews,
Grant & Jarrod

What wond'rous life is this I lead!

. . .

To a green Thought, in a green Shade.

—Andrew Marvell, *The Garden* (1681)

Contents

Introduction
Dancing with Pan

"Row on, Mole, row! For the music and the call must be for us."
— Kenneth Grahame, "The Piper at the Gates of Dawn,"
The Wind in the Willows

As a kid in the Aurora public schools, it was clear that any small gift I might possess was verbal rather than mathematical. At least, I loved words more than numbers. Armed with that and a precocious vocabulary I got from the readers and teachers in my family, I cruised to easy Bs and occasional As on writing that was facile and flashy if not good. I traded English busywork for math busywork with my numerically adept friend, Jack, to free up our time for butterflies, sports, and girls. I discovered that I could earn college money in essay contests sponsored by service clubs, by writing what they wanted to hear. I liked to read and writing came easy. But I liked nature more; and when a teacher asked what we aspired to be, I thought maybe forest ranger, nature photographer, or biologist—not writer.

I didn't really *care* about writing in school. I enjoyed jotting butterfly field notes and scribbling illegible letters to grandparents or girlfriends. But in English classes we were taught exposition, not essay. Expositions honed my compositional skills, but neither brooked nor evoked any personal passion. My eleventh-grade English teacher, Mrs. Braswell, introduced us to *Aida* and Shakespeare, which were great gifts, best appreciated later, but not to Montreux, Lamb, or White, who might have really caught my imagination. She also (unjustly) accused me of plagiarism, just about ruining any enthusiasm I might have had. I left high school in June 1965, never wanting to write another so-called essay, with no idea what fun it could really be. Not until that summer after graduation, stuck in a knotty pine cabin in a rainy canyon with a sheet of motel stationery and a pen, did I ever write because I felt I *must* write—for myself, not just to please Mrs. Braswell or anyone else. Which is why my motel manifesto opens this book, though it has never been published until now.

All the subsequent writings I have chosen for this collection are that kind of testimony—impassioned, personal essays that I *had to* write; all have come from the heart. So what else have I included, what have I not, and why impose such a collection on the unsuspecting and overbooked world in the first place?

Over the years, I have become increasingly aware that my occasional essays have been homeless. Of course, many of the lighter vehicles deserved this; others were quite happy on their own, buried in the periodical stacks in recondite libraries or recycling stations. But others whined about it, lobbying for some sort of group home for the ages, insisting they still had something to say. I came fairly close to compiling collections now and then, even at the invitation of publishers, but never quite did it. Finally, all those voices got to me, and realizing I was approaching a compelling (and appalling) anniversary—that is, *fifty years* since that first must-write essay—I resolved to comb the hundreds of occasional tracts I have inflicted on the serial press, to see if I could dowse from it a body of essays actually worth pulling together into a book.

It is easier to describe what this smorgasbord does not contain than what it does. You will search in vain for any strictly reportorial science writing or environmental journalism, which do not make the bar of personal essay. While there are some very short pieces, I've excluded others that I judged ephemeral. Book reviews are left out, essentially being about the writing of another. You will find none of my "Tangled Bank" columns from *Orion* magazine, since they are all collected in their own book (*The Tangled Bank: Writings from* Orion, OSU Press, 2012). Nor are there any chapters from my stand-alone books: a selection of these is forthcoming, as is a compilation of several longer, philosophical essays, excluded here. Except for minor corrections of grammar, spelling, scanning errors, and conformity, I have not edited the selections: they appear as they were originally published. Clearly, some decades were busier than others. The jobs and first books of the eighties, for example, left little time for outside essays.

Since childhood mine has been a life deeply connected to the more-than-human natural world. Ever since I learned about Pan, Puck, and Robin Goodfellow in grade school, I've felt I was dancing their dance, to their beguiled and beguiling music. Like Ratty and Mole looking for Baby Otter, I felt the sweet piping call must be for me. And ever since I found that I could write better and more happily than calculate, life's been a matter of the pen and the panpipes for me. I trust that placing these essays in the context of a life gives them the sense and movement that I see in them; like me, my writing has undergone change.

My trajectory as an essayist has been a long one, ranging through academia and activism, science and literature, nonprofits and government agencies. Much of my earliest writing came out of a conservation activist role in university and beyond. I've worked for the National Park Service, the US Forest Service, state parks and wildlife departments, and I've managed lands, projects, premises, and committees for various conservation groups, here and abroad. I've taught for any number of institutes, schools, and universities. Along the way I have committed some actual science, and still do, a little. Any one of these professional fields, in research, teaching, nature interpretation, or wildlife conservation, could have offered a safe career. But long ago I understood that my inner poet outweighs my scientist self. Whatever I did, it was always the actual field—the green one—and the writing that I most enjoyed and came back to. Every job, every professional prospect, threatened to bring me indoors and rein in my language. So in 1982 I opted for none of the above, went freelance, and dedicated my energies to natural history and writing in earnest. Most of the results have come as essays. No one would have been more surprised than Mrs. Braswell, except perhaps myself.

With this history, I have been witness to a broad arc of changes: from the optimism and rage of the days of Carson and Ehrlich, through the wisdom and rage of the era of Wilson and Abbey, to the cynicism and just plain rage in the time of tar sands and fracking—engaged as participant and observer all the way along. The journey has stretched from Roderick Nash and the pure fight for wilderness and national parks to this complicated era of the three Cs at the heart of current conservation and social change: Carbon, Climate, and Catastrophe. From John Lennon to Father John Misty, the panpipes have led me through it all. I've had the privilege and onus to experience a big slice of the second half of the twentieth century and the start of the next, and the essays that follow ought to furnish a singular window on it all.

That window opens onto a wide range of contents. There are butterflies here, of course, and echoing themes from the front to the back: kids and nature, special places, alienation versus intimacy, and the primacy of natural history to all endeavors. But there are also marshes and dumps, cities and ditches, wilderness and vacant lots, brambles and sex, islands and ethics, Bigfoot and toads, owls, otters, and apes, and outright outrage, alongside love songs for everything under the sun. One alternative title I considered was "Our Lovely World, Our Tardy Rage," and that about says it. Another one was "By-Catch"—what a fisher brings in that wasn't the main business of the net-set—true enough here, as the occasional prose is what cropped up between the books.

In what follows you will find polemic and rant, ode and encomium, rhetoric ranging from propaganda to elegy to jubilee (sensu Patti Smith). I hope there is something of popular science, of whimsy and laughter, of dark arts. While there is reporting of issues, it is always in a custom context: informed, opinionated, and refracted through this particular green lens of mine, scratched and rain-stained and ground to my own personal prescription. This is an activist's prose, from one embedded in the actual physical world. It would be overbold to suggest that readers will find a history of modern environmental thought and struggle in these pages. But I can promise a broad spectrum of reports from the field, growing out of deep involvement in many benchmark struggles and ideas of the era.

Naturally, some of the pieces respond to timely topics of the day, such as extinction, 9/11, and contempt for what we should take as sacred. Readers may also find that I have anticipated certain conditions that later became matter-of-course: the loss of small-scale life, for example, and the essential bond of children and nature, both rarely ever mentioned back then, but on many lips today. I have been fortunate to occupy the ground floor in many contemporary interactions between humans and the rest of nature, and to write about it from a front-row seat in essays such as "The Extinction of Experience," "Resurrection Ecology," "Las Monarcas," "The Rise and Fall of Natural History," and "Free Range Kids."

It would be a poor scrivener (or person) who failed to grow through five decades of steady scribbling. I hope I've grown not only in style, sensibility, and economy of expression, but also in subtlety of engagement and depth of love for my subjects. And if I haven't become a better naturalist along the way, then there hasn't been any point. I'd like to think there is a certain consistency of ethic, purpose, and devotion throughout, reflected in every piece, with an upward shift over time in the tools and refinement with which they are told. If there is one common theme throughout the book, let it be exaltation of the ordinary and actual connection with what Nabokov called "the individuating details" of a generous world.

Some might hear a less sanguine voice in recent essays such as "Evening Falls on the Maladaptive Ape" and "A Nat'rl Histerrical Feller in an Unwondering Age." Well, I am older. Darker times and deeper dangers take a starker voice, if one is honest. But I hope mine never grows cynical. Some faint rumor of hope remains for tomorrow, and all the hope in the world for the long run when, as Robinson Jeffers wrote in "November Surf," we'll regain "the dignity of room, the value of rareness."

Last summer, prowling our family's old ranches in Colorado with my sister Susan, I returned to the site where I had scribbled that first must-write essay in 1965. On a butterfly trip during that especially rainy summer, our mother and I had been blocked from returning to Denver by a landslide on US 40. Where we'd gone to ground, and where I wrote those words after a deeply affecting walk among the rain-wet aspens, was a motel in Silver Plume called the Millsite Lodge. Since then, the old highway, much of the canyon wall, and the west end of the village had been obliterated by the building of Interstate 70. Now, in 2015, along the remains of the former two-lane, Susan and I found the old watermill, and a flat below the freeway where the lodge must have stood. Above it, the place of my wet green epiphany was now nothing more than cast concrete. But later, behind an old log cabin in the town, where various historic bits and bobs had been stowed, I spotted an old, yellow-painted tin sign, with the rusty words just visible: Millsite Lodge. I knew then it hadn't all been a chimera, and I felt for a moment that ancient rush of urgency to put down on paper just what I'd felt that day. And so, ever since.

So what's next? Although lately I have been spending more time on poetry and fiction, I will always write essays. Only the essay, as E. B. White liked to say, allows one to don whatever suit of clothes he wishes to wear, every day. And what shall one write about, in what suit? In an onstage interview I once asked John McPhee how he decided what *not* to write about, since he writes about seemingly everything. "I write," he told me, "about whatever most fascinates me at the moment." That seemed right to me then, and it still does. And what I and any writer might hope for most earnestly is to be most fascinated by something new, something that has not grabbed one's attention before. I chuckle deeply at the fact that my sense of verbal facility grew largely out of my youthful antipathy for arithmetic, whereas the final selection in this book has to do mostly with mathematics, as it enters and colors our whole lives.

What else will grab me that I have neglected, rejected, or didn't even know about before? I can't wait to find out. There are things I know I want to write about, nothing more than the eventual establishment of a Dark Divide Wilderness Area in southwest Washington. But I suspect a good many surprises await as well. Some may think that such a book as this is bound to be a swan song, a sort of ceremonial wrapping it up before hanging it up. But I wouldn't be so sure. After all, even though this book spans half a century of my work, I am only 69—still a kid, when you think of writers like Norman MacLean, who didn't publish *A River Runs Through It* until he was 74; E. O. Wilson, who has just brought out his latest book at 86; one of my great mentors, Victor B. Scheffer, author of *Year of the Whale*, who compiled his last collection of short essays at 103; and Marjory Stoneman Douglas, who was still writing and fighting for the Everglades at 108. It could be that I am just getting started.   —*RMP, Gray's River, August 2016*

Reflections from Silver Plume

(unpublished; written on Millsite Lodge stationery, Silver Plume, Colorado; July 23, 1965)

That rainy summer, returning from a butterfly expedition, my mother and I were trapped in the mountains by a slide. Thus came the first piece I ever wrote from a deep desire to commit my honest thoughts and intense impressions to paper. Callow and mannered, overrich in adverbs, and no doubt modeling some of the nature writers I'd read by then, it nonetheless holds up beside my current thinking, and has a line or two I'd still be happy to write. When I read it now, I wonder whether I have been trying to write the same essay again and again, in different ways, for fifty years.

I cursed the mudslide that prevented my expedient return home from the mountains. I loved the mountains—but yet I wanted to attend to the many unfinished things awaiting me in the city. Therefore this impediment that led to an overnight stay in a second-rate motel was unwelcome.

Thus detained, and without enough of the day's work left to keep me occupied in the early evening hours, I spontaneously walked toward the nearest forested mountainside, which was behind the motel, and which, on first inspection, manifested old tin plates, a "tourist-made" fire, and other remains of what must have been some Easterner's encounter with the untamed wild of Colorado. A few feet farther on I found a new barbed-wire fence, at which point I almost turned to leave, but instead climbed through and continued walking leisurely. Very soon the terrain rose sharply and became a wooded mountain. Although I had climbed dozens of wooded mountains during my summer's work, and in spite of the fact that my shoes and pant legs were already soaked (the same downpour that closed the highway and ended my day's work had considerably dampened the undergrowth), I proceeded to climb, because I suddenly felt compelled to do so. A path led for some distance up the slope, terminating at a low, hurriedly built shelter by a rushing stream. This curious abode was the last I was to see of anything of man's for an hour.

The woods were not new to me, and I was no stranger to their verdant mysteries; but in my many sunlit rambles through the forest in search of its gossamer-winged denizens, I missed much that only the rains can instill and that only those who stay out the rains away from the fireplace can discover:

Everywhere, everything was painted with the green-beseeching brush of wet, wet rain. The ground of the forests in Colorado always seems out of keeping with the rest because it is brown—but here, in the misty drizzle of a thousand million instant dust removers and automatic life-givers, the floor was green to match the rest. The hundreds of insignificant shrubs, which we thank along with Smokey because they hold the soil but which we seldom look at, were each a glittering emerald. The low evergreens, which are always green and always needle-like, were somehow greener, and soft as the moisture that rendered them so.

As I lumbered slippingly up the mountain, each firm aspen I gripped gave me the strength it possessed in its supple sapling trunk. Eventually I heard a rushing rivulet and hurried to see it, lest it all run away before I got there; it hadn't. I always welcome a mountain stream, especially a white one, because it tastes so good when my thirst is great; and I wish I were a portion of it, hurrying over the uncomplaining stones and through the greenwood which is always greenest near it. But I had no thirst now, and I felt as though I was part of a very, very wet stream—but still I hurried, because I had to—and I was greeted with a sight I had not seen since I visited a rain forest in Washington a year prior: the brook plummeted over a moss-covered stone wall, and then contained itself in a smooth but boisterous pathway before me. Across the water lay a dead tree—but *not* dead, because it was covered with moss and ferns from which the color green must have been described.

By now my spirits were high, my mind was happy, and I was filled with the beauty of life around me. I groped through a twilight-hazened thicket and then hurried to find my next discovery. Unheeding of the telltale shredded feeling of dead and brittle wood, I placed my trust in an advantageous branch, which repaid me with a resounding *snap* and launched me on a rapid flight down a steep and long, moss-covered slide. When I landed, wedged between a rock and a branch, somewhat bruised but thoroughly exhilarated, I laughed in pure enjoyment.

Rather than righting my position, I remained on my back in the wet and clean mossy moisture, and watched, and listened. At that precise moment, a truth was revealed to me—a truth so simple that I felt I had always known it but needed only to have it revealed to me dramatically: *When one has love in his heart and the greenness of nature about him, no one or nothing can take away from him or despoil for him the very real beauty and wonder of life.*

As the sky darkened so that I could hardly see the clouds so near my head, I rambled back in the direction of my obligations. I bent my head toward the source of my wonderment and licked the glistening droplets of life from the aspen and spruce tips—sometimes bumping the tree and receiving not one drop on my tongue but a thousand on my head.

Even in the dusk the green remained, and deepened; even the single animal I saw—a moth—was green. I caught him, watched him, and let him go—he was perhaps the most beautiful green.

Very suddenly I came again to the barbed wire. I asked myself, quite naturally, if now I returned to reality. I answered, no—that I had just been a part of *real* reality, and now I was returning to the artificial world. The green, the wet, the freshness and wildness—they were beauty; they were idyllically, profoundly real. The barbed wire and the tin plates were not *my* reality, but the contrivances of man's complexly disordered mind.

I thanked the mudslide that prevented my expedient return from the mountains.

Conservation and Natural History
(*Northwest Conifer,* 1968)

When I got to the University of Washington, I leapt immediately into con-servation politics and, both in and out of class, read the great conservation and natural history writers. The purge of the naturalists was under way in the academy, and I could see that this trend would undermine conservation, as well as my own educational goals. Two of my most urgent concerns found expression in this early piece, to be developed later in "The Rise and Fall of Natural History" and "The Extinction of Experience." Polly Dyer, the great wilderness advocate, published the local Sierra Club journal, Northwest Conifer. *If I took part in stapling parties to get the magazine out, Polly would publish anything I wrote, including this and others of my earliest discur-sive essays. I sent this one to my inspiration, the great essayist Joseph Wood Krutch, and he returned an encouraging postcard.*

The entirety of conservation is uniquely and deeply intertwined with natural his-tory. So closely juxtaposed are the two that they are actually interdependent on one another. To say this implies that conservationists are, or should be, natural-ists, and the reverse, so that my premise may be familiar to many readers: natural history is waning in the face of modern, mechanistic biology, and if the trend continues, conservation will have suffered greatly.

Natural history and biology are no longer one and the same discipline. At the advent of organized thinking about life they were, and they continued as such until the present century. Linnaeus, Darwin, then Muir, each representing one of the three major centuries in the history of modern biology, were themselves biologists supreme and at the head of the mainstream of biological science for their respective eras. But they were described just as aptly by the term *naturalist.* Their biology was concerned with the discovery, description, and interpretation of the life forms about them.

The divergence began sometime after Muir, when biologists became inter-ested in the physical and chemical foundations of life and found they had the tools with which to ply nature for her deep secrets. Today, the divorce is no longer pending. A person can be both a naturalist and a biologist, just as he could be both a historian and an anthropologist. But some can be found who represent natural history or biology exclusively, and their studies have no more in common than the fact that they both utilize animals and plants as subjects for their inquiry. Examples are easily found, and credible. Donald Culross Peattie wrote, "Modern botany has almost ceased to concern itself with living plants. In many places . . . the 'amiable science,' as Goethe called it, is become an affair of titration tubes, spectroscopes, microtomes, chromosomes, and the mathematics of genetics. The botanical faculty are practically vassals of the physics and chemistry departments. Through their mills vegetable tissue passes as the raw materials of the laboratory. It is in many cases of so little apparent moment to know the names or the life habits of the living plant which furnishes forth the experimental material, that it is possible now to be a bespectacled young doctor of botany without having a speaking acquaintance with half a dozen plants where they grow."

The totality of the separation was brought home to me forcefully in a recent conversation with a zoology major at the University of Washington. I told him that I was seeking an education in natural history. "Why then," asked this modern young biologist, "aren't you in the history department, instead of biology?" A zoology major here also at first, I found myself a nineteenth-century naturalist in a twentieth-century university. Due to a great preponderance of required chemistry, physics, and molecular biology courses, there was no possibility for nature study as such. Now, because there is no established degree program in natural history, I am left to forage among the excellent nature courses that do exist, but are intended as electives for biochemically oriented botany and zoology majors. Because I would prefer observing frogs and turtles in a marsh to pithing them and recording the reflexes of their dead muscles on a smoked drum, I am a living example of the de-emphasis on natural history at the bastion of teaching and research, the university.

The purpose of this essay, however, is certainly not to disparage modern biology. The benefits of cellular biology and biochemistry to medicine are multifold, spectacular, and undeniable. In addition, vast quantities of knowledge concerning the basis for life have been gained and proliferated as a result of modern materials and methodology. Twentieth-century biology has acted to explain or elucidate many of the phenomena only observed or described by the old naturalists. So the emergence of modern biology in its own right was a positive occurence. But along with a deeper understanding and more sophisticated studies has come a mechanistic attitude that seeks to explain all factors of life in physical and chemical terms. Whether or not mechanism or vitalism is the answer to the life question (this writer is a professed vitalist) is not at issue here. What does count, concerning conservation, is the effect that this now-predominent mechanistic thinking has on natural history.

Joseph Wood Krutch wrote a marvelous article for the September-October 1967 *Audubon,* entitled "The Demise of Natural History," in which he expands upon many of the ideas expressed here. Let me use some words of his to illustrate my point: "The development of biology during the half century just past has led it farther and farther away from the methods and concerns of natural history. It has made the biologist less and less a man of the out-of-doors, more and more a man of the laboratories. He has retreated, not only from the woods and fields, but from everything that is, or can be, part of the everyday experience."

Frequently while manning a conservation literature table sponsored by the Conservation Council at the university, I am asked, "What is it you people are trying to save, anyway?" Or, "What GOOD are forests, rivers, and mountains if they aren't being USED?" How familiar these queries, to all of us. And herein lies the basis for my earlier statement, that conservation and natural history are interdependent: nature subjects must be preserved, obviously, if nature study is to proliferate. And for conservation projects to succeed, especially those not directly related to industrial resources, the public at large must be aware of the values inherent in a sacrosanct natural legacy. These values, necessarily, are not provided by a mechanistic, biochemical approach to life science. They must therefore come from a rejuvenated natural history concerned with living things themselves, their intrinsic aesthetic worth to mankind, and their welfare and per-petuation. Modern biologists do not disregard these concepts, and in fact often form a bulwark of support in conservation matters. But it is the naturalist in them that is speaking, most probably, not the professional dissector of the chemical and physical fiber of organisms.

The death knell has not yet rung for natural history, nor is the bellman ready. In fact, there are a good many persons in America who possess all the requisites, as lovers and learners of nature, to be termed naturalists. Some have combined superior intellectual capacity and such empathy for nature as to be not only our most sensitive naturalists, but also our finest biologists—for the two yet have a kinship and can be deployed together wonderfully. I speak of such people as Joseph Wood Krutch, Edwin Way Teale, and Marston Bates; others of this breed were the late Rachel Carson and Olaus Murie. One needs only to explore the well-stocked nature section in bookstores and libraries to envelop himself in the resurgence of pure and introspective natural history writings. Large organizations are dedicated to gaining knowledge of and assuring protection of wildlife and other manifestations of nature. These include Defenders of Wildlife, the Audubon Society, and the National Wildlife Federation, and of course all other conservation groups give natural aspects of the environment prime importance. Their publications are fonts of natural history illustration and writing. Perhaps it is the conservation movement itself that is drawing young writers to nature-ink.

Natural history is not languishing for want of literature or concern, it is true. It can reasonably be asked why, then, am I concerned for its future? I would answer thus: natural history today is riding the crest of the conservation movement. It was launched to that position by three factors: a new feeling for the land engendered in some by the crimes of laissez-faire despoliation; the writings and exemplary actions of John Burroughs, John Muir, and their contemporaries; and the prominent position once held by nature study in the public schools. It is different now. Great, dynamic naturalists we have. Reaction to destruction and endangerment flourishes. What has altered the scene is the passing of nature education, and I submit that it is this vacancy that threatens the fabric of the conservation–natural history symbiosis. In other words, nature study has peaked on the power of a grown generation's education; it can only decline without a fresh start. Given that decline, serious damage to the health of the conservation movement could result.

I cannot deny the great benefit that students headed for professional biological work can derive from preparatory schooling rich in modern biological concepts. But how much more the majority of elementary and high school students would gain from school exposure to real nature, to acquaint them not only with the internal workings of organisms, but also with the role, the beauty, the diversity, and that intrinsic aesthetic worth of living things of which I spoke earlier. We know that man cannot live apart from nature. We cannot, however, expect others to feel this way if their education leads them to believe that nature is to manipulate but not to know.

I wrote the bulk of these thoughts as I was sitting in Denny Park, a tiny but dear spot of green and autumn red in the center of busy, noisy downtown Seattle. The fall colors denoted something more to me than a chemical succession, and I experienced a most wonderful sensation when a wintering hermit thrush suddenly appeared on the patch of lawn among foraging fox sparrows. Just then a group of tiny children entered the park from one side. They paraded through, kept in rigid file on the pavement by teachers in front and behind. A little boy stooped to pick up a splendid maple leaf, and raised it toward his teacher with an excited "Look." Blank-faced, the teacher took the leaf and herded the child along without reply. I thought, can that child's nature wonder survive, or will it vanish like the summer green of the maple leaf? And when he is grown, will he care if a forest is saved?

Our Wilderness Anniversary
(*Living Wilderness*, 1968)

Scanning this young man's lush language, it's easy to believe that he was read-
ing a lot of John Muir at the time, and maybe channeling him a little. He
also had not yet given up referring to animals of no obvious gender by the
male pronoun, which had been the practice for nature writers forever, but
was about to change.

Throughout our engagement, my wife JoAnne and I had hoped to be married
in the woods, or in some high alpine place. We felt that the moment should be
sanctified by the prominent presence of nature. This wasn't to be, for church and
family reasons. So we made do with a lovely clematis-framed church in Denver,
a two-day mountain honeymoon, and a resolution for one year hence: that we
should spend our first anniversary in deep, wonderful wilderness.

As students at the University of Washington without a car, most of our weekend excursions during the intervening year were in the Puget Sound area. When
it came time to plan our anniversary jaunt, then, it occurred to us naturally to
visit the North Cascades, which we'd spoken about so often yet had seen so little
of. It wasn't a certainty, though, until JoAnne told me of reservations she had
made for one night in Stehekin, as a surprise.

Our bus left Seattle after midnight on July 29, and we turned all heads in the
station with our backpacks and our butterfly nets. We didn't sleep until just before
dawn, which came as golden reflections off the cliffs and hills of the Columbia.
At Chelan, we barely made connections with the boat, *Lady of the Lake*—the only
ready means of access to Stehekin, which lies fifty miles north at the head of Lake
Chelan. During the four-hour ride, we witnessed a remarkable transition from
arid hills and irrigated orchards to dry mountains of ponderosa pine to the first
startling eruption of the Cascade peaks from above the lake.

Tiny tarns, glittering high to the side after the halfway point, were slight indi-
cation of what was to come. The only unchanging aspects of the voyage were the
sky and the water, both of which were regally blue throughout.

Our Stehekin stop was short. We found our lodge for the second night, and
rented the last available old Chevy, since we hadn't sufficient time to walk the

Stehekin River Road to the trailhead. We drove the twenty miles slowly, stopping often to marvel at different sorts of natural things. The river was turquoise the likes of which no Navajo has ever worked. Greenness grew in intensity as we climbed the canyon. Butterflies were one objective of the trip, and waterfalls by the road were frequented by many of the gossamer wings. At one such wet spot, chestnut-and-cream mourning cloak butterflies were flying in the hundreds and lighting on crystal-dripping rock walls to imbibe Cascade water. Our attention was diverted by a moss-cup dipper's nest behind the spray. There were minuscule ouzel eyes peering out, and a tiny beak; it was certainly one of the most pleasant homes we've seen, all green and cool. Nearby a tawny Silenus anglewing sunned, but a wasp-gathering deterred me from taking this uncommon butterfly.

We bounced along and stopped again at a roadside meadow, where mariposa coppers were delighting in amethyst asters. Then, at last, we came to Cottonwood Camp—well named for its broad-leafed monoliths, which reminded me of my native Colorado prairie watercourses. But this was no prairie! We were at the base of great mountains, about to begin the foot ascent of the upper Stehekin Valley to Cascade Pass. And eager we were, not only to reach the alpine heights, but also to escape the abundant and aggressive black flies at Cottonwood Camp.

We were tired from lack of sleep but began fresh of spirit. The low valley was a world itself to enjoy, and we had only the afternoon, so we hiked along slowly and looked at things. The trail was clear, but violet-green swallows and western flycatchers led us up the valley anyway. Their colors were intensified by the afternoon rays bouncing off rock walls in three directions: the one became pearls joined with emeralds and amethysts in a setting of life, which transcended broad distances effortlessly, seeming to change dimension by the moment; the other was golden, but was lighter than any metal as it redefined movement magically.

Such became our thoughts as we entered the wilderness. If our surroundings were zoologic, botanic, and geologic, they were to an equal degree poetic and vital. I may be a very poor biologist, for when in the wilderness I seem to lose my scientific objectivity. But in doing so, I feel closer to nature itself, and perhaps the empathy I gain equips me more fully as a naturalist. One particularly delightful little cascade, framed with wildflowers, caused us to stop for refreshment and moved JoAnne to draw and me to write. The lupines, Sitka columbines, and penstemons were too much for us, so we both concentrated on the water. I seldom attempt poetry, but with the water flowed short verses:

Foaming over granite, you are soft,
It is hard

But you triumph. And the granite
Triumphs to have borne you.
Carve rock but harbor moss;
Flow through my hair
As if it were moss, indent my brain—
As if it were the stone.
Liquid of the ices immemorial,
And of fishes and ouzels,
You are no chemical
You are Water!

Evening wasn't far away when we came to Basin Creek. Here was a good campsite, but we wanted to get a bit higher before dusk. So we crossed the swaying suspension bridge and continued, while yellow pine chipmunks scampered and chittered and let us know that it was a good enough place for them. Shortly before we gave out, I beckoned JoAnne to examine a lovely clump of ferns, under which I had hidden a fern guide she wanted. Her laughter seemed a bit exaggerated for simple surprise; I understood her exuberance when she took another copy of the same book from her pack, which she had brought for me!

We were still far below the pass when the sun went down behind it, and we thought we should seize upon the first flat place we found for the night. The first flat place turned out to be the most wonderful camp we've ever had. It wasn't in a likely place. We were high above the valley floor, and the trail was merely a flattened granite slope between two talus slides. Doubtful Creek, coming down from the right, became a steep, broad cascade above the trail. As it intersected the trail, the creek spread over the rock, washing it in a shallow stream before splitting into two waterfalls that plunged into the valley. Below the trail, and between the waterfalls, was a granite shelf; here we made our camp. No sooner had we arrived than a dipper flew by, landed, dipped, and disappeared: a wonderful welcome, as we'd searched for them diligently without success. Battered firs had stocked the site well with dry wood, and water of the purest, coldest kind was on three sides. The rock was flat, but very hard, and we were glad we had brought our air mattresses. But the greatest glory of our anniversary camp was its view. With the last sun, we could see all the way down the valley and pretend we were riding the glacier that had so obviously been there at one time. And across the valley and at its head were hundreds of waterfalls, cataracting collectively many thousands of feet on their spectacular route to Lake Chelan. We had crystalline music to sleep by.

Sunday the thirtieth was our anniversary. There was no church to go to, but nature was our Mass, and we had a wonderful celebrant: a hermit thrush sang to us his "religious beatitude," as John Burroughs once described it. After pancakes, we took to the switchbacks, which began immediately uptrail. Cascade Pass actually lies above a hanging valley to the east, and so one must negotiate two valleys to reach it, crossing what is known as False Pass in between. These switchbacks were gentler than some we've tried, and several other things made their passage most pleasant. We were entering the Hudsonian life zone, and the fir-studded slopes were largely open and flower-covered. Of course, there were butterflies. Two species dominated the flowers and the sky—the large snow-and-scarlet parnassians, and the smaller orange-and-ebony western meadow fritillaries. Rufous hummingbirds darted all about, stopped momentarily to sip or sit, then darted again. I hung brass earrings from purple flowers for JoAnne to find.

In a short time we were at the False Pass; the Stehekin River valley below was a panorama unmatched in our memories, and worthy of the trip in itself. There was a short hike through a spruce forest, walking often in the last snowdrifts. Then we emerged onto the side of the Cascade Pass approach valley. Most of the way was on talus slides, and, as did the flowers, the noises of the wilderness changed. The river was below us, slow and boggy, not loud. We were above the hummingbirds. What we did hear, almost constantly, were the calls of the two common alpine rock-slide mammals—the hoary marmot and the pika. We were never far from one or the other, as was betrayed by the marmots' very loud, monotone whistle, or by the soft, shrill, ascending *weet* of the pika. Big, banded marmots could often be seen standing upright over a burrow, or lumbering across a snow field, if we followed our ears. But it was another matter to spot the little gray pikas among the big gray rocks, even when we heard them plainly nearby.

We weren't far from the pass when we saw the butterfly we were truly in search of—the warm brown, rust-banded Vidler's alpine—a resident only of these high slides and meadows. He eluded my net. Then, though the morning had been sunny, the clouds of the pass reclaimed it. Butterflies don't fly when the sun doesn't shine, so we saw no more alpines. We weren't particularly dismayed, however, probably due to incipient seeds of the thoughts that have since caused us to give up our nets for a camera. Butterflies will remain a major part of our wilderness experience, but they will also remain a part of the wilderness when we leave. [*Note: In fact, some collecting remained essential for study.*]

And so, magnificent Cascade Pass was foggy when we reached the top. We had been told to expect this. We had also been told to expect many people, but they, unlike the clouds, didn't materialize. Except for a few small and well-scattered parties, the pass was ours. After taking in the western vista, toward a valley only two miles of which is not violated by a road, we chose the trail up Sahale Arm for our afternoon's pleasure. Before starting, we gazed long at the peaks and crags and listened to the ice-avalanches, for we would miss these things.

The rest of the day belonged to the alpine meadows, which are perhaps my most beloved kind of wilderness, if one can gauge such things. Partway up the arm, we came upon a veritable lode of gold-glistening glacier lilies, exuding their loveliness from the foot of a snowfield. JoAnne was overcome and sat to sketch the lilies, wrapped around in lupines and buttercups. I was sorry she hadn't come when, a few moments later, I came upon a small flock of vesper sparrows on a boggy heath. I'd never seen them before. I climbed eventually to high mountain ridges clad in red mountain heath and overlooking Doubtful Lake. Of that pristine spectacle, I wrote in my journal: "Doubtful Lake was probably named such because its discoverer doubted that there could be such beauty in the world. A tarn of tarns, it is embraced by Sahale, which nurtures it with thousands of azure waterfalls. The ice and snow are not yet gone from one side, and form a sub-aqual vault of topaz beneath the surface. The place is paradisial, which, if not a word, should be. Heather of several colors pillows the granite and my mind, which has had all of this thrust upon it too quickly for comprehension."

The enveloping mist only enhanced the mood of seclusion and soft grandeur. I roamed heathered hillocks for a while, at one point surprising a pair of Oregon juncos and some water pipits in an isolated stand of firs. Later, I perched in a heather patch and watched a pika very closely. He ate a wilted lily, munching progressively the stalk and leaves and gobbling the flower for dessert. The diminutive rabbit relative was busy gathering green plants, which he would cure as "hay" and store for his cold winter to come.

JoAnne found me then; she had seen most of the things I had while searching for me. Her sketchbook was full of her wilderness impressions, which were good. Together we watched a big Clark's nutcracker flapping slowly through the mist, revealing a glorious display of white-on-black in tail and wing. Its long, sharp bill added measurably to the imposing sight; we were glad to be on the mountain with this outspoken bird.

Now we had only enough time to return. We left the high country reluctantly. We wished that, somehow, it could be our home. The five miles back to the car were taken rapidly (for us), but it was impossible to pass the strangely and beautifully banded gneisses down below without stopping to speculate on their origin. There were deer tracks all the way down the trail.

We wondered if the two very reddish mule deer does that we saw while driving back had been the deer on the trail. If so, we wondered why they had left the high meadows so early. *We* certainly would have stayed had we been able to, and spent another night in our granite "honeymoon suite." But in order to be sure of catching the boat the next morning, we stayed in a rustic cabin in Stehekin instead. There were bats to watch over the lakeshore that evening, and nature films and a talk by the ranger who built the Cascade Pass trail.

In the morning, there was just time for a walk along the lakeshore trail for a little way south. This path, which parallels the lake all the way to Chelan, is in ponderosa pine forest, very different from above. Pale brown wood nymph butterflies wafted into the open areas. A western tanager punctuated the treetops, along with one of the almost unidentifiable *Empidonax* flycatchers. I plunged into the lake, and plunged right out again—it was no warmer than the meltwater feeding it! A chipmunk and a western gray squirrel were the only others on the trail nearby; the latter lives no farther north. Though not wilderness itself, Stehekin is a most pleasant doorway to it. We hoped fervently as we left on the *Lady* that Stehekin would always have many miles of deep water between it and a road.

The long, cool ride back to Chelan provided a quiet period of deceleration from the titillating heights our senses had reached over the weekend. It was sad to leave those emotional peaks, but necessary, because we would soon be in the city. Nevertheless, we knew our experience would leave a good aftertaste and reclaimed minds, and would thus make city life better. While relaxing and dreaming on the boat, we contemplated the future of the Cascade Pass area, which had just uplifted us so. It is included in the North Cascades National Park bill, which conservationists are hopeful will soon clear the Congress. But we hope mightily that the future wilderness review in the North Cascades will include Cascade Pass in a legislative Wilderness Area. [*A North Cascades bill, including Cascade Pass, has been signed into law by the President.*—Editor.] Only seven miles separate the east and west roads, and even in a park, a highway over the pass might be an eventuality. There was a man on the boat complaining loudly to anyone who would listen that he wasn't allowed to use his trail bike to "get up in that country." Thank God that he can't.

From Chelan, we had to hitchhike home, as the bus didn't make connections in time to get us to work the next morning. The great good fortune of our short trip continued, as we were given a ride by a peach farmer on his way to market. "Help yourselves," he said as he opened a crate. We hopped aboard and did just that. The ripe peaches were reminiscent of the sweetness of our wilderness anniversary.

On Immensity and Usufruct

(*Northwest Conifer*, 1968)

The previous piece suggests how I was falling in love with big western spaces even more deeply than I already had as a kid of the Rockies. As soon as we set down in England on our hundred-day exploration of western Europe, thanks to one of the student charter flights prevalent in those days, JoAnne and I were confronted with a very different sense of size and compactness. In Professor Richard Cooley's influential conservation class, we'd been introduced to the concept of usufruct. Coming home, it occurred to me to put the two together—the idea and the experience.

During the summer of 1968 my wife, JoAnne, and I were privileged to travel freely and widely around west-central Europe. Inevitably much of our time and energy went into nature study and conservation comparison. From the experience of one hundred days devoted largely to such pastimes, several ideas emerged in our minds regarding European nature attitudes and situations in relation to our own. Perhaps the most striking of these were the powerful realizations that we retain immensity, in acres and landscapes, that is unavailable in Europe, and that certain European attitudes and patterns of land usufruct might give us insight into how and how not to foster our own precious immensity.

Our first two weeks were spent in Great Britain, traveling by rail. After that we drove, spending half of our time in West Germany and Austria and something under two weeks each in Italy, Switzerland, and France. Though we visited briefly many major cities, including London, Hamburg, Salzburg, Vienna, Venice, Rome, Naples, Munich, Paris, and others, we actually rather slighted the cities and concentrated on the countryside. Driving lanes instead of autobahns, walking trails instead of sidewalks, we saw 104 species of birds, fifteen of mammals, photographed many butterflies, fungi, and other small-scale wildlife, and visited many nature reserves of different kinds. In this way, we felt that we were able to sense something of the essence of the land, of the wildlife, and of the peoples' attitudes toward and problems with both.

Aside from cultural and architectural traits, three things assailed us almost immediately in the countryside of each region we visited. First, the extremely parceled, fragmentary ownership and management of the land seemed evident nearly everywhere. The pleasing rural *landschaft* that dominates so much of western Europe gave evidence of this fragmentation, with miles of intersecting shale fences and hedgerows in England and wood and wire barricades in other nations, and by the numerous farmhouses scattered over small areas. This is not to say that there are no large farms, nor that such patterns are unattractive (the hedgerows, in fact, are one of England's most interesting and valuable habitats.) It is to say, rather, that ancient systems of land tenure and inheritance have persevered to create rather motley management. Building such systems into orderly and effective land-use units presents immense problems. The effect that is pertinent here is that they tend to give the impression of smallness and disunity of the landscape. One can imagine the problematical nature of park establishment or large-scale reservation of land for aesthetic purposes.

Second, we were continually dismayed by the tininess of the forests; for though patches of woods are common, they are seldom at all extensive. One enters a forest and exits within moments. Indeed, sometimes the forest promised on a map by the regional name is never found, because it has long been cut, leaving only the name behind. Thus we drove into the Steigerwald of Bavaria and out again with scarcely a chance to identify the forest type. The famed Black Forest in southwest Germany was much more expansive, but still the strips of uncut timber were narrow in comparison with the broad clearings. Surprisingly, the Vienna Woods constituted one of the largest intact forests we encountered. Marshes, heaths, and plains suffer the same loss-in-reality-but-not-on-the-map fate. We searched the northwest corner of Germany for certain moors that no longer existed. And the Luneburger Heide, a great region to the south of Hamburg, which in feudal times was carpeted for hundreds of square miles with purple heather, retains its natural integrity today only in two small *naturschutzgebiets* (nature-protection areas). This is not a condition peculiar to Europe, if one considers our own prairies and eastern hardwoods, but it does serve to intensify the feeling of compartmentalization and minuteness.

Finally, we never escaped the feeling that no matter where we roamed, we could find no place in any of these countries that was truly wild. In fact, this wasn't just a sensation, but a reality. This is a basic premise that one must work with when comparing American and European preservation: there is virtually *no* wilderness, as we know it, in western Europe today. In a loose sense, there is wild country: land that the natives regard as hostile and that hasn't been used in a generation or two, or land that has for one reason or another been set aside. But not even Brock Evans could dig up many areas that would qualify for the "Wilderness System" here.

These three factors bear upon one's consciousness as he enjoys the great beauty of the pastoral European countryside. Juxtaposed with the actual scale of the land, the minuscule mileages, the perpetual villages at five-kilometer intervals, the tiny countries, these components of the European land situation finally blended and made us understand what it was that Europe lacked and we were used to from our native Rockies and adopted Northwest—immensity!

Now that we had that settled, we might have settled comfortably into the envelopment of the unique European pleasure, which seems almost to make immensity superfluous. However, hung up as we are on uses and abuses of land and wildlife, we persisted in our informal investigation along other lines.

We had come to Europe essentially believing that the people of that continent possessed something of a land ethic akin to that of Aldo Leopold (*Sand County Almanac, Round River Essays*); that their attitudes and actions would reflect centuries of growing up with often destroyed and renovated land; and that the state of nature and the land would in turn reflect such attitudes. What we wanted to find out was, do these people with the alpenstocks understand nature better than our shopping-cart culture does? And do they actually have a better concept of land usufruct, or the right of use with concern?

If land and game management on a grand scale can be equated with usufruct, then perhaps Europeans have such a concept. But the man who said that every animal bigger than a polecat and every tree worth cutting in Europe is in a logbook somewhere wasn't far from right. Stand after stand of single-species, uniform-aged trees, and row after row of boar tusks and deer antlers from hand-picked animals on hunters' walls disenchanted us with the European super-management. We often remarked that European logging was almost inoffensive, there being next to no clear-cutting. This may have been due to widespread concern over attractive timber harvest; more likely, it is because lumber trees are largely imported. So while European land use is quite efficient, we found that it could not be equated with a deep-seated conscientious concern for nature and the integrity of the land.

Our hikes and rambles at first confirmed some of our preconceptions of public outdoor attitudes. Everywhere were people walking and riding. On country roads we passed many, many old people on bicycles. On passes and high trails, city people and very old people kept the same pace as the young and native Tirolers and Bavarians. Everyone *did* carry an alpenstock, and most were used on frequent walks. Buoyed by this initial evidence of an outdoor breed, we looked deeper and found that we had been misled in our generalities. Many of the hikers, for example, got up the mountain (as we did when time restrictions dictated) by means of the trams, trains, and lifts that "grace" so very many peaks across Europe. When they got there, regrettably, the people picked as many wildflowers, left almost as much trash, demanded as much or more incongruous develop-ment, and made as much noise as Americans do.

We should not have been surprised to discover that these traits are interna-tional. But having been told again and again that "the Europeans *respect* their nature," we felt impelled to find wherein this respect lay. As we saw, it does indeed exist; but it was not a special, universally imbued quality that permeated all of European society. For instance, no extraordinary respect for the century-tortured land is shown by hikers, as I mentioned; they walk more, but care no more than we as a group. I will say that the nature-consumers in Europe *enjoy* their natural heritage immensely, perhaps more so as a people than do we. But this enjoyment does not seem to be matched by a commensurate ethic. If it were, perhaps we would have been spared the sight of dams on every single river and stream we explored.

Or perhaps our greatest disappointment in all of Europe might have been diminished: overgrazing. I doubt that John Muir, when he spoke of "hooved locusts," the sheep of the Sierra, saw meadows more ravaged than is the majority of the over-timberline expanse in the Alps. While one of my goals was butterfly photography, at the famed Jungfrau I had to walk a cog railroad track to find a single specimen: there were no flowers elsewhere. And almost no grasses or sedges were left on the trampled, shaven turf. Meadows at the Matterhorn were nearly as bad, and the whole of the alpine zone differed little in its condition. Between the cattle, sheep, and people, the wildflowers stand no chance. We never did find a living edelweiss to photograph.

Of course the deeply indented land rights and the near-impossibility of con-trolling them are bases for this problem. There is no appreciable public land, cared for in the public interest. This also underlies the vast dilemma of inappro-priate development in much of the high country, which is typified by the Italian national park Dello Stevio. Within the boundaries of this large "park" we found commercial helicopters, particularly ugly ski developments, large power lines, gaudy souvenir stands, many villages and town sites, heavy grazing, agriculture, logging, a huge dam, and factories. Just across the border lies the Swiss National Park, a tremendous contrast. The Swiss park, only ninety thousand acres large, was established with nature and the renovation of wilderness in mind, and with people-use considered important but peripheral to its goals. Regulations are so stringent, the policies so firm, and both so well accepted by the public, that here lies a truly sacrosanct piece of land.

It was, in fact, the Swiss National Park and its very capable and articulate director, Dr. Robert Schloeth, that gave us our best clue of where the European land ethic lies. We had found that it does not lie in a widespread appreciation for immensity or pure wildness, for few European landscapes are either vast or untouched. And it does not lie in overall usership patterns, because this can be as frightening and biologically sterile as ours. Nor does it exist in a heritage of well-established and large public lands, although the several national parks (the Swiss being privately run), the German and Austrian *naturschutzgebiets*, the British Nature Conservancy sites, and other similar attempts at land protection herald a growing trend in this direction. We think, rather, that the conservation ethic in Europe is emerging in a responsive, concerned movement just as is our own—the difference being that we have much more to work with at the outset.

The point of this essay is not to detail our entire experience with European conservation, for it was an incomplete and incohesive experience at best. It is merely to put forth an idea that occurred to us while making probably unfair comparisons: that we do have wildness, ungrazed alpine heights, and untrammed peaks. Above all, we do have some portion of wild immensity—and we have it to *begin with*. We don't have to experience the centuries of land abuse and depreciation that were required for our European friends to arrive at the same state of nature appreciation that we now have. And that, given the proper formula for usufruct, we will be able to retain immensity—not just in miles, but also in spirit and life—and all the intrinsic values that come with it.

Union Bay

A Life-After-Death Plant-In

(*Ecotactics*, 1970)

As I stumbled over the DMZ between natural history and the hard sciences, I evaded chemistry by birding in the university marsh-cum-dump, almost flunking out in the process. When the remnants of that marsh came under threat, our conservation cadres fought back. While fellow students protesting the Vietnam War took over the president's office and demanded peace and justice, our group took over the Montlake Fill, demanded soil and trees, and (easier to provide than peace and justice) got them. Today the Fill is one of the great urban habitats in the country. I was asked to write this tale of a classic sixties action for the Sierra Club paperback Ecotactics, *and it became my first writing to appear between the covers of a book.*

Union Bay is a tiny appendage of Lake Washington, on Seattle's east side. A half century ago, when canals and locks were constructed to join Union Bay with Lake Union and that lake with saltwater Puget Sound, the water level of the bay fell and vast marshes emerged along its gently sloping shores. In time, these marshes evolved into one of the finest wildlife habitats in western Washington. The diversity and abundance of life forms in the area soon inspired a book, *Union Bay: The Life of a City Marsh*, by Seattle naturalists Harry Higman and Earl Larrison. When the book was published in 1951 more than 125 species of birds could be found there, as well as substantial populations of weasel, mink, beaver, muskrat, and otter.

For a time, Union Bay remained undisturbed. To the east opened the broad, uncluttered expanse of Lake Washington, and beyond the Seattle skyline rose the incomparable Cascades. The northern shores attracted residential neighborhoods of pleasing quality. On the west, the largest and most renowned educational institution in the region, the University of Washington. Beyond the academic buildings, the Montlake Ship Canal merged the waters of the two Unions, its high sides draped with ivy and studded with holly and birches. And above the gothic, copper-cupola towers of the Montlake Bridge, beyond the yachts and houseboats of Lake Union, rose the profile of the magnificent Olympic Mountains on their distant peninsula. Finally, to the south, on a fogless day, Mount Rainier dominated the horizon.

When I came to the university as a student in 1965, I was immediately attracted to the marsh below the campus. Crossing an enormous parking lot that had been implanted beside the bay, I sometimes paused to watch the mallards or the mountains. Occasionally, I also canoed along the watercourses of the university arboretum, passing in and out of stark pillars that supported a freeway approach to the new, concrete Evergreen Point Floating Bridge. I was less surprised by the pillars than by what seemed to be a surfeit of nature remaining in a modern city of more than half a million people.

As my appreciation for the whole of the natural and wild scene deepened, I began to wonder what the bay might have been like before the freeway. And I found part of the answer in the book *Union Bay*. Now, I walked and paddled in the same places as before, but with different eyes. Now the swampy edges of the bay shrank into their proper perspective: mere fragments they were, tattered and incomplete, barely reminiscent of the great refuge of the previous decade. Now the freeway in the arboretum zoomed into sharp focus. This road was not a positive thing that, by the beneficence of its engineers, had preserved something of the green scene; rather it was a callous intrusion, a preposterous travesty that subverted totally the purposes of the arboretum. Looking for once beyond the small, reedy islands and the sparsely grown shoreline, I realized that the monolithic blight of the Montlake Dump had once been marsh. It had taken three years and a telling book, but now I recognized Union Bay for what it was: not a fortuitous condition of values preserved but rather a condition of heinous disturbance, where some small vestige of the natural ecology still struggled to maintain its integrity.

How could the university have allowed this to happen? Perhaps government pressures to route the freeway through the arboretum had been too great to combat in those days of an unaroused public. Still, the sanitary fill that had supplanted so viciously the superb north marsh had been sanctioned, even encouraged, by the university. While many colleges spend large sums to acquire accessible study areas where biological instruction and investigation can be carried out in the field, the University of Washington already had an ecological wonderland literally on its back doorstep—but had rejected it.

It was no coincidence that the deplorable condition of Union Bay soon inspired new interest in conservation at the university. Under the leadership of

Terry Cornelius, the membership of the old Conservation Education and Action Council increased 200 percent and the name of the organization was changed to the Committee for the Environmental Crisis (CEC). The campus, at last, was discovered to be a very real part of the environment, and one that had had its full measure of the crisis.

The climate was right for a confrontation. On campus, construction was being rushed to keep pace with mushrooming enrollment (which hit thirty-three thousand in September 1969). There was immense dissatisfaction with a gargantuan excavation that had destroyed the largest open green area on campus. It came to be nicknamed hatefully "The Pit." In general, people in the university community, and lots of them, were becoming disgusted with the decline of environmental quality and seemed ready to do something personal for their part of nature.

How this latent energy could be harnessed to benefit Union Bay was a question of much concern to us. It answered itself spontaneously one night at a meeting of a new off-campus group called Ecology Action of Puget Sound. We forged a coalition to work together on a common project: an environmental learn-in and fair to be held at the university. While Ecology Action, under the direction of founder David Soucher, was to carry out most of the planning and execution of the event, the CEC was to serve as sponsor and to provide an action event on campus for public participation.

It occurred to me during a campus rap session that a logical and highly demonstrative event might be the establishment of a park on the Union Bay dump. Response to this idea was enthusiastic and heartening. Right then I named it the Union Bay Life-After-Death Resurrection Park, or, for short, the Life Park.

With Jim Lachiotus, details chairman, and several other volunteers, I began working toward the day of the fair and the plant-in. First, we consulted university officials weeks prior to the event to head off the possibility of a student-administration confrontation. We did not, however, construe this consultation as "permission" to carry out the plant-in. I informed the university departments affected that though the plant-in constituted severe public censure of previous management of the land, and though we firmly intended to carry out the plan regardless of university policy, we would nevertheless appreciate their cooperation. Then we circulated a general statement:

> The University failed those of us inside of nature badly when it allowed . . . the ruination of Union Bay Marsh. It has the opportunity now to reclaim some portion . . . of good environmental conscience as well as our respect by supporting and sanctioning the Life

Park. If it should be so very insensitive as to resist us in our effort to bring back to the ugly blight of the dump some natural beauty, then . . . the University will be indicted as one of the great, malevolent environmental villains of our time, along with Georgia-Pacific, Kennecott Copper, the pesticide industry, the Vatican and the no-return bottle.

Fortunately, no callousness was encountered. Instead, we were delighted to receive the full cooperation of university officials.

The second matter was to locate a supply of plants. Since it was to be an affair of creation rather than depredation, we could hardly encourage people to dig plants out of their own backyards. Our problem was soon solved by state lands commissioner Bert Cole. With Cole's help we were able to purchase conifer seedlings from the state nursery, which normally sells only to commercial growers.

Dave had color silk-screen posters made to publicize the fair and an additional set especially for the plant-in. Numerous press releases were cranked out and announcements were broadcast by the local radio. By the day of the learn-in plant-in, nearly everyone had been alerted.

The Total Environmental Learn-In Fair (sardonically subtitled "No Deposit-No Return") was a monumental success. It featured a variety of exhibits. A duck decoy bobbed in a tub of crude oil; participants were invited to touch the oil, try to remove it from their hands, then imagine the plight of seabirds with oiled feathers. Displays provided by the Sierra Club, the Seattle Audubon Society, and other organizations vied for attention with graphic slide-shows of defoliation in Vietnam and other environmental crises. The speakers were dynamic and depressingly convincing. They included Brock Evans, Northwest regional Sierra Club representative; Professor Gordan Orians, prominent University of Washington ecologist; and Cliff Humphrey, founder of Ecology Action in Berkeley, among others.

Outside the Husky Union Building (HUB), I mounted the speaker's platform. I did so not without some trepidation, for not once in five years had the subject of a speech from that platform concerned nature's ills. Yet I was buoyed by the fact that the University of Washington *Daily*, which had long shunned conservation as a proper issue for campus concern, had just devoted several columns and an editorial to the fair and the park. So I rapped about the university environment, and in concluding, I invited the people to march with me to the dump, to help establish our incipient Life Park. Nearly everyone accepted the invitation. The trees, one hundred each of Douglas-fir, grand fir, and ponderosa pine, were handed out. Then we began our half-mile march.

As we crossed intramural playfields, sterile parking lots, and the fetid canal that borders the dump, we were met by more marchers. Our ranks included students, faculty, housewives, and businessmen, even a high school biology class. Some marchers brought their own plants, including willows, Oregon grape, white pines, and one incongruous but welcome bamboo plant. Professor Frank Richardson, resident naturalist, arrived with dozens of shrubs.

We—nearly four hundred of us—arrived at the dump at three o'clock in the afternoon. Our negotiations with university personnel had been profitable, for we were greeted with a truckload of topsoil and a couple of dozen shovels. Heads and straights, political activists and ROTC cadets dug in to plant their own trees, to get their hands in the soil (that topsoil *was* needed, for digging into the cruddy dump dirt a few inches unearthed everything from beer bottles to funny papers to a pair of red panties). It was heartening to see differences forgotten as one person dug and another lightly tamped fresh soil around fragile roots.

The "resurrection" of Union Bay was over in a couple of hours. Though it seemed to me then that the stench of the dump was less malodorous than before, I realized that our efforts could not end here. Already there were plans for a new university parking lot, an asphalt coffin for a large parklike area next to the ship canal and behind the stadium. We would have to inform the university that the *Sequoias* and cedars and grass that grace that green expanse could not be sacrificed. And after Life Park, I began to think that the university might listen.

Willapa Bay

(*Audubon*, 1970)

The previous essay in Ecotactics *led to this assignment from* Audubon— *my first writing about Willapa, the region that would become my home for most of my life and the subject of* Wintergreen, *and also my first publication in a national magazine of* Audubon's *stature. Willapa Bay, though subject to a great many stresses since, is essentially protected today in the Willapa National Wildlife Refuge.*

There are still a few precious places where the salt sea is met by and mingles with the sweet freshwater of the land. These are the estuaries, the richest communities in the biotic matrix. Fewer yet, and even more precious, are fully living estuaries, those not yet buried by economic defecation. And according to the National Estuary Study, prepared by the Department of the Interior, "Willapa Bay is probably the least affected by man's adverse industrial and agricultural activities of all the major bays on the West Coast of the United States."

Such a declaration of environmental health would seem to constitute a mandate for vigilant protection of a remarkable estuarine resource that has been accidentally left alone. Yet a barrage of destructive projects—that depressingly familiar pattern—are planned.

Willapa Bay is a unique pocket of the Washington coastline, entirely different in character from both the stack-studded wilderness beach of the north and the resort and salmon-charter sprawl of the middle.

Just north of the Columbia River's mouth, the doglegged bay runs east into the Willapa River for twenty miles, and a like distance south along the inner shore of the Long Beach Peninsula. It encompasses 70,400 acres of open water at mean high tide, with depths exceeding seventy feet; at low water, more than half of that area becomes a swirl of mud, sand, and gravel flats. Because of the excellent circulation in the shallow waters, immense natural populations of wildlife thrive in Willapa Bay.

Within the waters and substratum of the bay are nurtured extensive fisheries for native and Pacific oysters, hard-shell and soft-shell clams, and Dungeness crabs. Five species of salmonoid fish migrate, spawn, feed, and acclimate in Willapa Bay and its eight tributary streams. Rock and bottom fishes, including sole, flounder, and perch; forage fishes such as herring, anchovies, and smelt; and both green and white sturgeon utilize Willapa Bay for part or all of their lives.

Here, in the strange crinkly community of the *Salicornia* salt marsh and the intertidal eelgrass, vast flocks of migrating birds are nurtured (about 210 species). Rare is the birding party that does not encounter huge assemblages of ducks, grebes, loons, shorebirds, raptors, and land birds. Native mammals, terrestrial, freshwater, and saltwater species, are similarly abundant.

Now, the imminent threats to Willapa Bay's integrity are multifold and terrifying: destruction of tidelands and marshlands by filling and diking at public expense; drainage of freshwater marshes for construction of lagoon housing; dredging for navigation, and dumping of the spoilage; construction of bulkhead, pier, and shoreline facilities, including a jetty across the mouth of the bay; industrial, community, and agricultural pollution; offshore oil drilling; sedimentation from upstream activities; and radioactive and thermal pollution from a proposed nuclear power plant at the mouth of the North River.

If this catalog of horrors seems oppressive, contemplate this: there are three county, twelve state, and eleven federal agencies involved in the administration of Willapa Bay, many of which are oriented solely toward manipulation and alteration of the resource for commercial and political purposes. In addition to the diffuse bureaucratic controls over Willapa Bay, private interests from crabs to cranberries complicate the picture.

Since the Willapa environs contain several navigable routes, the Army Corps of Engineers has been preeminent in the planning. Not surprisingly, that agency figures very high on the list of potential destroyers, along with the Washington Department of Natural Resources (oil leases) and the Pacific County Public Utility District (nuclear power plant).

In contrast, the efforts of the Department of the Interior have been in the direction of saving the bay. Following administration scuttling of the National Estuarine System, which would have included Willapa Bay, a codified planning approach has been adopted in order to foil the numerous plots to disembowel the bay.

Robert E. Ratcliffe, regional solicitor of the Department of the Interior, has written that uses of the bay should be considered unreasonable "because they pollute, or because they offend our sense of aesthetics or natural beauty, or because they interfere with the right of the public to enjoy a natural resource of national significance, or because they threaten in a harmful way to upset the ecological balance of nature, or simply—if you please—because to permit the occupance would confer a valuable privilege without either necessity therefore or a fair return to the public in whose name the privilege would be bestowed."

The Department of the Interior has been directed by the Estuary Protection Act of 1968 to execute this enlightened policy. If it succeeds, Willapa Bay could retain its character. Otherwise, chaos is inevitable.

Today, the marsh-slogger, beach-walker, or canal-canoer is bedazzled by the prospect of variegated life offered at Willapa. Public concern can cause Willapa Bay to remain the abode of hundreds of herons, of a countless bounty of intertidal creatures, of wild strawberries on the dunes, and turnstones in the sloughs. Let it be.

A Colorado Yankee in Cromwell Country

(*Cambs, Hunts, & Peterborough Life*, 1972)

As the grass is always greener, the mysterious is always more so on the other side of the fence—or sea. Cowboys and Indians, the Rocky Mountains, and the Colorado desert may conjure exciting images in the minds of East Anglians, for whom hedgerows, the fens, the Wash, and Cambridge are familiar fixtures. It was just the reverse for me, a native of lofty Denver, Colorado. So when I learned I would be living in Huntingdonshire for a year, my anticipation was high. I was not to be let down.

Everyone said it was the best autumn in years when I came to Monks Wood, which was just beginning to reflect the sun's generous gold in its aspens, birches, hawthorns, and maples. I had come to The Nature Conservancy's Monks Wood Experimental Station as a US Fulbright-Hays scholar to study the conservation of rare and endangered butterflies, a science especially far advanced in Britain.

My supervisor, Mr. John Heath of the Biological Records Centre, broke me in quickly to the historic fenland scene by taking me to a steam traction rally at Roxton. After the chrome behemoths that clog our American freeways, I couldn't decide which were more novel to me: the beautifully crafted, brass-fitted steam tractors or the sensible small cars in the parking area.

Joan Heath had long been looking for lodging for me, but found most places already occupied by my countrymen from Alconbury Air Force Base. When she finally did score on a house, I was incredulous at my good fortune. My wife, JoAnne, arrived from her summer job as a national park ranger in Alaska shortly thereafter, and it was thrilling to be able to take her home to a 1648 black-and-white cottage, partly thatched and full of ancient oaken beams inside.

We'd thought such places existed only in storybooks; certainly not within our reach. Imagine our pleasure in writing home that we actually lived in a place that quaint, and older than the American republic by more than a century! We didn't forget to mention that there was a real English pub two doors down, with the charming name of the Three Jolly Butchers.

So in the idyllic setting of our listed yeoman farmer's house, with the ancient church behind and fairy-tale thatch all around, we passed our English autumn in Wyton. We discovered the wealth of footpaths and enchanted places in our neighborhood, which JoAnne was to haunt frequently with camera and sketch pad while I was at the laboratory: Houghton Mill and locks, the Great Ouse maze and meadows, the pretty Hemingfords, the Thicket path to St. Ives.

About the time the beeches bronzed along the Thicket, rose hips reddened along the disused railway line to Godmanchester. The redwings were not alone in harvesting the rose hips, and we found they made a good winter jam.

Soon the blackbirds, redwings, and song thrushes in the field over our road were joined by great winter waves of mistle thrushes and fieldfares. I watched them worming just below the fog level as I caught the early morning coach to Monks Wood.

Once there, I was introduced to various aspects of nature conservation in Britain by the scientists who carry out the actual research behind the policy. "My" section, the Biological Records Centre, is responsible for mapping the fauna and flora of the country. Special sections level inquiries into the nature of chemical poisons in the environment, the ecology of native woodlands and grasslands, and other fields. All this made a fascinating backdrop to my butterfly studies.

Fens and hedgerows became more than romantic images when their actual character was shown me through research and management centered on Monks Wood. By the same token, rushes meant more when I learned to work with them in an evening class, and the exotic-looking fen reeds took on a deeper perspective when we saw them exquisitely shaped by local thatcher Steve Morley.

Back in Wyton, Stuart House was growing chilly. By Yule it was downright cold; but at its coldest and dampest, we wouldn't have swapped our village idyll for the central-heated suburbs we'd always known. Before a coal fire, we weathered the winter and the power cuts with English amenity: tea, digestive biscuits, *Mort d'Arthur* on the wireless and blue tits out in the frost-dusted garden.

On weekends, we got about in Cromwell country. Ely Cathedral in a rare fen blizzard was frigid, but impressive. The trip back across the fens, through March, provided the picture of a roan pony blowing steam clouds from a snowy muzzle in a bleak and frozen fen. A warmer but wetter day's trip was made to two places our curiosity would not let us miss: Boston and Denver.

The former, though much smaller than its American counterpart, was uniquely flavourful with its famed Stump poking into the winter mist and its docks green and quiet. But when we saw Denver, where the Ouse Washes sluice into the Ouse proper, we wondered if our big hometown at the base of the Rockies could possibly have been named for this tiny, fenny flatland hamlet. Other excursions took us to the saltings of the Wash and Tattershall Castle on the outskirts of the region, and to the medieval maze at Hilton and Hinchingbrook Castle closer to home.

On Boxing Day we walked the Thicket to St. Ives, the river to The Olde Ferry Boat, and beyond to Brownshill Staunch, and back through the meadows to Fenstanton and the Hemingfords—and counted thirty sorts of birds in an effort to emulate an old American tradition, the Christmas Bird Count.

We traveled by foot, by bicycle, and with the ancient Morris Traveller we picked up. After the petrol prices at home, the bicycles seemed most attractive here, and after the elevation and relief of Colorado, fenland bicycling was even more inviting. Tucked-away villages like Oldhurst and Woodhurst were favorite destinations nearby, but we went as far afield as Cambridge under our own power.

Cambridge, of course, astounded us more and more with each visit. Even after we came to know it a bit, we never came to take the city for granted. But although Kings was lovely when the October horse chestnut echoed the mellow hue of its stone, and the winter starkness of the Gothic turrets had its beauty, still our favorite time in Cambridge was the fabled spring. One very sharp picture we will retain is that of the pale green drape of early willows over the Cam; another is carpets of crocuses over the Backs.

Came the tide of spring wildflowers. Primroses blanketed Brampton Wood, while Monks Wood was studded with cowslips and Knapwell Wood with oxslips. The latter, we thought during one especially fine vernal walk, smelt of apricots. By now the waters had receded from the vast water meadows of our vicinity. The hay was already rising and the skylarks rose as well in their seemingly perpetual aerial song. The stridulation of the skylark would have to be reckoned as the emblematic sound of our year here, contested only by the roar of the omnipresent F-4 Phantoms.

We had vowed to boat frequently on the Great Ouse, which sinuated virtually through our back garden. We never made it until JoAnne's last day. Then the meadows opposite Hartford Church were gilded with buttercups. It was the only bright day of a foggy fortnight, and it seemed to concentrate all the fullness and promise of May into that one riverine experience.

Then, too soon, JoAnne returned to Alaska. And as the greenest season swept over the land, my fieldwork took me away as well. But not before my Gomcestrian friend Peter Harris and I found the tracks and spoor of an otter—and glimpsed their maker briefly—in the river by Godmanchester Common.

A summer's field research and symposia drew me to Saarbrucken and Somerset, to Surrey and San Antonio, to Cornwall and the Lakes, to Scotland and

Wales. I felt I had a visitor's experience atypical in its richness and diversity. Yet each time I dropped back into Wyton to rest or repack, I felt that I regretted the summertime away from the village as much as I enjoyed it. The season progressed from green grain and cardamine to yellow grain and poppies.

When I finally came back to Huntingdonshire to relax and write up, it looked as it did when I first came: the flower boxes outside the pub were bountiful, the Michaelmas daisies were visited by tortoiseshell butterflies preparing for hibernation, the thatched cornstacks near Wyton airfield had been erected. After traveling, it was good to live out the late summer in the warmth of this one place. And now that the sumac by the ivied wall behind Stuart House has gone vermilion, it's about time to move on.

After a year in Cromwell country, Colorado will be the same—but my perception of it will have changed. It will seem strange indeed to see the big, red-breasted birds we call robins, and to see tits, which we call chickadees, in black-and-white instead of in colorful blue and yellow. Distances will seem very great, as I've come to think of Cambridge as a fairly long journey and London as a downright trek. I was impressed by high schools in castles and abbeys, but intimidated by an inflation rate that has elevated most prices to or above the level of those in the states.

I will miss the myriad public footpaths through the rural countryside, the lanes and hedges, the meadows and swanny river walks; but I will welcome the public mountain vastness with its wilderness trails. I will deeply miss the pubs, such as the Three Jolly Butchers, the Royal Oak, the Axe and Compass, the Three Horseshoes, the Black Bull, and the Catworth Fox; but I will be glad to have a real hamburger again. I will long for the rich matrix of culture, history, and age I have become accustomed to here (the native Colorado culture was just as old and rich, but ephemeral, and we colonials erased what was left).

Most of all I will miss the warm people who stripped away their "English reserve" to deepen and broaden my experience immeasurably. Publicans and landladies, neighbors and colleagues, a thatcher and a rush worker, butterfly people and penguin people, scientists and shopkeepers, fenmen and research students, and many others provided the human part, while the fens and the clays provided the setting.

I am told that this is a subtle, unspectacular corner of England. In contrast, Colorado is spectacular on any scale. But to this Colorado Yankee, Cromwell country and cowboy country compare very favourably. And isn't that a cowboy hat on old Oliver's statue in the St. Ives Market Place?

Silk Moth of the Railroad Yards

(Natural History, 1975)

During my doctoral studies at Yale, I had hoped to study with William Zinsser, author of the classic guide to writing nonfiction, On Writing Well, *but his famous class was reserved for undergraduates. I didn't have much time for extracurricular writing, but I wanted to keep my hand in. My major professor, Charles Remington, suggested I look into the remarkable situation of the ultra-urban cynthia moth and write a popular piece about it. Having bought a new suit for my first visit with New York editors, I pitched it to* Natural History *in person and was thrilled when they accepted it. As part of the research I reared the moths in my lab. The article was graced by gorgeous photographs of the living creatures in all their life stages taken by Andrew Skolnick, but I hope my word-pictures alone will paint a picture of this beautiful animal in readers' minds.*

There is nothing readily apparent about the cynthia moth that should single it out for ecological favors. Yet this lovely insect, one of the giant silk moths, may be the only member of the family Saturniidae to survive this century in much of the eastern United States. Among the sixty members of the family that inhabit North America, *Samia cynthia* is the only one that is not indigenous. Of the native species, many are endemic to the eastern hardwood belt, while others inhabit narrow West Coast ranges. The family has a worldwide distribution—an Asian representative *(Attacus atlas)* is the largest moth or butterfly in the world, with a wingspan of almost a foot.

For the last ten years, entomologists and conservationists have been concerned about the vast general decline in numbers of giant silk moths. Formerly abundant species such as luna, cecropia, promethea, and polyphemus moths are now scarce. The demise of this moth family is not unique; many populations of Lepidoptera (butterflies and moths) have diminished in the last few decades, and an entire latter-day offshoot of the wildlife conservation movement has focused around these insects. But the plight of the giant silk moths, with the exception of the cynthia moth, seems to be more severe and more pervasive than that of most other moths and butterflies.

In the past, researchers have put forward several theories to account for the severe diminution of saturniid moths. Some blame habitat destruction, by far the biggest culprit in most cases of insect decline; but silk moth populations are low even where the land remains undisturbed. Others suggest that pesticides are the principal cause of devastation; yet while local extermination occurs in areas of heavy spraying, the general levels of chemicals in the environment have not been positively correlated with silk moth disappearance. Besides, many other moths and butterflies have maintained fairly high populations in districts now devoid of saturniids. The ornithologist Roger Tory Peterson suggests that smog might affect the reproductive ability of the moths by masking the sex pheromones by which they locate mates. The success of captive cynthia females in attracting males even in New York City, however, contradicts this idea.

Most lepidopterists now subscribe to an altogether different theory, advanced by Douglas Ferguson, which blames the wide use of mercury vapor streetlights. The large moths, powerfully dazzled by the ultraviolet emitted by these lamps, may be killed by predators or by cars traveling under the lights. But more likely, the moths are drawn by the lights far from their usual habitat and are unable to find larval food in an unknown area. Finally, since males seem to be more strongly attracted to the lights than are females, the normal courtship behavior may be interrupted, resulting in nonfertilization of eggs.

Whatever the actual cause of silk moth disappearance may be, the cynthia moth does not seem to be seriously affected. The moth flies on broad vanes of warm olive tan blending into buckskin margins. Each of the four long wings bears a creamy central lunule edged with golden scales. The points of these crescents just reach the pale mauve band that traverses the wings. One of the most subtly pleasing features of the moth's beauty is the wrinkled lilac patch, punctuated by a blue eyespot, in the apex of each forewing. These hues and patterns, made up of thousands of tiny scales, color a set of wings that may spread six inches on a large female.

The cynthia moth was introduced to France from China and India in the last century, and from there to Philadelphia in 1861. Numerous other introductions were made in eastern seaboard cities, the motive being to boost the failing American silk industry. For a number of years the industry in this country had been based on the cocoons of *Bombyx mori,* the silk moth traditionally used for silk manufacture. The particular mulberry trees upon which *B. mori* fed, which had been introduced with the moth, however, could not withstand the repeatedly harsh New England winters. The silk industry in America seemed doomed until the cynthia moth arrived, along with its principal food source, now variously known as tree of heaven, paradise tree, and stinkweed (*Ailanthus altissima*). The big new moths were easily raised and made large cocoons. Their food plant proliferated.

As much silk as the cynthia moth cocoons contained, however, it could not be successfully harvested. The silk of the *B. mori* cocoon can be easily unwound into several miles of unbroken thread, but the fiber of the cynthia moth's cocoon is thinner, weaker, and cemented together at many points. The glue can be dissolved, but not without a strong probability of breakage. The complex machinery invented in Europe to circumvent this difficulty proved uneconomical, and the whole venture was dropped before 1900.

The collapse of their commercial usefulness did not mean the end of the cynthia moth and the ailanthus tree in the New World. They both adapted readily to the Northeast and extended their ranges. They now occur abundantly in cities from Boston to Washington, DC, and as far west as Chicago. Further range expansions will depend on the ability of both the moth and the stinkweed to disperse to large cities.

These trees are the exclusive host of the cynthia moth in North America. When the insect first came to this country, observers thought it would exploit many other kinds of broad-leaved trees and shrubs. An entomologist reported in 1881 that cynthia larvae were feeding on nearly all the trees and shrubs in New York's Central Park. But the lack of discrimination by egg-laying females proved deleterious, the moth apparently having a physiological requirement that only the ailanthus tree will satisfy. The same entomologist found that the diverse diet in Central Park caused unusually small caterpillars, most of which died before pupating.

When not thus aborted, the life history of the cynthia moth constitutes a remarkable sequence. In July the female oviposits small rows of oval eggs usually on the undersides of leaflets. Upon hatching, two to three weeks later, the quarter-inch-long yellow larvae cluster by the dozen or more as they grow and molt, turning green and developing blue tubercles and yellow tips. Highly conspicuous in such form and numbers, they are at this time especially liable to predation. Upon discovering a caterpillar colony, birds may feed upon the larvae until the entire colony is gone. But if they are not detected and survive to the sixth and final molt, a month or so after hatching from the eggs, the four-inch caterpillars resemble miniature distended turquoise serpents. They are blue-jeweled, yellow-pawed lions, rampant as they rear up toward a virgin leaf—and they are eating machines supreme.

Toward the end of summer this efficient foraging terminates. The bloated caterpillar pupates, usually by spinning a cocoon around a leaflet of the ailanthus. Before doing this, however, it performs a remarkable feat by actually lashing the chosen leaflet to the tree. As the ailanthus tree bears compound leaves, anchoring the leaflet is not enough, since the entire leaf, and thus the cocoon, will fall to the ground in the autumn. The larva therefore spins a silken cord from the leaflet along the leaf's long petiole to the place where it joins the branch. Here, the larva anchors the cord, which may be as long as eighteen inches.

When the leaf falls in the autumn, it, together with the cocoon, will dangle in the air. As Long Island lepidopterist John Cryan has found, the long lash serves a protective purpose beyond mere attachment. When struck—by a bird's beak, for example—the cocoon swings like a pendulum, absorbing the blow.

In its final hours as a caterpillar, the moth wraps itself inside a leaflet and spins a double-walled cocoon. Thousands of yards of silk go into the powerful mesh construction, which forms first an outer, looser sack and then an encasement within, like hard-pressed cardboard. The final molt takes place within this two-inch, blimplike chamber. Out of the shriveled and split larval skin wriggles a stout, brown pupa with the suggestions of the moth's form—wings, antennae, body segments—sculpted in its shiny surface. No idle sarcophagous, this thin case encloses one of the most incredible transformations in nature.

Through autumn, winter, and spring, the creature dangles quietly, its unexpected splendor hidden by a grim shroud. Then on a summer evening, the finished moth secretes a clear drop of solvent from its head to clear an exit from one end of the cocoon. With damp, folded, and compressed wings, the adult crawls into the air.

After hanging from a leaf or twig to spread and dry their massive wings, female moths release pheromones. Males, sensing these perfumes with their large, feathery antennae, may be drawn from five or ten miles away to mate with the females. Courtship and pairing often go on until dawn.

Like all saturniid moths, cynthias have no functional mouth parts. All adult activity must be sustained on energy stored by the caterpillar, so the life of the moth is short—perhaps only a few days. But sometime during those days new chalky eggs will have been fertilized and laid.

This cyclic miracle takes place only where ailanthus trees grow, but only if they are in the neglected and denigrated corners of eastern cities. In spite of one of its common names, tree of heaven, the ailanthus prospers in the least heavenly niche of all. It competes poorly with native trees and shrubs in woodlands and has limited use as an ornamental in gardens and parks. But wherever the growing is tough, this adaptable plant spreads its roots, capable of vegetative reproduction, to find bits of soil to exploit. And where the tree of heaven strikes a claim among concrete and broken bricks, the cynthia moth follows.

An abundance of evidence corroborates the moth's unwholesome preferences. Sandy and Paul Russell, amateur saturniid researchers in Brooklyn, find the largest numbers of cocoons between the bases of the Manhattan and Brooklyn Bridges, among garbage dumps, abandoned factories, and warehouses. Lepidopterist Cryan seeks the species in old air bases and shipyards and in alleyways. My own experience suggests that railroad yards are especially suitable havens for the insect, an impression reiterated by many students of cynthia distribution. This seems not to be a new association. New York naturalist Bernard Sherak earned spending money during the Depression by providing quantities of cynthia pupae, gleaned from Brooklyn railroad yards, to biological supply houses. But while Sherak knew enough to leave pockets of cocoons unexploited for repropagation, the cynthia moth's habit of clustering makes it easy prey for unscrupulous collectors. A selfish market collector recently removed every cocoon, about five hundred, from a dismal New Haven, Connecticut, railroad yard.

Some sites are favored over others. In an effort to further characterize the features of cynthia's habitat, I compared two stretches of ailanthus-lined railroad track in New Haven. The first section I examined is an old spur line, which, while littered, makes a rather pleasant green strip through the city. The flora along the tracks, which run along an abandoned canal bed, grew densely and variously. Where maples were backed up against the bank, shards of broken glass were hidden by a carpet of yellow leaves. Locust and catalpa trees lined other sections, while mullein spread its furry rosettes among the rock ballast, and milkweed broadcast silky seeds into the autumn wind.

These trees, shrubs, and herbs created a great deal of cover, which was exploited by a surprising amount of wildlife. Mourning doves crowded on overhead wires. Blue jays, never out of earshot and seldom out of sight, lurked among the scrub. English and white-throated sparrows hopped ahead of me in foraging flocks. A crow lumbered overhead, while a gray squirrel ran along a rail and a rat slunk up the side of an embankment. Starlings were my constant companions.

Trees of heaven grew all along the spur, having sprung from rock and brick and concrete. Their leaves fell away with the wind. But the loss of foliage revealed not a single cynthia moth cocoon along this stretch of the road.

I next visited the New Haven railroad yards, where city senescence meets railway decay in a very bleak setting. Here were all those aspects of the city that make urban existence so difficult for the naturalist. Stark parallel patterns of tracks, wires, roads, and pipes blocked the view, while traffic dinned and fumes filled the air, a sterile scene, yet the cynthia was there in abundance.

Scores of sleeping moths were suspended in a skeleton of stinkweeds along a soiled wall. Compositions in silk and soot, the new cocoons looked fresh and pink next to the previous year's discarded gray ones. But the scenario hardly sparkled with life. Fingerlike ailanthus grew prolifically, but practically the only other growth was a stand of reeds, which partially concealed the snout of a steaming locomotive. I began to understand the moths' remarkable adaptive strategies. To live in this habitat at all is an achievement; but the moth did more than that—it lived well.

Swaying from nearly every limb, woven into one another in the absence of a better substrate, even set into the diamonds of a chain-link fence, the cocoons offered a rich and vulnerable food resource for would-be predators. Even with their tough shells and swinging suspension, some of them would certainly fall victim to birds or mammals that happened upon them.

And yet here, I suspect, lies the secret of the cynthia moth's success in the inner cities: there are virtually no predators here. For, unlike the well-vegetated spur line, this railroad yard evidenced no vertebrate life. Even the wasp and fly parasitoids that attack many Lepidoptera larvae were not observed in a sample of cocoons from the site. Parasitism of the cynthia seems to be infrequent in many other populations as well.

The low incidence of predation in certain habitats emerges as a theory for the prolific existence of cynthia moths. While few populations are actually controlled by predators, the survival of these saturniid moths appears to get a significant boost from lack of enemies. This could be especially important in the hostile environment of the inner city, where pressures such as the removal of ailanthus trees, vehicle-caused mortality, and occasional overcollecting by humans act against the moths.

Assuming, however, that a few predators stalk the urban wasteland, the cynthia moth may already be evolving into an even better urban strategist. Nineteenth-century entomologists noted that the species was genetically very plastic, capable of rapid evolutionary change. American cynthia moths were reputed to be noticeably different from the French and Chinese stock after being here only a few years. Now, subjected to twentieth-century pollution, the moth appears to be evolving a degree of melanism.

Charles Remington, a Yale University biologist specializing in insect evolution, has watched New Haven and other urban cynthia moth populations for more than twenty years. Certain color mutations are quite evident, one of them producing a striking black insect. In New York City, the Russells have discerned a strongly gray-flecked form, which predominates among the moths they rear for experiments. Of all the mutations that could arise, melanism would be one of the most advantageous in the sooty environment of the railroad yard if there were just enough predators to select for it.

One big question remains to be answered in this portrait of a moth and its curious distribution. If mercury vapor lights are indeed the principal factor in the depletion of saturniid moth faunas, why does the cynthia remain abundant in places where mercury vapor lights glow intensely? Elaborate experiments might give the answer; in the meantime, lepidopterists can only speculate. My own speculation is that lights, ordinarily situated close to the cynthia's habitat, might serve to concentrate the moth in places with a high probability of ailanthus occurring—the cities. Since the drawing power of female pheromones is almost certainly more far-reaching than that of the streetlights, mercury vapor lights are not likely to remove male moths from the vicinity of females. The immunity of city cynthias to modern lighting seems to be rooted in the very nature of the moths' urban habitat. Once again, the cynthia moth demonstrates its elegant adaptation to urban existence.

While many forms of wildlife perish before expanding human populations, other animals and plants have adapted well to the marginal habitats spurned by people. Foxes breed commonly in London, raccoons populate New York City parks, and beavers are at home in Seattle waterways. The cynthia moth appears to be another creature adroitly adapted to the rigorous urban environment. Whatever the cynthia is doing, it is doing it right. For while giant silk moths of other species disappear, the cynthia thrives in the cities. And the cities are richer for it.

The Death of a Moth
Rejoinder to Virginia Woolf
(News of the Lepidopterists' Society, 1976)

Not long after this note came out, Annie Dillard published an essay by the same name, describing a moth that flew into her campfire, in the Atlantic. *I sent her mine from the rather less illustrious* News of the Lepidopterists' Society, *and she sent me a kind postcard in return, acknowledging our mutual debt to the moths and to Ms. Woolf.*

In her essay "The Death of a Moth," Virginia Woolf dwelt upon her feelings at watching the futile struggle of a "little hay-coloured moth" against its ultimate demise. They may not have been the kinds of feelings that many of us would experience, let alone be able to express in so evocative a manner. Yet Ms. Woolf's perceptions will not be lost on the sensitive lepidopterist who, like her, can say that in a moth "one saw life, a pure bead."

I had occasion last summer to think more about the dying of a particular moth than I might normally have done. She was a *Cecropia* moth, which my father found and brought to me on an early summer evening in Denver. She came in the rain, with damp shine on her furry spiracles and moist spots on her salmon bands. Later, after her cocoa-skim wings had dried, she spread them and broadcast the pheromones we could faintly smell.

Placing her in a screened window, I hoped that a male might come to her. She called, and not a male but perhaps twenty or thirty came brushing and banging at the screen at three-thirty that dawn. I captured a few, all my killing bottles would hold, and watched the rest in genuine awe (for this was my first time)—great, fluttering bigwings over and under the eaves, in and out of the porchlight, slow and strong and altogether too easy to net. Unable to get through to the female, the males tried windows all over the house—her pheromones must have spread down the halls, and out each sleeper's window. Two I took to her, one fresh, one less. "The books" often say that the more wizened males achieve the mating. But two days later, it was the perfect male I found *in copulo* with the female. For that, he became a satisfied specimen; the rejected tatty one flew free for his few more hours.

The newly gravid *Cecropia* traveled west with us to Washington, laying more than two hundred eggs along the way. Each evening under her netting she shook and fluttered—calling again those twenty? No western moths ever heeded her aroma on the wind.

Then one night we left her in a Corvallis hotel room as we joined our fellow lovers of moths at the reception for the Pacific Slope meeting of the Lepidopterists' Society. I thought perhaps I should have brought her along for friends to see, but decided against it: *Cecropia* is a common animal, and by then she was quite battered. When we returned, I found that she had died that night. I regarded her. The lilac wingtips were gone, victims of the incessant nocturnal quivering and the abortive flight attempts. But the chestnut, mouthless face was still downy. Since she died in our absence I was unable to see the last movements, could not try to cipher meaning in them, a la Woolf. Yet, reflecting on her longevity as an adult moth, I found that I agreed with the poet: "when there was no one to care or to know, against a power of such magnitude, to retain what no one else valued or desired to keep, moved one strangely."

"The books" say that saturniid moths, unable to feed, live but a few days. This female *Cecropia* came in the rain on May 30, and she died, after long hot and cold travels, on June 22. I spent nearly three and one-half weeks in her company. As I packed her away into a paper envelope and wrote on it the dry facts that said little about her, a nighthawk called outside the hotel window. It struck me that this hunting bird would enjoy my moth no more than I had done.

The Bramble Patch Trap

(*Horticulture*, 1976)

I submitted this essay for an anthology of ordeals from the field, but the editors rejected it in the belief that it must be hyperbolic fiction. Elsewhere it was mistaken for a noir fable. Finally I convinced Paul Trachtman at Horticulture *that it was unvarnished true life experience, and if anything, understated. How exciting it was when he engaged the great* New Yorker *cartoonist, Edward Koren (still drawing after all these years!) to do the illustrations of monster thorns and stickers. I wrote him my thanks afterward, and he sent me a splendid illustrated letter in response. At the time of this ordeal, I labored under the misbelief that my hayfever stemmed from the very obvious foxglove, which is really insect pollinated and doesn't cast its pollen on the wind. The actual culprits were the grasses flowering at the same time. In fact, foxglove turns out to be an alternative foodplant for the heath fritillary. Thanks to research by Dr. Martin Warren, the species is now doing much better on a small number of managed preserves in southern England.*

As I eased the Morris Traveller down off the moor, the Devon coastal village emerged from the fog, and whitewashed cottage walls shone through an English summer mist. Capped figures in shabby tweeds tramped along alleyways and by closed back doors. The scene struck me as an improbable idyll, though it was no more unlikely than my situation; I was a Fulbright scholar studying the conservation of endangered species of butterflies. And after nine months at a British government ecology laboratory, living in a fenland cottage built in 1648 and venturing frequently into corners of this "green and pleasant land," I often had a feeling of unreality.

For the past week my research travels had been delightful, but not entirely successful. I had explored the dark hollows of Dartmoor and the clefts of Bodmin Moor, the wild Cornish coast and the purple heaths of Somerset's Exmoor. But the explicit object of my "hunt" eluded me again and again. I was seeking the heath fritillary, rarest of the West Country butterflies, next to the nearly extinct large blue. The Nature Conservancy's distribution maps showed drastic reductions in the range of this bright, checkered creature over the past few decades.

It was the intent of Her Majesty's government to arrest the decline and prevent an apparent extinction. As the culmination of my year's studies at Monks Wood Experimental Station, I sought ecological reasons for the ebb and political means for protecting those colonies that might remain. Before *Melitaea athalia* could be conserved, we had to know where it was—and where it wasn't.

Mostly, so far, it wasn't. But a brilliant Devonshire morning now seemed to bode success.

I drove along a lane of thatched houses, where women swept doorsteps and worked cottage gardens; men rode bicycles to odd jobs, drove small herds of sheep, and stood huddled awaiting the opening of a public house. This hamlet lacked a quaint name such as many English villages possess, names such as Frisby-on-the-Wreake, Christmas Common, Molesworth, or nearby Woolsfardisworthy (abbreviated Woolsery). It went instead by the simple and solid English name of "Lee." Parking outside a small shop, I entered and bought a bar of Cadbury's chocolate for the hike, and inquired of the confectioner whether he knew the way to the Vale of Mortehoe. "Ye falla thet stone wall dun at the bot'om," he said. "Backalong aways ye'll come by the track up the combe. But Mortehoe is a good, longish ramble. Ye'll be some glad when ye get there, and the pub ought jest be op'nin!"

I could have told the man that I would be turning off to climb Windcutter Hill in search of butterflies, but I was anxious to get on and knew it would require a lengthy explanation. Country folk are more aware of butterflies than city people, but they don't understand why they need to be studied. As it turned out, I should have taken the time.

I left the village through a bower of scarlet fuschias. The greenwood loomed ahead and my way lay beyond—steeply up a green slot through the verdure of high summer. The trail narrowed to a path alongside a stream. I paced easily, shirtless now above the chilly sea mist. The day was warm and sunny, just right for butterfly activity. And the glimpse of open country up ahead seemed promising. For the heath fritillary is a particular beast. Although the food plant of its caterpillar, the plantain, grows all over England, the butterfly frequents few of the seemingly appropriate habitats. So far I had worked out a rough formula for its range: edges of woodlands and open spaces that have been recently disturbed, near heathland but where the plantain grows vigorously and the bracken and brambles have yet to dominate. I came into the sun, stood by the brook, and looked across to a vast hillside that seemed to fit this description well. Oh, there might be a few brambles lower down, but they seemed to thin out. Or so I thought.

Windcutter Hill, according to the Ordnance Survey map, had been planted up as a conifer plantation. An increasingly common sight in the British countryside, such forestry ventures exclude most wildlife when they grow tall and close and dank. But in their early years, they provide the perfect kind of "edge" preferred by many beneficial insects, including the picky heath fritillary. My supervisor at the Biological Records Centre, appropriately named John Heath, was especially anxious to locate sites that might be managed to perpetuate the creature. The butterfly's range map showed a dot in this ten-kilometer square, based on a very old record. I felt sure, as I sloshed across the cool, mossy stream, that I would be able to find the heath fritillary—possibly in one of its last stands in the British Isles.

But I could see that Windcutter would not be a simple prominence to negotiate. The forty-five-degree slope rolled upward like a loose carpet of thick pile. Slipping in unstable duff, I grabbed the crown of one of the little conifers for support. Ouch! Sitka Spruce! I knew these trees and their needles, like steel pins, from the Olympic Coast of Washington.

I had hardly expected to encounter them in Devonshire.

All right then, dodge the spruces. But there were more than a few brambles, too, that I could see (and feel) now. In the autumn, British brambles become Blackberry Bushes, Bearers of Ambrosia. But for the rest of the year they are just plain brambles. They pluck and tear with a vengeance, and cannot be disengaged without further inflictions. And for a victim of plant allergies, like me, bramble wounds are all the worse because they swell and sting and itch.

But once through this, I figured, the going will be easier. It was, for a bit. Just far enough to lure me much deeper into the briers. I did not realize it yet, but once inside, there was no ready exit from *this* bramble patch.

I forged ahead, more slowly. I had hit a couple of false summits and the tangle showed no signs of thinning out. In fact, the thorns were closing in around me. I abandoned my transect—it was too thick for the butterflies anyway, but maybe higher—and struck straight upward for the moor. But I was repulsed. All sides, suddenly, were great walls of spike and barb. I put on my shirt and shoved against the armed cataract. For a way I persisted like this, treading on the higher serpent coils of blackberries to break a pathway. I certainly couldn't turn back; after all, the cool, open moors lay just a short bramble-bash ahead. Retreating would mean duplicating an ordeal that had already been quite painful.

Soon my heavy work shirt made no protection, as the chambray shredded before the vines. My Levi's helped little more. One wanted *armor,* I thought, as a slight misstep sent woody weapons into my knees and thighs, or the backlash of an escaping cable kicked my shins like a hobnailed boot. I cursed at that, and clutched at stickers that stuck again every time my jeans brushed my skin. The sweat ran hard. But when the first blood came, my enthusiasm of that morning burst like a balloon among the brambles.

The gradient increased even more now, and the blackberry vines began to give out—to be replaced by a regiment of blackthorn, hawthorn, and wild roses. Each plant, I learned, held its own brand of attack. The roses acted like hypodermic needles, puncturing belly and elbows quickly and painlessly for a second—then hurting devilishly. The hawthorns, in contrast, an ancient deterrent to strays and trespassers still employed in miles of hedgerows, bore broad blades that bored large holes. The blackthorns struck like ice picks into my chest and buttocks. I stopped comparing these offenses when the first nettle slapped my fingers with a thousand hot lancets. Recoiling, I shrieked and backed hard into . . . a holly bush!

Standing still and feeling very foolish, I tried to regather my composure. Irrationally, I found that I hated the foliage. The ecologist in me protested, for I've eaten many blackberries in my time, and certain rare butterflies in Monks Wood depend on blackthorn leaves. Besides, I am the intruder. Bramble scrub like this makes excellent habitat for small wildlife. I repeated consoling thoughts like that, finding that they did not improve my condition. What was it Peter Rabbit did when Reddy Fox was on his tail? He made his escape into a brier patch. Surely he must have had some way of getting around in there. I dropped to my knees and tried crawling, forgetting that I was several times larger than any rabbit. I made, predictably, about two yards of progress. Mostly, I punctured my palms and my knees. And in trying to stand up again, I lacerated my back on a patch of thorns.

Now I was scared.

How far did this thorny trap extend? Could I make it to the moor, or must I relive this torture? A few feet away grew a gnarled hawthorn, perhaps twenty feet high. If I could climb it, I might find respite for a moment and also get a bearing. Wrestling through a small patch of nettles and roses, I reached the tree and shinnied up its trunk. This was studded with its own horns and wrapped around with spiny vines. Reaching daylight meant forcing my shoulders up through an upside-down bed of nails. I wiped the sweat from my eyes and forehead and gazed out, dreading what I might see. The moor lay still half a mile above me. No one, clearly, could make it through that botanical booby-trap. So I looked back whence I'd come—and almost despaired at what I saw. For in spite of the slow, wracked pace of my progress, I already had advanced a thousand yards.

As my feet met the ground, I found myself pinned up against the bark like a mounted insect. Rosethorns pressed into my thorax like fine German insect pins. There might have been some humorous irony in this had I been pursuing butterflies with intent to kill. But there was little humor in it, for by now my pain was extreme. There seemed no way out. Even my route of entrance was sealed. I simply could not move without being cut from every side. Most Britons will tell you they prefer the countryside to the problems and the violence of London; yet here I was, up against a wall of holly with hawthorn switchblades in my ribs. And now my energy ebbed as I got more desperate. Shaking weakly, I realized that I *had* to move. It is possible after all, to succumb to the dread challenge of equatorial jungles and blazing deserts. But to be beaten by a mere tangle of scrub in tame, benign Devon, land of clotted cream and strawberry teas—that seemed absurd and laughable. Yet I was in greater danger of physical and mental collapse than I have been when stuck in sucking quicksand or flailing in deep water.

Now, however, I spotted a possible reprieve—a log lying astride a shallow ravine. If I could only beat the next bramble thicket, then negotiate the nettles beyond it, I could use the log as a bridge to the clearing I'd spied from the tree. No gesture could be made now, not an elbow lifted nor a step taken, without fresh incision. But with great pain I made it to the log. Inching along its narrow back afforded my first relief in hours, since it lifted my face and chest at least above the needles. But now, on the middle of my bridge, I looked down and recognized a massive clump of the most notorious of all British thorns: gorse! This tall, rounded shrub, similar to Scotch broom, bears hundreds of very long, stiff, super-sharp sabres on each branch—each one a real toad-stabber, as my friend used to call his pocketknife, to my displeasure as I liked toads. Now, like the hapless toad caught by my friend, I was at the mercy of the gorse.

Resuming my course along the log, I shuddered as I heard above my own heavy breathing a crack, a rending of rotten wood. And just as one has barely a moment to dread the crash of falling through ice, I felt the stabs of gorse even before I was plunged full-square onto the bush. Two hundred pounds falling six feet make gorse quills go rather deep. I think I screamed at that point. I know I did when, falling off the gorse, my momentum carried me a few yards farther down the ravine, rolling over blackberry vines as I went. Once I saw in a western how the cowboys wrapped up a range-fencing farmer in barbed wire and rolled him down a hill into a gully. It must have been something like that.

Tumped up against a little spruce, I lay groaning. No one to hear but a hedge sparrow, which scurried past unconcerned. When I could stand I took reconnaissance. By less than the best route, certainly, I had at least gained the open meadow. What an unspeakable pleasure, to step out of the barbed-wire butterfly net and into an open field!

In a rush of exuberance, I stepped more quickly, and kicked hard, right into a low-lying bed of thistles! With its beneedled, stiff leaves, the Scottish emblem may be less formidable than the other tormentors. But whacked in full stride, thistles slice right through jeans into knees, leaving a special sting. I could hardly see these new aggressors to avoid them, wrapped up as they were and tied together with bracken ferns and foxglove. Foxglove! I might at least have been spared that. I am highly allergic to the beautiful purple trumpet flowers of *Digitalis,* and hayfever is funny only to those who are not afflicted by it. I started sneezing violently. My eyes, already swollen from cuts, swelled more and itched maddeningly, and blood ran all down my body. There were tears, as well.

By now it was midday, the hottest part, and the blackflies came out. Perhaps they weren't as fierce as flies of the Yukon, nor as numerous as the scourge of the Scottish Highlands. But they swarmed and bit nonetheless. The blackflies located my wounds (no difficult task) and bit me where the flesh was already broken. I slapped at them, only making my skin sting more. Then I cracked. I felt absolutely picked upon. In a sort of delirium I began to curse over and over again, "Stick a fly, thorn! Bite a thorn, fly! *Atchoo!*"

I guess the black comedy of it all refreshed me slightly, or perhaps a cloud came over the sun and brought a breeze. Anyway, I somehow scrambled back into the brambles. The sneezing ceased, the blackflies departed, and all I had to contend with was the original barrier of a million miniature daggers. Defeating the Scottish dirks gave me courage to continue. For another hour I struggled, and the perpetual shredding continued, the unrelenting pricking and piercing—the nearest to torture I ever want to be. My wish for a machete, or even a butterfly net to thrash with, was not granted. Swinging my camera in front of me only tore the case, and made scarcely a dent in the barrier of foliage.

But at last only a drapery of nettles as high as my head separated me from the brook and the open path. I hadn't the energy left to carefully trod at the base of each stinging nettle, so I plunged through in a final, searing shower, landing on my chest in the shallow brook. I never did eat my Cadbury's, though I could have used it for energy. It had melted, and now ran in a brown stream, mixed with blood and water. I had run the gruesome gauntlet of the bramble jungle.

When I was able, some minutes later, I trundled back down the shadowed path, sort of whimpering. Seaside holidaymakers spilled their tea at the sight, as

I passed them sitting in a cottage garden. One gent called me a "bloody" something, and I don't believe he was swearing. The red fuschias that I had seen when I set out now seemed like gory omens. By now my cuts and scratches had all swelled into massive welts so that I looked like a gladiator who had faced the lions and lost. I was very conspicuous, and in no mood to be stared upon. So I chose to drive (I could barely sit) down the coast to Braunton Burrows, a little-frequented nature reserve. There I stripped and floated in the natural epsom salts of the sea. The salt, of course, stung sharply. But the water soothed.

That evening I did not have the strength or patience to seek out the sort of pretty farmhouse or bed-and-breakfast place in which I usually spent the nights; nor even to visit a congenial country pub: it was too soon and too painful to begin telling the tale. So when I came to Barnstaple and spotted an American motel, I gratefully checked in and, once installed, ran a deep, hot bath.

The heath fritillary, I mused, may or may not be making its last stand on Windcutter Hill. But I very nearly made mine up there! In my report, I proposed changing the name to Fleshcutter Hill, and logged another failure.

I did not know it then, but two days later in Exeter I was to play a part in arranging for the acquisition of a heath fritillary reserve elsewhere in Devon. My studies eventually aided in the conservation management of this rare and lovely creature. Perhaps crowns of thorns have their recompense after all.

The Extinction of Experience
(*Horticulture*, 1978)

Probably nothing I have written has been more quoted, anthologized, or used in college classes than "The Extinction of Experience." It was a lucky pick of a phrase for a concept that came right out of my own experience and seems to relate to that of many others. Most have quoted or used the longer rendition, a chapter in my book The Thunder Tree. *This is the original version, which grew from a talk I gave at an AAAS panel, "Wildlife in the Year 2000," in Boston in 1975. I wrote it, and three other essays, for* Horticulture *in exchange for the $800 I needed for a VW bus. Richard Louv has been generous in his recognition of this essay as an inspiration for his important book,* Last Child in the Woods: Saving Our Children from Nature-Deficit Disorder.

As a young naturalist, I roamed a century-old irrigation ditch called the Highline Canal, which snakes along the foothills of the Rockies out onto the plains east of Denver. In ten years of wandering the canal, as prairie dog colonies became condominiums and the sandy flats vanished before the developers' advance, we succeeded in maintaining an intraurban trail as a preserve for a wide variety of wildlife. But I doubt that a child wandering the Highline Canal today could be so readily reached by its wonders. The goatweed emperor and the Olympia marble no longer fly there.

These species of butterflies have become extinct, but hardly in the generally accepted sense of the word. When we think of extinction, we usually think of the elimination of entire species on a global scale. Biologists agree that these extinction rates have risen sharply since the introduction of agriculture and industry upon the landscape. The trend is abundant reason for ethical as well as ecological concern. As land managers, we can succeed in preserving species threatened with complete elimination if they give us pleasure or other benefits. We can compile lists of threatened species, based on current trends and future projections. But it is a game best left to the professionals of such management, with the information and charts at their command. Another approach, more valuable for the rest of us, is to consider the particular kinds of extinction we can see all around us, and more important, the kinds we may be able to do something about.

The majority of extinctions involve not the eradication of species on a global scale, but the disappearance of portions of them wherever we look. A colony goes extinct here, a subspecies drops out there—two varieties of butterflies vanish from the Highline Canal. They add up, and the consequence is a drastically undermined flora and fauna. It seems to me that the impact of these partial extinctions upon our natural base and collective psyche, as well as our ability to withstand future assaults on the environment, is very great indeed. In the long run they may affect more of us than will the disappearance of entire species. For what these local extinctions represent is the loss of opportunities—the extinction of experience.

"Between German chickens and Irish hogs," wrote H. H. Behr to Herman Strecker in 1875, "no insect can exist besides louse and flea." Behr, a pioneer West Coast entomologist, was referring to the diminution of native insects in the environs of San Francisco. His particular concern was the coastal habitat of the Xerces blue butterfly, which was giving way to building lots. Xerces, peculiar to the San Francisco peninsula, held out for several more decades, finally disappearing altogether when its last habitat was altered by military construction in the early 1940s. Two or three striking subspecies of San Francisco butterflies preceded Xerces into oblivion and several now seem ready to follow. So far, the Xerces blue is the only entire species of American butterfly that has been eliminated by human impact. It is not the only cause for concern.

My own specialty in wildlife conservation has been butterflies and other beneficial and benign insects. Terrestrial arthropods make up perhaps 75 percent of the world's animal species. Relatively few insect species actually compete with us for food and fiber, and by far the greatest number serve a useful role. Butterflies, moths, and bees pollinate our crops and flowers, while caterpillars form a large part of the diet of songbirds. Conspicuous yet sensitive to environmental change, butterflies can be excellent indicators of both the vitality of an ecosystem and the specialness of communities. Yet in spite of this, insects and other invertebrates have not received the attention that their ecological importance should command. In fact, little happened in the realm of local insect conservation in this country in the 101 years following Behr's sardonic warning about the San Francisco Bay region—until, that is, some of his predictions of extinction began to come true. In the wake of diminishing butterfly populations, an entire school of wildlife conservation devoted to insects and their habitats has surfaced.

It may be that the Xerces did not die out altogether in vain, for this small indigo insect left a legacy in the form of the Xerces Society. This six-year-old organization works internationally to conserve habitats of rare terrestrial arthropods. Through the Xerces Society, something of the power of the wildlife conservation lobby has been extended to the "lower" realm of the most numerous animals—some of the species of which are very rare indeed. In one recent case, the Xerces Society assured the continued existence of a shabby but vital bit of duneland in Southern California that happens to be home for the El Segundo blue. Now restricted to two sites in the Los Angeles–area community of El Segundo, *Shijimiaeoides battoides allyni,* a butterfly much smaller than its name suggests, is considered endangered. One of the two habitats lies at the end of a runway at LA International Airport, the other beside a Standard Oil Company refinery. Jeannine Oppewall, a Xerces activist, convinced Standard that it would be in the nation's, the community's, and its own interest to conserve the site. The corporation subsequently fenced the dunes to protect them from dune buggies, and guaranteed access to the reserve by lepidopterists who wish to study the remarkable local butterfly. Further measures were necessary to restore the right conditions for the blues. An exotic, invading ice plant *(Mesembryanthemum edulis)* threatened to crowd out the native buckwheat *(Eriogonum parvifolium),* the host plant for the butterflies' caterpillars. Standard removed the ice plant. Might a similar concern have saved Xerces blue?

The El Segundo blue is just one of six California butterflies of the family Lycaenidae (the blues, coppers, hairstreaks, and metalmarks) that have been placed on the current federal list of threatened and endangered species. Two Florida swallowtails were the first insects to be named as "threatened" by the Office of Endangered Species of the Department of the Interior.

The two rare residents of the Keys are the Schaus' swallowtail *(Papilio aristodemus ponceanus)* and the Bahaman swallowtail *(P. andraemon bonhotei).* Both fly on long, elegant wings of cream, ebony, and tangerine. Research suggests that Schaus' swallowtail still survives in fair numbers on Biscayne National Monument. But housing and other developments have usurped most of its former habitat in the Miami area, and hurricanes could represent a major threat if populations become too dense. The official listing of threatened species by the government provides for the critical determination of habitats and regulations to maintain them. Such action may prevent this superb butterfly from going the way of another (former) member of the Florida fauna, the brilliant green atala *(Eumaeus atala).* The extinction of this tropical hairstreak in the United

States may be attributable to overdevelopment and the alteration of its water-side habitat.

People frequently use the word "rare," when some other adjective might be more appropriate. The six California lycaenid butterflies typify creatures that can be called genuinely rare. Their range is highly restricted, and their total number is never particularly high, even though there may be more than a few on the wing for a few days each year. Population biologists recognize a threshold below which the numbers of these organisms should not drop, lest extinction of the entire species follow. That level is a critical mass of sorts, the minimum number necessary to maintain mating and other functions essential for the colony's survival. The problem comes when a population is rare enough to be near that threshold.

But just as often, rarity is a matter of the relative distribution of a species over time and space. And it is in this sense that even a common species can become so rare as to result in the extinction of experience. The monarch butterfly, *Danaus plexippus,* is an example. It can be enormously abundant at the right times and places; 1975 was a good year in Rhode Island but was less so in New York; 1973 seemed to be an abundant year all over the East. During the peak of the southerly migration in October, I saw hundreds of thousands of the cinnamon-colored monarchs milling about on Cape May, along with the birds that give this New Jersey peninsula its fame. In Washington State, by contrast, the monarch is never numerous due to complex biogeographical patterns. Suitable habitats seldom yield larvae, and only a few fliers are seen coming through each year. Yet the monarch as a *species* cannot be said to be rare, nor is it endangered in Washington; it just never has been abundant there to our knowledge.

Similarly, in some years the painted lady butterfly appears in the north by the millions. In other years, when its Mexican winter habitat has been unfavorable for nectar production or other functions, nary a *Cynthia cardui* may be seen in the temperate regions come summertime. Nevertheless, this orange-and-black thistle feeder is so widespread that it is also called, alternatively, the cosmopolitan butterfly. What are we to make of this? Is the painted lady common, or rare? Clearly, it can be either.

One more case of relative rarity is that in which "inaccessible" describes the insect more clearly than "rare." For example, arctic-alpine butterflies of the genera *Oeneis* and *Erebia* display their dun, lichenous colors in the high, montane reaches of the northern hemisphere. Often, colonies of these high-altitude animals, prized by collectors, inhabit places exceedingly difficult to reach, let alone to run about and swing a net in. Hence, lepidopterists often call these creatures rare, even though they may be quite numerous in season.

The kinds of stresses that humans apply to ecosystems are all too well known by most of us. The first that comes to mind is direct killing. Insects, which are mobile and reproduce rapidly, can seldom be reduced in the long run by the destruction of individuals. For that reason, butterfly collecting doesn't worry conservationists except in a few unusual cases in which the population has already been seriously depleted. In fact, a great deal of research is still necessary before we can develop truly comprehensive butterfly conservation programs, and thus careful collecting can actually be an aid to insect conservation.

Hunting is seldom a threat to whole populations, because game managers set bag and harvest limits designed to ensure a healthy supply. Even the vicious and unwarranted persecution of predators in the West, while it takes a terrible toll in nontarget wildlife, doesn't stand to eliminate its chief target. The coyote is frequently the scapegoat for an uneconomic and highly subsidized sheep industry, for which it suffers a diabolical trial-by-poison at the hands of frustrated wool-shepherds. Still, the coyote is an astonishingly adaptable animal, and I suspect that one of them will be sniffing around the tombstone of the last human being in Wyoming. Certainly direct killing of wildlife can bring about extinctions, especially on a market-hunting scale: it happened with the sea otter on the West Coast of the lower states, except for a small part of California, and it happened with its counterpart of the northern Pacific seas, the Steller's sea cow, altogether. Wolves, pumas, and grizzly bears occupy little of their former ranges, and California did away with its state mammal, the golden grizzly, many years ago.

The golden bear of California was not wiped out entirely by hunting and trapping. Like so many other extinct or endangered members of this state's fauna, it succumbed in part to more subtle factors. If California seems to come up disproportionately in discussions of wildlife extinction, it is because it exemplifies, even embodies, a simple formula: Endemicity + Overpopulation = Extinction. Endemicity refers to a high number of organisms limited to one area and nowhere else. Overpopulation refers to *Homo sapiens*. This formula applies to much of California, and the result may be found in the state's list of extinct and endangered species. And so the cumulative effects of human population represent a graver total threat than simply killing wildlife outright. The key word is habitat: destroy one habitat, and you can obliterate a great variety of flora and fauna with a single stroke.

Washington State, where I have done much of my own research, and neighboring Oregon, are considered by many to be model states with regard to environmental conditions and regulations. Yet even in the Pacific Northwest I have observed far too many examples of local extinctions through habitat alteration. When the great short-grass prairies of the Palouse region of eastern Washington were transformed into a vast wheat monoculture, uncounted plants and animals were lost. These amber waves of grain are beautiful, productive, and strategic, but in such overwhelming uniformity they support little diversity. Polyculture farming can provide a good deal of wildlife, as well as a profit.

Nearby, fifteen dams on the Columbia and Snake Rivers have all but erased the riparian habitats that made these watercourses the great biogeographical corridors of the Northwest. Oregon swallowtail butterflies *(Papilio oregonius)* have lost many former habitats, due to the slackwater drowning of the black basalt coulees where their wormwood host plant grew. The loss of the last free-flowing portion of the Columbia would be the price of the proposed Benjamin Franklin dam. Northwest conservationists have determined that this shall not pass; for naturalists, the legacy of deadened rivers is as bitter to take as the swallowtail's wormwood. [*Editors' Note: Bill Clinton's establishment of the Hanford Reach National Monument in 2000 ended the threat of such a dam.*]

To preserve the world's diversity of species, I believe it is necessary for us to retain a rich matrix of local wildlife habitats nearby. We can and should try to head off the global extinction of endangered species that we wish to retain as part of our world. But we must also save the endangered experience of precious contact with wildlife in our own communities. If a species that exists elsewhere becomes extinct within our own reach, the result is the same, in one sense, as complete eradication. Since the young are the least mobile, their opportunities vanish first. And they are the ones whose sensibilities must be touched by the magic reaction with wildlife if biologists, conservationists, and concerned citizens are not to become endangered themselves. What is the extinction of the condor to a child who has never seen a wren?

The Particular Pleasures of Small Islands
(*Pacific Search*, 1979)

Visiting the San Juan Islands with family on an expense advance, I hired a speedboat to get us out to Matia Island. Never having handled a motorboat on open saltwater, eager to get there before sunset, and oblivious to how much driftwood lay just beneath the surface, I goosed the boat to a nutty rate of knots. We were lucky to get back at all. The other islands mentioned I knew from my work as northwest land steward for The Nature Conservancy.

"An island, if it is big enough, is no better than a continent. It has to be really quite small, before it feels like an island." So thought D. H. Lawrence's "Man Who Loved Islands." I agree with him. For many people, all of the San Juan Islands may fit this criterion, as opposed to England or Manhattan, for example. For others, only the truly tiny San Juans seem wholly island-like in Lawrence's sense. However one regards them, the islets are surely less known than the big, ferry islands; and that is probably as it should be, for small islands are special places, easily changed.

What is to be done with little islands? Should they be homesites for the privileged, or for private souls such as the subject of Lawrence's tale? Many are, and that's that. Should they be bird and marine mammal refuges? The US Fish and Wildlife Service has dedicated several rocks and minor islands for this purpose. Can even these wild refuges remain unaffected by the island development boom? And what about the remaining dots on the map—the understated islands, large enough to live on but not to make a living from—how should these finally be allocated?

Because I am concerned about the preservation of such places, and because I am another "man who loves islands," I have visited some of the smaller, more obscure San Juans to see for myself what they are like, and to ask how they might best be used. Each time, I have returned filled with images and questions and one certain conviction: an island's importance cannot be measured by its acreage.

One of the minor isles in Wasp Passage is Yellow Island. Yellow is eleven acres of seduction. Island-lovers as diverse as biologists and landscape painters deem

Yellow a favorite within the archipelago. Upon beaching there, among magenta blood currants glowing against a soft, spring-green backdrop, I understood why. A mere mound upon the surface of the sea, a mossy hump above the waves, Yellow is clothed in a lush, low fabric of stonecrop and snowberry with a topknot of fir. The texture is softly tomentose, like an animal covered with matted hair. Unlike the salal carpets of some islands, which beckon then repel the walker, Yellow's rich floral sward invites gentle rambling. Small trails wind through the flowers and mossy knolls to minute coves, sunny slopes, cool green glades, or rocks where the harlequin ducks come ashore.

The glory of Yellow Island lies in its wildflowers. Some of the rarer species are less than spectacular—native grasses and subtle saxifrages, for example. But here bloom also "tropical-looking" shooting stars, exuberant fawn lilies, surprising orchids, even a cactus species, native, but far from its normal desert range. More remarkable than the diversity may be the virtually unaltered nature of the plant communities. True, some English ivy clambers around the bole of a fir, and a substantial holly gives away the island's settled history. A few European plants have struggled outward a short distance from the small garden. For the most part, however, the lichens and mosses, grasses and herbs, shrubs and trees of Yellow Island are as they were before human occupation.

The main cabin, a hobbit-house of wood and stone, bespeaks a gentle way of life for the islanders. The chimney might have grown right out of the island stone; to my eye it resembles a bottle-shaped cup fungus, such as those whose minute fruiting bodies clung to last year's nettle stalks near the cabin dooryard. The nettles, which other occupants might have cleared as a matter of course, will mean red admiral and tortoise-shell butterflies in summertime. And at the end of my last visit, I watched at sunset a wave of golden moths rise out of the snowberry thicket in their courtship flight. Perhaps they were never noticed before; they may not be again. But to me, yellow wings against the sun-struck waters of the sound were evocative of the island's spirit. Often, it is the smallest things that distinguish a place.

Such is not always the case. Upon my first arrival at Sentinel Island, six bald eagles arose from an offshore rock, two more from the island itself. Sentinel supports an active nest of this federally listed threatened species. I had gone in late winter, before they were nesting. My way ashore led through an enchanted, elfin forest of scraggly Garry oaks above, dense licorice ferns on the ground beneath. Runways through the ferns led to a thick moss pile, where bits of abalone, scallop, cockle, and urchin lay scattered about. Otter? Raccoon? Very different, this wild creatures' island, from adjacent Spieden Island. Spieden, once renamed Safari Island, was the grim scene of "hunts" whereby wealthy day-trippers stalked imported African wildlife, until the whole sordid affair mercifully went out of business. Not soon enough, however, to prevent severe overgrazing of the sunny south slopes by the doomed ungulates.

Resting against sun-warmed granite on Sentinel, immersed in a rich turf of native grasses and herbs, I could see over my shoulder strange sheep and fallow deer still haunting and chewing at Spieden's remains. The striking contrast in island-sides gave me pause to be thankful for small favors. Then I noticed a russet rain around me: the bracts of fir cones, tossed away by foraging chickadees. I watched the efficient chippers for a while. But chickadees, unlike eagles, occur in many places. I had to admit that Sentinel was probably not a good place to go to watch them feed, if it meant possibly disturbing the eyrie. If Yellow Island can handle visitors who comport themselves lightly upon the land, perhaps Sentinel should be a strict preserve, at least during nesting season. A few months later I passed Sentinel on the ferry and spotted two eagles bathing offshore, another on the nest. I reckoned I'd been right before. Chickadees and chocolate lilies can be seen elsewhere. Sentinel should be left for the eagles.

It is not always so easy to designate appropriate island uses. Matia Island punctuates the northern rim of the archipelago. Unlike its near neighbors, horseshoe-shaped Sucia and Orcas Islands, Matia has not been relegated chiefly to human purposes. Of its 145 acres, 140 make up a National Wildlife Refuge, the rest a concession to recreation in the form of a state park with dock and campsites. This means Matia is trying to be both park and preserve—a tall order for a small island. I visited Matia to see how well it works.

Plying the waters around Matia, one passes beneath cliffs of wildly honeycombed sandstone. In the late afternoon sun they were the color of the wild-honey bark of three old madronas on a prominence above. Where the rock runs flat out toward Puffin Island, a coal-shiny black oystercatcher preened with its lobster-red bill, as cormorants hunched on the rimrock like befrocked country vicars. Around on the Canadian exposure, straggling firs ran down to sloping stone, grizzled, flecked, and knobbed by salty tides. Roots of firs ran recumbent along the rocks almost down to glistening algae, which looked like roots of the rocks themselves. A gibbous moon rose over Rolfe Cove, where kelp aligned like eels and boats bobbed.

I went ashore onto paths penetrating virgin cedar swamps. Pileated woodpeckers, bishop-mitred powers of the woods, worked the cedar snags with their pentagonal holes; a brown creeper scaled a grand fir, stripping it of insect life. A gray moth flew from the charred sanctum of a hollow cedar. Across a well-chewed bracket fungus ran the glassy trail of a great banana slug. I felt the wildness of large and small things. Yet each path ran down to a cove-side campsite, far from the designated spaces. And from a woodpecker's hole, I extracted the wrappers of chewing gum. I found no solid answer to the paradox of Matia's best use. The slugs will adapt to moderate human presence. As I left, I spotted that telltale gossamer stripe across the door of the privy, shining in the sunset. Whether the pileated woodpecker and the pigeon guillemot will remain as people visit more frequently, I cannot say. Clearly, the managers of Matia face a challenge in stewardship.

What was clear to me indeed was the singular character of Matia Island. People ask why we need to protect any more islands. With the Fish and Wildlife Service wilderness islands, The Nature Conservancy's preserves on Waldron, Chuckanut, Goose, Deadman, and now (if all goes well), Yellow and Sentinel Islands, why should Matia not be left to the recreationists, like Sucia? It is a good question, this—what does make an island different from all the rest, worth the considerable sacrifice of setting it aside?

One could name species of special plants, of course. Goose has plants lacking on Deadman; Yellow nurtures flowers absent on either. I found a saprophytic heath on Matia, beneath the dark firs, which I have seen on no other island—a witchy gray bouquet of funereal heather bells, on which browsed a tiny gray caterpillar. Was it the progenitor of the moth of the hollow cedar? Perhaps both plant and animal owe their existence in the San Juans to the refuge.

Yet in the end, it is not just rare species of which we must speak, nor plant communities, nor occupied eyries. These are important, for in nature, diversity is all. But surely it is a *feeling* about an island that renders it truly distinct from all others: the same sort of feeling Lawrence wrote about in "The Man Who Loved Islands." Matia gives me that feeling; so do Yellow and Sentinel. Each is wholly, fundamentally, refreshingly different. In a world of gathering sameness, can we afford to forsake small islands such as these—places that still retain their special, separate faces?

Butterflies
Now You See Them . . .
(International Wildlife, 1981)

I began writing about butterfly conservation in 1967, with an article called "Conservation and the Lepidopterist." This was an unsung topic in those days. The Xerces Society came along in 1971, and invertebrate conservation is now commonplace. This piece touches on its early days, and on my most remarkable opportunity as a young naturalist, working in Papua New Guinea.

Always when we entered a village, friendly Melanesians gave us a boisterous welcome. Not this time. As we approached the tiny tropical island of Nimoa by canoe, no one stood on the shore. Not even a pig could be seen among the huts behind the beach. The ghostly scene made us feel uneasy.

There was another reason for our apprehension, too. We'd received a warning the day before: "Do not come." Five years earlier, we knew, these villagers had been cheated by foreigners looking for a large and extremely rare butterfly. Here in Papua New Guinea, the response to such crimes is frequently vengeance, and now we were searching for exactly the same insect.

My wife Sarah and I had journeyed to this remote area with Angus Hutton, a tea planter and explorer. Our mission was innocent enough. We wanted to check on an ingenious butterfly repopulation scheme Hutton had begun on the island the year before.

The particular species in question, an exquisite greenish-blue variety of the green birdwing (*Ornithoptera priamus caelestis*), lives only on Nimoa. Birdwings are the giants of the insect realm, and some measure nearly a foot across or more. Because they do not reproduce as quickly as other butterflies, birdwings are vulnerable to collectors, particularly if their ranges are highly restricted, as they are here on Nimoa. For years, collectors have coveted them, and as a result the demand has long exceeded supply.

As we tugged our dugout up onto the beach, we spotted a single old man sitting quietly on a log, whittling, beneath a palm. This, it turned out, was the

Big Man of the village. Coolly, he greeted us in pidgin, and then, at the urging of Hutton, he told us the tale of Nimoa's stolen butterflies. One day, a German butterfly dealer arrived on Nimoa and hired some young villagers to help collect hundreds of adult birdwings and chrysalides, the intermediate stage of the butterfly as it changes from a caterpillar. These came from a small part of the forest where the caterpillars' food plant grows. The dealer paid the people one Australian dollar. Elated, he remarked to his foreign companion, "That was an easy day's five thousand dollars."

The collector's aside was understood by one of the villagers. He told the others and, not surprisingly, they felt exploited. The next season and the one after, not a single birdwing was seen in the forest. And since then, whites with an interest in butterflies have not been welcome. That is why, when word reached the village about our party, we were warned to stay away.

Angus Hutton managed to convince the village Big Man that we were on Nimoa to help conserve, not to catch, the butterflies. Only then, at some secret signal, did more people appear, silently and mysteriously, from the bush. We made friends. Any crisis, real or imagined, was over, and not long after, a small party of us set out for the butterfly forest. On a previous visit, Hutton had secretly reintroduced this butterfly from a colony across the island. The transplant's success was as yet uncertain, but as soon as we entered the right grove, our companions began to cheer. The celestial birdwings were back for the first time in several years. Females, with ten-inch wings of chalky-white and coffee-black, floated delicately among the vines. Males, resplendent in emerald and sapphire, sailed imperiously above the tops of the bushes in search of mates and nectar. One particular male flirted with a purple vervain, then alighted on a twig. I simply watched, transfixed.

It was easy to see why the people here had been bitter, but the loss of butterflies is far from a local problem. From Britain to Brazil, these insects have come under siege. In California, half a dozen coastal butterflies have been lost since the 1860s, and an equal number are now endangered. In Madagascar and Rwanda, endemic swallowtails and other butterflies occurring nowhere else are being sacrificed to clear forests. In Europe, perhaps one-third of all butterfly species are in trouble, due chiefly to the drainage of wetlands and possibly to acid rain. In Sri Lanka, aerial pesticide spraying will kill millions of native butterflies along with the targeted crop pests. Worldwide, nearly all butterflies have suffered shrunken ranges, and an estimated half of the world's local butterfly populations face threats from development. The losses are much more than esthetic, for nearly all butterflies are beneficial to people. As effective pollinators of crops and flowers, sensitive indicators of ecological health, and a major link in the food chain, butterflies benefit plants, songbirds, and people equally.

The easy answer is to blame collectors and a butterfly trade that has reached an estimated $10 to $20 million worldwide each year, and in cases like the one at Nimoa, collectors *are* at fault. But all too often, butterfly traders are scapegoats. The real problem is more likely to be the bulldozer and the chainsaw, as butterfly living space is transformed to farms and plantations, parking lots and houses. We were to experience that problem just a few hundred miles farther north.

Again in the company of Hutton, Sarah and I visited the Duke of York Islands, a small cluster of islets in the northeastern part of the country. This is the home of the Mioko birdwing, a shimmering, velvet-blue butterfly (*O. p. mioensis*). Yet when we searched the island of Mioko, for which it is named, we could not find a single one. The story repeated itself on neighboring islands until at last we found one remnant colony.

The Mioko birdwing, it turned out, was not the target of overzealous marketeers. The culprits were coconut farmers. Nearly all of this butterfly's prime habitat had been converted to plantations unsuitable for the Mioko. The lone colony that we discovered occupied fewer than a hundred acres. No other suitable habitat remains on these islands, and the Mioko's prospects for survival are therefore not promising.

Of the two problems—overcollecting and habitat loss—the first appears to offer the simplest solution. Many conservationists would simply stop butterfly collecting altogether, or at least curb the trade. Dealing with collectors is cheaper and far more manageable than setting aside large blocks of land.

The trade itself takes two forms. One deals in low volumes and high values, like the Swiss commerce in watches and chocolates. Papua New Guinea has traditionally followed this high-quality approach. The second type of trade involves high volume at low value—like Hong Kong novelties. Taiwan's butterfly business typifies this.

The Taiwanese butterfly trade takes place on a vast scale. Estimates vary from fifteen million to five hundred million butterflies annually. At least a dozen factories employ scores of workers. Butterfly wings pasted onto paper bodies with pig-bristle antennae go into ornaments and objects ranging from table coasters to clear-plastic toilet seats. The bodies are recycled as pig feed. Similar but smaller industries trafficking in butterflies are found in Korea, Malaysia, Honduras, Hong Kong, and several African nations.

As repugnant as this trade may seem, though, it cannot be clearly linked to declining numbers in nature, except with birdwings and a handful of other rare species. In the first place, the reproductive abilities of most insects enable them to replace vast losses in nature. In this, the birdwings are exceptions. With most butterflies, the most efficient collectors could never remove more than a minute fraction of the number that will fall prey to birds, spiders, parasites, and disease. Furthermore, males—which have brighter colors and are more in demand—are usually more expendable than females, as each male can fertilize several mates. The famous blue *Morpho* butterflies of the American tropics enter the trade at the rate of some fifty million per year. Nearly all of these are the incredibly metallic males, and biologists figure the number could be doubled without harming the overall population. In the case of Taiwan's butterflies, the kinds and numbers seem to remain steady despite the massive trade. Thus, regulating collecting of these insects usually misses the basic problem altogether.

Of course, genuine collecting threats should be headed off. In order to monitor traffic that might be damaging, for instance, conservationists have placed the Apollo parnassian butterfly of the Alps, along with all of the birdwings, on Appendix II of the Convention on International Trade in Endangered Species of Flora and Fauna, a treaty for regulating the trade in rare animals and plants.

Very often, though, trade regulation or collecting laws tend to become smoke screens for serious habitat issues. In Malaysia, Raja Brooke's birdwing, a gorgeous black-and-jade creature, receives paper protection from the government. Meanwhile, its crucial forest habitats have been progressively destroyed, largely by government-approved projects. Having passed laws restricting collecting, officials feel they have discharged their responsibilities for butterfly conservation. Then, they turn a blind eye to habitat loss. Habitat loss is by far the more critical issue. All animals depend on habitat.

If habitats change, the animals must change as well, or leave, or die. Usually they die, since suitable alternative habitat may be occupied or out of reach. Today, butterflies are losing ground daily, but the first butterfly extinction caused and recorded by people was that of the English large copper. A glorious, fiery creature of the fens, it died a slow death over the fifteen hundred years it took to drain the vast marshes of East Anglia. The large copper finally passed from the English scene in the mid-1800s. At about the same time, American entomologists were lamenting the decline of the Xerces blue and other dune butterflies of the San Francisco peninsula. "Between German chickens and Irish hogs," wrote a California lepidopterist to his counterpart in the Midwest, "no insect can exist besides louse or flea." Now the large copper is considered threatened throughout its range in Europe, and the Xerces blue became extinct altogether during the 1940s due to urban development.

Even saving habitat may not be enough, however. The US Fish and Wildlife Service recently purchased some of the last San Francisco Bay dune habitats for an endangered butterfly, Lange's metalmark, but experience elsewhere shows that this laudable step is no guarantee that the species will survive. Scientists in England, the birthplace of butterfly conservation, had a hard lesson in this just two years ago. To save a species called the large blue, they set aside several of this butterfly's prime habitats as reserves. These areas were fenced, protected from grazing, and wardened against collectors. Yet the English large blue became extinct in 1979.

What went wrong? The bizarre life history of the large blue has long been known. The caterpillars of the blue feed on wild thyme at first, then drop to the ground where ants find them and carry them to their nests. Then the larvae of the butterflies become carnivorous, feeding upon the larvae of the ants. In exchange, the butterfly larvae secrete a honeydew that the ants devour. The rest of the life cycle occurs underground until the adult butterfly crawls to the surface, mates, and deposits her eggs on thyme the following summer. The species therefore relies upon both the ants and the thyme.

Recently, Jeremy Thomas of the Institute of Terrestrial Ecology (ITE) in Dorset, England, probed this life history more deeply and found some surprises. Earlier observers, he found, failed to appreciate two facts: only one kind of red ant was suitable, and the thyme had to grow in a particular density. In the old days, grazing by sheep and rabbits kept the vegetation in the right condition for the right ants. But the sheep were fenced out, the rabbits died of myxomatosis, and the turf was taken over by coarse grasses. Under these conditions, the wrong species of ants prospered, and the caterpillars of the large blue failed to survive. By the time the proper management formula had been worked out, the large blue was so scarce that two consecutive years of unfavorable weather resulted in its extinction.

Such studies have led to the salvation of other English butterflies, but before research can begin, it is necessary to know just where a rare butterfly lives. Collectors are commonly secretive and old records are unreliable. In England, a Butterfly Recording Scheme, begun by John Heath of ITE, maps the known distribution of all native species in great detail. Hundreds of amateur recorders help to chart the changing fortunes of British butterflies. Surveys of rare species always begin with these maps.

For all their value, though, surveys and research are hardly enough to offset habitat loss. With the odds stacked in favor of agriculture and development, what can be done to help? Fortunately, several conservation groups are working to save habitats. Among them is the International Union for Conservation of Nature and Natural Resources (IUCN), which identifies top priorities in international butterfly and moth conservation. Its highest priority of all: saving the Mexican wintering grounds of the monarch butterfly.

Such attempts to conserve habitat or, for that matter, to regulate trade, are doomed, however, unless they also consider the needs of people. Where human problems get attention, a great deal can be accomplished, and Papua New Guinea is a good case in point. Since independence in 1975, sweeping reforms have completely changed the butterfly trade there. Now, the seven rarest birdwing species are protected by law, and any collectors are heavily fined. Sale of other insects for profit is limited to citizens, and foreign collectors have even been deported. All insect sales are managed by the government-sponsored Insect Farming and Trading Agency, which returns all profits to the villagers without middleman charges. This income provides incentive to save the forest.

Finally, reserves are being set aside for special insects as well as other plants and animals. Managed by local people with professional guidance, these areas permit traditional resource use but protect the resource at the same time. One reserve benefits the Queen Alexandra's birdwing, the largest butterfly in the world, with a wingspan that sometimes exceeds one foot. Oil palm plantations are banned there, and so are timber concessions.

Papua New Guinea's marketing system is especially notable. Professional extension agents and ecologists serve the native participants while seeking ways to conserve the insect resource. Two birdwings, which are still legal to sell, along with many other species, are now exclusively raised instead of caught. Butterfly farmers grow caterpillar food plants in their own gardens, attract the females to lay on them and rear the offspring with care. Half are released, the other half sold to the agency. Eventually, the seven rare birdwings may also be farmed and made available on this basis, but only after their life cycles are understood.

Perhaps it is not so surprising to find these progressive actions on behalf of butterflies in a place so remote and undeveloped as Papua New Guinea. The island's butterflies are the most fabulous anywhere, and here the people have a special intimacy with nature in their village life. To my knowledge, Papua New Guinea is the only country in the world to specify insect conservation as a national objective in its constitution.

Shortly before we left, Sarah, Angus, and I stopped at the remote island of Misima where we visited the local butterfly farmer, a lad of seventeen named Isakiel. So successful was Isakiel in rearing the beautiful blue-green birdwing that inhabits Misima, that he was able to buy a brand-new bicycle, one of only a few on the island. After displaying his carefully tended caterpillar vines, he took us to see the birdwing habitat above his village. It was one of a dozen sites we were to recommend as reserves. In these protected enclaves, wild female birdwings will always be available to lay eggs on Isakiel's vines.

On Misima, as on Nimoa, butterflies have changed human lives for the better.

They are a cultural and economic resource, and because of that, they will survive.

The Niche of a Naturalist

(Orion, 1982)

When the Orion Nature Book Review *first became* Orion *magazine, I proposed a column to serve as a regular voice for natural history. The idea was adopted, but there were too many cooks at the pot, each with a different idea as to what the column should be. This first one expressed my thoughts on overcoming alienation, and suggested where the column might go. But it never got a chance. After the third dispiriting effort, which satisfied none of us, the column died a natural death. All the more surprising was that I was many years later again asked to write a column for* Orion. *This time I was given my head, and it ran for fifty-two consecutive issues over ten years, before being collected in the OSU Press book* The Tangled Bank: Writings from Orion.

I grew up on the wrong side of town. From the looks of the neighborhood, one might not have thought so. For me, though, the distinction was not one of class. I was a young butterfly hunter, and the Front Range canyons to the west of Denver are the scene of a butterfly ball, all summer long. But I lived on the prairie side of town, and those canyons might as well have been in Tibet. How I envied a friend who lived in a foothills suburb. He had only to walk out his door to see green hairstreak butterflies on Green Mountain.

I had to take my Rockies when I could get them. Mountain excursions had to be fitted into my father's fishing trips or family drives, which usually started so late in the afternoon that thundershowers already threatened to put the butterflies down. I drooled over the mountain ecology dioramas in the Denver Museum of Natural History and wistfully watched Mount Evans, which loomed ever so far away across the city. Unable to visit the mountains at will, I regarded myself as truly remote from nature.

After a few summers of such frustration, I discovered that the prairie ditches and leftover patches of grassland near my home offered their own attractions. Olympia marble wings, goatweed emperors, and chocolate, eye-spotted, wood nymphs dwelt there, along with other plains butterflies. The nearby Highline Canal infected me with a prairie mystique that I have carried with me ever since.

In later teen years when mountain trips became more practical, I would even worry, while in the mountains, about what I was missing back home on the plains. These early experiences taught me a lesson I have always valued: remoteness from nature is mostly a state of mind.

Of course, some conditions do isolate people from wildlife and natural landscapes. But I believe that almost anyone can get close to nature, given the will, and that everyone will benefit from doing so.

Barriers between people and nature seem to be of five kinds: distance, physical disability, poverty, lack of time, and attitude. Let's look at each of these, to see how high the walls really are, and how they might best be overcome.

Distance can seem to represent an obstacle, but, as I have shown, separation from major wild areas need not prevent us from communing with nature close to home. It is often just a matter of subtle versus more spectacular rewards. Virtually all kinds of landscapes, urban as well as rural or wild, constitute habitats for some kinds of wildlife. Wherever you are, you should be able to make contact.

Take the city environment. Urban wildlife is becoming a major topic of study and interpretation in many cities, and the townscape is being appreciated for what it is: a complex, if highly disturbed, ecosystem. In his modern classic, *The Unofficial Countryside,* Richard Mabey celebrated the natural pleasures to be found in the postindustrial wastelands, old canals, bomb craters, and vacant lots of London. His thesis is that the city-dweller need only look around with imagination to discover sights normally thought to be reserved for the country rambler. In *Enchanted Streets,* Leonard Dubkin tells how he experienced the same truth when, as a depressed and unemployed Chicagoan, he found mental solace in observing the insects and birds of the city's parks and shorelines. A third volume in this vein, John Kieran's *Natural History of New York,* reveals the New World's largest city as a reasonable niche for a discriminating naturalist, and others have come to the same conclusion. A noted entomologist, Frank E. Lutz, wrote in *A Lot of Insects* about the more than fourteen hundred species inhabiting his urban New York garden. Recently, butterfly counters have tallied over forty species in a rocky, weedy enclave of Manhattan known as Inman Hill Park. Birdwatchers abound in Central Park, and Jamaica Bay in Queens offers birders not only numerous birds, but also a dash of the flavor of the mid-Atlantic coastal marsh.

Some of my most memorable nature rambles have taken place in cities. No park is so manicured as to be without interest, and every urban waterfront holds adventure for the naturalist. Rafts of western grebes and rhinoceros auklets bob among the ships in Seattle's harbor. All Puget Sound is in the waves that lap against the wharves. Canoeing among the docks reveals an astonishing array of marine creatures that defy the pollution and abrasion of the busy port. Starfish and anemones cling to the pilings, and jellyfish balloon in the wake of the great ferries.

Of course city floras and faunas are impoverished, compared to those of wildlands, and the urban ethos never entirely retreats into the background. But even the settings of the natural world may be found in some towns. From the tallgrass remnant of Wolf Road Prairie in South Chicago to the boreal birchwoods of Moscow's parks and periphery, the green gestalt of nature makes itself apparent in unlikely places the world over. The unofficial countryside can never replace the real thing, but no city-bound soul is completely cut off from the natural world.

Physical disability may cause a more real separation from nature. For the deaf, there is no dawn chorus; for the blind, no fall color. The paraplegic cannot sally forth at will, and the spastic may need help with a handlens. Help is the operative word. It is available for the disabled seeking contact with nature, but they must be aware of it, and ask for and accept it. For those who do, like my legally blind friend who bicycles through the national parks of the world, the barriers tumble to a surprising degree. Naturalists generally take keen pleasure in aiding others. The Year of the Disabled (1981) saw many new outdoor programs and facilities introduced.

To appreciate nature as fully as possible, the disabled need to learn to use those abilities and senses they have. That which cannot be seen can sometimes be felt, heard, tasted, or smelled. Jewelweed, for example, audibly pops its seeds into the air, and certain ants taste like lemon drops. Many butterflies are scented (male mountain parnassians smell like Fritos), and their tarsi tickle; I use these features to interpret butterflies for the blind.

It is harder for the bedridden or very ill to get close to nature. Yet they can have something of nature brought to them, or perhaps they can be taken outdoors just to breathe, hear, or feel the breeze. All nature exists on a zephyr, for those attuned to her.

Like the unwell, the financially disadvantaged may be unable to make contact with nature, but not for reasons of accessibility. For the very poor, pursuit of nature ceases to be a priority. Indeed, where people must confront natural disasters and animal competitors in order to get their food, nature becomes the adversary. (This is an important concern for naturalists, for as long as a part of society has inadequate resources, the survival of natural areas will be in jeopardy. The growth of a viable world land ethic will require a closeness to nature that economic injustice denies.) For those, however, who are at least adequately fed, clothed, and sheltered, nature study still offers the last great, free entertainment, and it is good for a lifetime.

Of all the isolates from nature, it is the time-paupers for whom I have least sympathy. Conservation agencies and groups are full of martyrs who no longer "have time" for the field. If activism, or any other pursuit, becomes so all-consuming that it comes between nature and the naturalist, it isn't worth it. Not surprisingly, conservationists who make time for nature are far more effective at their work and lives than those who do not. Workaholics in any field always benefit in health and mind by trading an hour at their desks for one out of doors. This is a problem for self-help, and it can be easily overcome.

Inner remoteness from nature is an attitude that is harder to change. The nub of the problem is the same everywhere and for everyone: The world is too much with us. We are too preoccupied to hear nature's music. During a recent visit to Lake Louise in Banff National Park, I was struck by the sharp differences in visitors' attitudes. Some were clearly swept away by the scene. But a surprising number scanned the superb lake-and-glacier vista, snapped the obligatory photos, and then, as their eyes glazed over, resumed conversations about the attributes of their rental cars or about the distance from their room to the ice machine. The only solution for this kind of alienation is consciously to clear the mind and make it ready for natural stimuli. For some, it takes a major spectacle to bring home nature's reality—a visit to the Serengeti, the Great Barrier Reef, or a monarch butterfly grove. For others, subtler treatment may help: an experience entirely new and fresh to the senses, such as watching for the first time the sun set over the sea, getting dripping wet with the moss in a rain forest glade, or settling into the hollow of a cottonwood tree in a hailstorm, or stroking a snake or smelling a flower. The important thing is purposefully to expose oneself to such stimuli. Thoreau knew that it did not take big thrills to set one free, but simple sensations—such as the minor adventure of which he confessed, "There is no use reporting it to the Royal Society."

In most instances, we create our own remoteness from nature. Overcoming isolation from the real world—that of glaciers, petals, feathers—presents a challenge. Barriers must be surmounted, nictitating eyelids opened for good, imagination stoked and fanned. The wonder in all this is that nature is the best cure for all the conditions that keep us apart from her. We need only once to experience nature with any sense at all to know that we never need grow remote from her again.

Close Encounters
A Naturalist Looks at the Ethics of First Contact
(*Seattle, 1988*)

The Bigfoot phenomenon and traditions intrigued me ever since I took Bill Holm's Northwest Indian art and culture classes at the University of Washington. Eventually this led to my book Where Bigfoot Walks: Crossing the Dark Divide. *But well before that, I was concerned with the hypothetical moral and ethical questions of our behavior upon meeting the hitherto unknown. Grover Krantz was professor of anthropology at Washington State University.*

You've all seen the movie. An unknown life form arrives stage left—space alien, subterranean, mermaid, whatever—and the reaction of the authorities is . . . well, reactionary. The sympathies of the audience lie firmly with the interloper, who tragically perishes at the hands of the army, science, or villagers with pitchforks and shotguns. In the end we feel a communal sense of moral indignation and pity for a harmless creature misunderstood and feared. And the conclusion, every time, is that it didn't have to happen. The lucky ones, such as E.T. and the mermaid in *Splash*, escape, but only after hair-raising episodes of cloth-headed persecution.

After a half century of movies with the same basic script, we still suspect that our baser motivations would prevail and we would extend pitchforks instead of open arms to any alien who had the misfortune to land in our midst. I suppose the theme survives because it never ceases to jerk tears and sell tickets, but does anyone doubt that we really would react this way, given a genuine opportunity? Or that we would feel any regret about it afterward?

The issue has been one for scriptwriters and dreamers so far, since no outrageous species have dared to show up, so it has been a matter of no real consequence. Now we are presented with the very real possibility of the discovery of a hitherto unknown presence. And how do you suppose we shall behave?

Unlike Grover Krantz, I cannot say that I believe in Sasquatch outright. My biologist's background makes me wait for evidence to be sure. Nor can I say that

I would be willing to kill a Sasquatch in order to acquire evidence. Like Krantz, I believe that the balance of available facts suggests the presence of a large primate in the Northwest, and I would like to know for sure. But I would rather stick with plaster casts and hopes and dreams than plug one. Here's why.

One night in 1968, I camped near the Plains of Abraham on Mount St. Helens, in the vicinity of Ape Canyon, site of one of the first (and most dramatic) reported encounters with Bigfoot. I planned to look for tracks in the snow in the morning. That night, unable to sleep because of a muscle injury, I lay awake listening to the night. I was comfortable with all of the sounds, confident that I knew their makers. Then a soft cluster of howls arose, becoming a string of piercing yips, finally a plangent array of cries and whistles. I listened, rapt, and I remembered. When I arrived home, I found a copy of *National Wildlife* in my mail with the report of a recent St. Helens expedition in search of Sasquatch. Tracks had been found and recordings made, believed to be of the beast in question. The description of the sounds matched what I'd heard. Now, we might have heard the same owl, felid, or canid, but I knew the owls, the cats, the dogs, the other sounds of the Northwest forest at night. This was something new.

Later, when I took Bill Holm's classes in Northwest Indian art at the University of Washington, I was deeply struck by something he said: that, while the Kwakiutls, the Haida, the Bella Bellas, and the rest had given up literal belief in most of their "supernatural" totems such as Sisiutl the sea monster, they retain uniformly a belief in two forest creatures that you won't find in the field guides—Bokbokwallinooksiway (or Dzonokwa) and Bukwus, the Wild Woman and the Wild Man of the woods. Many feel that these represent Sasquatch.

Finally, once in The Dalles, Oregon, I met Peter Byrne at his Bigfoot Information Center (now defunct). The former tiger hunter and Yeti tracker, an Irishman from India via Britain, had documented many of the sounder Sasquatch reports in recent years, much as Krantz has done. I was so impressed with his approach and his evidence that I invited him to speak at the Yale School of Forestry and Environmental Studies (I was on the seminar committee that year). We had to get the permission of not only the dean, but Vice President Chauncey as well. He gave it, Byrne came, and when he had finished, a whole family unit of distinguished Yale primatologists, anthropologists, and biologists went out scratching their heads, unwilling to admit that they were completely skeptical about a large hominoid in the West.

They did agree, however, that if the animal exists, it is probably just that: a hominoid. A hominid, even—a member of the same family we belong to, the

Hominidae. Therein lies the rub, or the worst of it. We have already proved ourselves capable of truly bestial acts against creatures with whom we share most of our DNA—chimps and gorillas. But we define them (probably artificially) as Pongidae—the great apes—a different family. Sasquatch is likely even more closely related to us.

Should we kill one Bigfoot, there will be a blood-rush for specimens: museums, zoos, roadside attractions, labs—all will want their own. And like the great auk, Sasquatch might not survive this flood of lethal attention, once we learned that it did indeed exist, and where to find it. Already, bands of California fortune hunter–types are said to be gearing up to "get Bigfoot" with a survivalist's arsenal of heavy weapons.

On the other hand, capture or killing of a specimen would cause the Endangered Species Act (ESA) to kick in almost certainly. This would require federal habitat protection and complication of logging that would make the spotted owl seem like a gnat. So far, the Office of Endangered Species (nearly moribund under Reagan anyway) has refused to list Sasquatch pending proof of its existence, despite petitions to do so. But there is a federal precedent. The Army Corps of Engineers, in a surprisingly progressive turn, listed Sasquatch as a probable member of the state's fauna in an *Environmental Atlas of Washington*. So why can't the Department of the Interior follow that lead?

Here's the main point: if we proscribe the killing of humans, what about hominids? Professor Krantz may resent the professional opprobrium he receives as a Bigfoot believer, fallout that simply demonstrates the pre-Copernican attitudes of many scientists. He doesn't deserve their closed-minded contempt. But if Krantz dislikes the appellation of crank, he would appreciate even less that of murderer. For if he kills, or causes to be killed, a hominid, then a murderer he will surely be in the minds of many people.

I favor preventive listing by the ESA, and protective state and local regulations such as the statute enacted by Skamania County commissioners to protect Bigfoot in the region of most sightings. The penalties would have to be harsh enough to prevent the act being worthwhile. Even a $20,000 fine under the ESA would easily be recouped by media rights and museum sales. I favor calling the crime what it would certainly be: manslaughter.

Once such measures were taken, then we might seek dead specimens or photo documentation. Tranquilization and capture with release in mind could be considered, but that would be risky, since many animals are lost in such studies; and what about the creature's rights? Following widespread acceptance that Sasquatch existed, we should then act to determine and protectively manage the critical habitat. At the very least, a protocol should be adopted for the possible eventual encounter of remarkable new species of life. Otherwise, we might as well ask Hollywood to script the news release in advance, for we know the ending.

We have here, if we have anything, the greatest gift of evolution in our time, just as Mount St. Helens was the greatest gift of geology, and in the same place. If Sasquatches exist, we should cherish them. Perhaps in that manner, we might learn how to treat one another better. Or shall we begin this new relationship through the sights of a high-powered rifle, or the jaws of a great steel trap? And, finally, if we condone the murder of our ancestors, how far can we be from the brink?

No Soil Required

(Left Bank, 1993)

Sometimes all it takes is a word or a phrase to kick off an essay. It wasn't long after George H. W. Bush's invasion of Iraq, and logging was again intensifying in the hills of home. Mortality was much on our minds, and when I learned of Weyerhaeuser's bogus bonsai, which "eliminates the need for water, light, or nutrients," I knew I had to write about it.

Time was when we were fairly clear about the difference between life and death. Always the artificial has been with us, but without pretense. The plastic flower in the graveyard fools no one, nor is it meant to. So it is with the lumps underneath; we may speak of "afterlives," and some feel spirits among them, but there is no doubt really: the people we plant, like the fake flowers that mark the spot, are dead. We who remain, and the weeds that creep over the graves in spite, are alive. The line has always seemed, to me, a sharp one.

Now, as we rush to embrace death in so many ways, that once-clean distinction is blurring. Of course there are the so-called heroic measures for supporting the life of the living dead. There is the titanic battle to position the moment human life bestirs, at conception or birth or somewhere in between. These are not new. But now we find muddy ground as well when it comes to defining what, indeed, constitutes an organism—a living thing. Some say viruses are lifeless until they kill; others insist computers are alive and will soon reproduce. Is the earth a living thing? Is an anthill an organism, like a colonial jellyfish? And what about shopping malls? I've heard it proposed that these are the coming evolutionary units, with consumers as cells and products as nutrients.

Actually, it was in a shopping mall that I lost my footing in the slick and fuzzy DMZ beyond life as we knew it. Waiting for a tire change at Sears, I roamed the dreary aisles, seeking a manner of spending the afternoon that wouldn't offend the ghost of Thoreau, who said, "As if you could waste time without injuring eternity." Giving cursory inspection to a vendor's table of Southwestern figurines and other dross, my eye raked something that looked alive. Tucked among the song dogs and shamans, there were plants—cacti, succulents, bromeliads. They offered a moment's diversion to this fish out of water, but their removal from their habitats to this space station seemed even bleaker than my own.

Then I noticed a basket of what looked like skinny, greenish, dried-out spiders, or curly urchins. The sign read "AIR PLANTS—Tillandsias—a living plant that needs no soil. Just a little mist a couple of times a week and your love and they will grow and have babies." A suitable plant for malls, I thought—nature reduced to little parcels of weirdness, like lava lamps and fiber-optic sculptures—trophies for jaded shoppers to take home and love, with no care required, no messy soil. Well, who was I to sneer? At least they were alive, and we can all use more life around us. But what a life, I couldn't help thinking: stuffed into an ashtray on someone's TV or perched among the seashells atop the toilet, sharing the shower's spray.

The air plants reminded me of something else, and it picked at me until, back home, I found it in a file: a color brochure advertising "The Windswept Bonsai—a great gift idea!" The flyer pictured a little juniper rooted in a pot of gravel, atop a grand piano. "This incredible real bonsai stays beautiful without water or light," it read, "yet retains a carefree, natural look and fragrance." The trees, after being grown and sculpted in a nursery, are treated with a cell-replacement process that eliminates the need for water, light, or nutrients. In other words, they kill and pickle it. But nowhere does the brochure mention that your authentic bonsai is not alive. It does quote Joyce Kilmer on trees ("I think that I shall never see / a poem lovely as a tree"). The Windswept Bonsai Interiorized™ by Infinitree International. It is a product of the Weyerhaeuser Company, the Tree-Growing People, creator of Incredible Real Forests. And it is dead.

Now, I've always thought that the desire to have plants around one had something to do with the need, or at least the urge, to consort with other living things. We, the living, have traditionally sought life for company: friends, neighbors, pets, houseplants, gardens, yard birds, wildlife; even zoos and aquaria present the spectacle and the comfort of life, however out of context. Surrounding ourselves with active organisms of our own and other species, it seems to me, is both a means of staving off the morbidity that awaits us all, and a way to affirm our passing citizenship in the country of the living. But if you can make a strange plant reproduce out of any context of nature whatever, then why do you need such a context at all? Apparently you don't: you can have Incredible Real Trees in your living room or boardroom that needn't even transpire. Which implies that you could have animals that don't respire. Then the mannequins and shoppers at the mall could become fully interchangeable at last.

I remember in the vestibule of the huge gymnasium at Yale the original bull-dog mascot, Handsome Dan, is preserved, stuffed in a glass cabinet: "Bulldog, Bulldog, Rah Rah Rah, E-li-Yale." With the help of Weyerhaeuser, or perhaps Hormel, some future mascot could be preserved in such a way as to present a more lifelike visage than that moth-eaten relic. Rah.

Home from the mall, I sit on my front porch and try to regain the sense of a border I can believe. Here, it isn't hard. I am surrounded by the stuff of that which is living, the stiffness of that which is not. This iron trap, for example, is not alive. This poor mole, squeezed nearly in half but still soft velvet taupe, pink-tipped at both blunt ends, its massive digger's hands still pliable—it's Incredibly Real, but it is dead too. Love in the mist will not make it have babies, which is the point of its being in the trap. But the blowfly that keeps trying to land on the mole to lay its eggs is alive. Its maggots, too, will be living, for it can make babies with nothing but love and flesh.

Beside the mole is a cactus; it's out of context too, but at least in soil and sur-rounded by other plants; and just now, it's making a wave of big rose flowers. It is undeniably alive. In this lifeless tank, feeding on brambles that are dead but were recently living, is a giant Australian leaf insect: alive, and making babies—or at least eggs, that need to be hot and misted to hatch but don't care about love. This iridescent wood-boring beetle, emerald and gold against the white pillar, the wis-teria climbing the pillar from below, and the cat sleeping at the base of the pillar, are all alive. But the pillar is dead as a post.

As for me, I am alive and breathing the mist still, if not making babies. I have not been Interiorized™ yet. Nor have I been fooled. I am surrounded by life and death, and it is all as it should be: death is seldom obscene unless out of season, or masquerading as something else. It is clear to me which is which.

Still, there is the compost pile . . . beneath the living hornbeam trees, bounded by a roundel of dead bricks. Only here, where the mole will go, do I lose my bear-ings—where the slugs and the eggshells, the clippings and bacteria, the moles and the maggots, the worms and the dirt all mingle in such a maze that the gelid breath of Death itself goes hot and the stillness of the quick comes fluid and lithe. The compost heap: region of resurrection, where the living soil arises from the wreckage of what went before. That is where I lose all sense of sides.

Yes, they argue over whether the earth is alive or not. In the end, perhaps it is only earth that is both living and dead all at once, where that mortal boundary at last dissolves. In the soil—which, it seems, we shall no longer need.

Receding from Grief

(*Orion*, 1994)

I'd been traveling with other writers on several of the Orion Society's Forgotten Language Tours. It seemed that everywhere we went, we met people mourning places that they'd loved and lost, and we were no different. So when Orion *magazine's editors decided to focus an issue on the theme of loss and grief, I chose to address this universal hurt on behalf of damaged lands. Years later, when I lost Thea, I realized that I had also been practicing for expressing the deepest griefs we can know. The final line echoes a favorite sentence of mine from Bill Kittredge's great memoir* Hole in the Sky: *"Out, away to the world with hope."*

Some of the keenest love I've ever known has been that I've felt for damaged lands. It seems easy to love a wild place whose essential complexion differs little from its state before we found it. Broken country—polluted, raked, and scraped, and changed in light and heavy ways—demands a different kind of ardor that few seem eager to give. Yet we cannot throw the land away, and without our attention amounting to affection, the used places stack up like so many auto bodies: abandoned, cauterized by asphalt, or fenced off as Superfund sites. After all, these are the very places where many of us first connected with nature. They deserve something better, like love.

My attachment to battered land has led me to write about some subtle places: a range of modest hills, once thickly wooded, the site of heavy timber harvest for generations; the ragged hems of the High Plains on Denver's backside, where overeager, underwatered agriculture beat back the prairie, and where I grew up among millions of other latter-day settlers. I have known many places of greater beauty, wildness, and ecological wholeness than these secondhand lands. I am often asked why I chose to focus my attention on soggy, logged-off hills and a muddy flatland ditch, instead of the high Rockies or the wild Olympics.

My reply stammers about in the territory of responsibility, murmurs our duty to care for the landscapes that have nurtured us at their own great expense. But that is a purely intellectual response; there is more to it than that. My penchant

for so-called waste ground also involves at least three reactions of an emotional
nature.

First, I am struck that these injured spots are the very places where people
have lived, loved, reproduced, and made a living off the body of the land. Like
any other species, we consume elements of our own surroundings. We are learning to live more lightly, but up until now the marks of our successful habitation
have been mine tailings, clear-cuts, smokestacks, and turgid streams, as much as
pleasant parks and nice neighborhoods. True, some livelihoods (such as high-
elevation pastorage in the Alps) have sustained both beauty and diversity. But
since the industrial revolution, nearly all of our livings have created and depended
on desolated landscapes. This offends and repels us—yet, how is it possible to
hate the very land that has given rise to families, schools, and communities? I
think it is this stamp of humanity that first attracts me to hand-me-down habitats
like the Willapa Hills and the High Line Canal.

My second thought comes from a sense of the commonality of loss. The pain
felt by naturalists when habitats are ruined differs little from that experienced
by working residents of such places, when the living sours and they must leave.
This goes nowhere toward resolving land-use battles, but admitting it might help
soften the deep distrust between rivals for the land's love.

Third, I have always felt that when we grieve for a tree or a canyon or a hillside
or a marsh that we particularly loved and lost, the feeling is scarcely distinguish-
able from mourning the passing of loved ones of our own kind. Call it landlorn.
A heresy, this, in some circles, leading to charges that one cares more for animals and plants than people. That simple reaction misses the point. Grief is grief.
When something's gone that mattered, the hole hurts. How are degrees of loss to
be compared?

You'd think that such a conviction would steer me away from damaged lands,
where one confronts a constant legacy of loss. In fact, we face that everywhere: no
place is immune to change, much of it human-sponsored, most of it depreciative.
The hermit ensconced on the edge of the Olympics or Canyonlands will keen all
the shriller for that which is taken, because it was thought to be safe; whereas the
admirer of the humbler localities, where we've already done our worst, sees every
act of survival and regeneration as miraculous, every grassblade a gift.

This does not argue for stoic acceptance of the erosion of diversity—far from
it. Rather it counsels to look up from our activism long enough to appreciate
what's left. Loving blighted locales does not insulate the lover from loss; but, like
embracing the community of our own species with all its inherent tragedy, it

helps maintain perspective. If that view is downhill, comfort can at least be found in the knowledge that today's vacant lot will be tomorrow's wilderness—as in Robinson Jeffers's "November Surf":

The cities gone down, the people fewer and the hawks more numerous
The rivers mouth to source pure; when the two-footed
Mammal, being some ways one of the nobler animals, regains
The dignity of room, the value of rareness.

If the land and the people come together in our feelings over the loss of each, then how we treat our grief over both should bear some connection. Although frustrated by modern interment procedures, what could demonstrate this more than returning the body to enrich the soil while sanctifying the life of the beloved lost? When a dear friend died way too soon not long ago, a true gardener of plants and people, her husband offered portions of her ashes to those who came to honor and mourn her. The little seed packets went away to many gardens, paths, and wild spots, helping to heal her friends' loss as Elaine nourished the next plants and animals in line to live.

I was completely taken by surprise at one way my own grieving for persons and places came together. *The Thunder Tree* celebrates the urban wildland that made me who I am. Spontaneously, entirely ex-outline, the essays devoted to vanishing habitats and their butterflies became the same pieces in which I confronted the deaths of my parents. As I wrote, I came to realize the absence of any clear distinction between the extension of love and the reconciliation of loss, whether for places or people.

I believe that all the sadness in the world belongs to us. The land does not grieve. But as long as we live on the land, and among others, we shall know a state of permanent grief, for loss is continual, and always with us. After all, we are mortal. And as Aldo Leopold reminded us, the penalty of knowing nature is to live in a "world of wounds."

Yet there is a balm, and it comes from the same source. F. Scott Fitzgerald, in *Tender Is the Night*, wrote that "Receding from a grief, it seems necessary to retrace the same steps that brought us there." That way is out, to the land, and love.

In Praise of the Tangled Bank
(*Illahee*, 1994)

The title of this piece foreshadowed the name of my second regular column for Orion *and the subsequent book comprising those essays. It was also the first of four columns I wrote for the magazine* Illahee, *under the title "Gray's River Almanac." It was a good, free form for me, and I include all four here. University of Washington politics cut the magazine, and the column, short, a sad fact on which I express my opinion in the fourth and final column, "Elegy Written in a Country Farmyard."*

There is danger in diversity. Whenever we invite the different to dinner, we risk the discomfiture of confrontation and the possible need to change—our views, our habits, our strategies for life. And there is comfort in homogeneity. If we can keep or contrive to have everything the same, we avoid the need to adapt. Institutions seek to impose standardization for just this reason: when there are no surprises, you can keep things in hand—expenses, employees, products, profits.

Homogenization, however, flouts the second law of thermodynamics. Particles love a vacuum, and entropy will increase. Keeping the lid on through control and conformity always fails in the end. Entities that stifle variety tend to collapse from without or revolt from within. It works that way with business, with people, and with ecosystems. Selection will out. The inability to change, after all, is the stuff of evolution.

It is often said the other way around—that natural selection is premised on the ability to change. But if all organisms were equally adept at meeting the challenges of change, evolution would stop; or at least progress with only a change of costume instead of cast. As I see things, it is those who will not or cannot change who provide nature with its opportunities for elaboration.

It all goes back to the tangled bank. In one of the loveliest passages in natural history literature, Charles Darwin began and ended the final paragraph of *The Origin of Species* thus:

> It is interesting to contemplate a tangled bank, clothed with many plants of many kinds, with birds singing on the bushes, with various insects flitting about, and with worms

crawling through the damp earth, and to reflect that these elaborately constructed forms, so different from each other, and dependent upon each other in so complex a manner, have all been produced by laws acting around us . . . and that, whilst this planet has gone cycling on according to the fixed law of gravity, from so simple a beginning endless forms most beautiful and most wonderful have been, and are being, evolved.

In my simplemindedness, I have never doubted the virtue of the tangled bank. Quite literally, few visions have ever moved, intrigued, and attracted me as much as a chaotic slab of habitat. Vladimir Nabokov, novelist and lepidopterist, put it this way in his memoir *Speak, Memory*:

> And the highest enjoyment of timelessness—in a landscape selected at random—is when I stand among rare butterflies and their foodplants. This is ecstasy, and behind the ecstasy is something else, which is hard to explain. It is like a momentary vacuum into which rushes all that I love. A sense of oneness with sun and stone. A thrill of gratitude to whom it may concern—to the contrapuntal genius of human fate or to tender ghosts humoring a lucky mortal.

The style and the terms of reference vary (diversity being its own reward, after all), but the elements are as constant as gravity: plants, animals, and substrate in all their glorious variety.

The tangled bank, however, is not universally beloved. Spring is the season when that sad fact becomes literally apparent: the growth season, when the richness of the flora once again flaunts its fervor and its power to clothe the damaged lands. The season, too, when spray trucks roll, blurting their venomous vapors onto roadside verges, causing the sensitive to roll up their windows and shut their vents, and twisting the plants of the banks into a bleached and contorted parody of growth.

Of course, the managers have their reasons, and most people agree that careful use of herbicides can be a tool for conservation. But according to a 1988 poll by the American Association of Highway and Transportation Officials, the Washington Department of Transportation (WDOT) ranked number one in the nation in chemical use. WDOT was also rated first in the reduction of acres of roadside treated mechanically. The agency refused to take part in the survey in 1989.

WDOT recently underwent an environmental review of its roadside spray program. The environmental impact statement promised reform and greater care, and WDOT's new management has embraced the principles of integrated pest management. An initiative has also been announced to make the state's right-of-ways more "wildlife friendly" in cooperation with Audubon chapters. All this is much to be applauded and encouraged.

Yet, again this spring I watched as spray crews blasted banks of native herbs and shrubs twenty feet and more from the actual roadside along State Route 4. Bad enough that the poison killed red flowering currant, oceanspray, and other desirable plants, but the herbicide shot right past as well, directly into the Columbia River and its productive sloughs west of Longview. This act violates state and federal law, for the product labels clearly warn against using the chemicals where runoff into fish waters might occur.

While everyone else is trying to save salmon and wetlands, WDOT routinely sprays ditches and waterways draining into fish-bearing rivers: this I observe, painfully, each spring. The old "brownout" spray line, promised by WDOT to be a thing of the past in favor of selective application, lives on in Cowlitz County and elsewhere. Along Highway 101 near Crescent Lake, in the Okanogan, and all over the state, I see banks of native flowers, shrubs, and trees herbicided where they represent no serious threat to the roadway or its users. We can only hope that WDOT's promises bring actual reform on the ground, not just in memos, speeches, and press releases.

Meanwhile, the growth season also brings helicopters swarming over commercial timberlands, loosing from their booms more clouds of herbicides to quell competing vegetation among the short-rotation pulp plantations euphemistically called "forests." Even these frequently denounced monocultures of dog-hair Douglas-fir and western hemlock clones could arrive at some ecologically meaningful structure, given time and natural recruitment of understory. Yet in the three or four decades they may stand, floristically cleansed with 2,4-D and other powerful preparations, they have no chance of diversification.

So when I roam the Willapa Hills around Gray's River and see the brown stripes across the miles of Cavenham, Hancock, Longfibre, and Weyerhaeuser timberlands, I see woods stripped of nitrogen-fixing alders in a nitrogen-poor region. I see fiber farms that hold as little potential for long-term, steady jobs for workers in the woods as they do for natural diversity. And I see a crime. You or I can shoot a single song sparrow or Wilson's warbler with a BB gun and be guilty of both a state misdemeanor and a federal violation. Yet Plum Creek, the "inventors of environmental forestry" according to company ads, can spray hundreds of acres of hardwoods and shrubs in peak songbird breeding season, displacing and killing numbers of protected birds and their food sources, with impunity.

These benighted forms of management by toxin remain among the embarrassments of an age when more sensitive land use is widely touted and sometimes even adopted. Vermont, a state of lush green growth like ours, controls roadside vegetation by judicious cutting. Manual brush control, where practiced, guarantees jobs and a selective approach to site preparation for reforestation. But commonsense approaches such as these mean lesser rewards for individuals and institutions whose bulk and bloat flow from an ever growing chemical dependency, who view plants as mere material backdrops ("good" or "bad"), and who resist diversity as if it were anathema. For them, the word herbicide should be recast to mean not only a substance but an act, like homicide: murder of the tangled bank.

I choose these examples to illustrate my point since they are particularly blatant and hurtful (spoiling, as they do, entire chunks of inoffensive habitat), but the signs of our collective fear of variety rune the landscape all around. Consider the fuss surrounding our tardy attempts to celebrate human diversity in public institutions. Admittedly, this process involves discomfort and the risk of error, as when entire canons are tossed onto the ash heap. Such a reaction can be just as destructive as the cultural myopia that brought it about. Yet the fact that anyone can still question the reality of social multiplicity—when the alternative is the sort of tribalism that is ripping up the world—shows that we have a long way to go before embracing the rich tangle of our own descent.

So it is with our more distant relatives, the other species. As the Endangered Species Act comes up for reauthorization, promising months of tedious hearings and tendentious rhetoric, we can only wonder that there are those who miss (or avoid) its basic intent. Naturally the impact of any sweeping legislation on human communities and economies should be examined and the results accommodated or ameliorated by all available remedies. But these "remedies" must not include enfeebling the act itself, or undermining its best possible results. The current rapture over "ecosystem management" (as opposed to "species management") will not sweeten the medicine. You cannot conserve ecosystems without identifying and caring for their individual components, which are species. Neither can you save species without attending to their habitats. The two goals are inseparable and their methods nearly identical, never mind the popular language of avoidance.

Shortly before writing this essay, I had the extreme and humbling pleasure of assisting a northern spotted owl researcher in a survey of nest sites in unprotected old-growth forest. The depth of black in the eyes of the owls, before they disappeared with their mice back into the shadows of the forest, mirrored the bottomlessness of our ignorance.

At breakfast in a nearby cafe before going afield, I'd overheard regulars sharing consternation over owls, murrelets, and the likes of me. A denizen of a turned-down timber town myself, I empathize with neighbors whose world is rapidly changing, their livelihoods dropping out from under them. But when one of the coffee drinkers summed his plaints, he said that soon the Gifford Pinchot National Forest would be dedicated to nothing but recreation and aesthetics— never mind that the president's forest plan will free up quite a bit of timber, if not as much as flowed downhill before Judge Dwyer's injunction. What disturbed me was not the exaggeration, which has an understandable basis in fear and real frustration. It was the lack of any recognition that the main reason for curtailing the harvest of old growth is the perpetuation of natural diversity.

Diversity just doesn't enter the picture for most people, and if it did, it wouldn't be fully understood. Recreation and aesthetics at least ring a bell. But natural variety for its own sake? The fact that disenchanted rural residents seldom share that value—and the fact that Congress can seriously question the very premises and tools of the strongest law ever passed to protect diversity—means that biologists and conservationists have done a rotten job of communicating their profound conviction that diversity is, indeed, its own reward.

Or perhaps such a thing cannot be communicated; perhaps it can only be felt. Darwin felt it; Nabokov felt it, and so did Rachel Carson. The logger who chooses to live in a wooded landscape and to work in a place that he rightfully expects to remain a working forest with all its parts intact (if not all in the same place at the same time) feels it. But the forces that drive standardization—of peoples, book-stores, and breweries; of forests, towns, and countrysides; of architectures and roadsides—just don't feel the love of the tangled bank.

Atop my ancient computer sits a bumper sticker sent me by a friend who spotted the Darwin fish on the back of my ancient car: "Honk if you love Darwin," it says. Regardless of our personal creation myth, whether it be found in sacred texts, native traditions, Western science, or Eastern mysticism, we should all honk and honk for the love of Darwin—or at least, for his love of nature's sublime complexity. For the danger of diversity is in its absence. As deep as forever and as dark as extinction, it lies in the shadow of sameness. Long live diversity's rainbow; long live the tangled bank.

Damning the Sacred

(Illahee, 1994)

Ellen Chu, editor of Illahee: Journal for the Northwest Environment, *and her colleague, Professor James Karr of the University of Washington's Institute for Environmental Studies, encouraged me to take on whatever issues were on my mind in "Gray's River Almanac." As a member of the Natural Heritage Advisory Council, I came up against acute conflicts between urban and rural ideas of conservation and land use. Together with the rise of the "green theology" movement, these differing values suggested the title, and the essay followed.*

"So what's the big deal 'bout this goddamn snail sniffer?"

Big Bill Rose, my brother Tom's redheaded boyhood friend, works for Union Pacific and lives in a mountain canyon west of Denver. Tom and I were visiting him some years ago, and the talk came around to Two Forks Dam. This proposed behemoth, since canceled, would have flooded the nearby canyons and mountain villages. Bill wasn't sure he was for it because places and trout waters and people he knew would be affected. But he couldn't see why the Tellico Dam in Tennessee should be derailed by a dumb little fish, the snail darter—or "snail sniffer," as he called it. "Hell, you can't even eat it," he snorted.

I thought of Bill and his snail sniffer recently on a visit to a sage-steppe remnant in eastern Washington known as Sagebrush Flat. The thirty-six-hundred-acre site is considered the largest and best piece of habitat left in Washington for the pygmy rabbit. This regional endemic and state endangered species formerly occupied a wide region of sagelands, but agricultural changes have edited the small lagomorph out of most of its former range. Our group, the state-appointed Natural Heritage Advisory Council, was surveying the area as a proposed state natural area preserve. We were accompanied by resource agency officials familiar with local cattlemen who would lose their grazing leases if a preserve were established. I asked a man from the Department of Natural Resources how the pygmy rabbit is regarded in local cafes and bars. I wondered if it drew the same blend of bemused contempt and outright derision that the northern spotted owl evokes in turned-down timber towns. "How do you think?" he asked. "To most folks around here, some damn little rabbit is a lot less important than a steer, to put it mildly. Bunnies don't pay the bills."

I've heard similar attitudes toward federally endangered Columbia white-tailed deer in Wahkiakum County, where good bottomlands were taken out of farming for a national wildlife refuge; toward endangered butterflies in the way of development on the Clatsop Plains of Oregon or on San Bruno Mountain in California; and many another creature caught in the cross-fire of human needs and desires. I will never forget a frustrated mall developer stomping back and forth outside a hearing room in Albany, New York, where the future of the endangered Karner blue butterfly was under debate. Jamming his foot-long cigar in and out of his mouth and pacing, he muttered, "I can't believe it—all this trouble for a goddamn *butterfly!*"

I hate to think how developers, businesses, and resource-dependent country people would respond to an ecologist's concern for still "lesser" forms of life than pygmy rabbits and Oregon silverspots. For example, there lives in the old-growth forests of the Northwest a remarkable creature called the wood roach (*Cryptocercus* spp.). An evolutionary enigma, it is the object of great biological interest. Wood roaches have not been found in Washington for more than half a century and should by all rights receive at least as much attention as the northern spotted owl. But I can just imagine the uproar if a single timber sale were suspended on behalf of a creature that shares the traits of both roaches and termites. Already timber lobbyists have expressed bitter chagrin over the decision to include mollusks—or as one astonished landowner put it, "a bunch of damned slugs!"—in the management mix for the Northwest timber plan.

Or how about the Oregon giant earthworm? When I worked for The Nature Conservancy, I learned about relict populations of these highly attenuated annelids—up to ten or twelve feet when relaxed—in remnant forest soils of the Willamette Valley. We considered launching a fund-raising campaign to purchase critical habitat for the species and the system it represents. Our slogan was to be "Save the Oregon giant earthworm: can you dig it?" But we never pursued the idea. I've always cherished the imagined notion of an indignant legislator rising in the Salem statehouse to denounce the insanity of taking land off the tax rolls for the sole benefit of a bunch of big worms—too big even to use for fishing!

Yet, to many people, such arcane animals—and similarly esoteric endangered plants with unhelpful names like Furbish's lousewort—really matter. To them the question is not one of putting critters before people. It is an issue of respecting and caring for people and the rest of nature together; of recognizing the innate sense of poet Robinson Jeffers's line, "Not man apart." It is believing, and acting as if, resource use can and must accommodate the rational maintenance of diversity and that failure to protect diversity is fundamentally irrational.

We often try to explain away these radically differing perceptions as the product of profound ignorance on the part of one side or the other—ignorance of biological functions, say, or of economic systems. Without a doubt, we all have our blind spots. The millwright is likely unaware of the essential role of mollusks in maintaining forest health while the urban environmentalist might be innocent of the facts of real human life in a mill town. But the yawning gulfs between our understandings cannot all be explained by lack of facts, or lack of empathy. We must finally recognize that we are waging, on the battlefield of species' graveyards, a war of ideologies. The lack of shared values, the dogmatic refusal to even consider sharing common values, is such that a word like ideology is none too strong.

Environmentalism—like abortion, population control, sexual orientation, immigration, affirmative action, and growth management—has become anathema for certain people. The rabbits and roaches are of no real consequence to them but serve as visible targets for their wrath. Indeed, that seemingly useless animals and plants have no particular consequence, except as unwelcome agents of unwanted change, is a tenet of this creed. Its values extend well beyond species conservation, running into mining and grazing on public lands, the use of all-terrain vehicles on the commons, even the very concept of a commons as embodied in the public lands. As I write on the shores of Lake Crescent, jet skiers shatter the national park serenity, taking up the auditory space of a hundred quiet walkers, swimmers, riders, or rowers. I am a nonviolent person, but when jet skis appear in such a setting, I look about wildly for the nearest bazooka.

At Sagebrush Flat we saw no rabbits but plenty of sign, these being the only North American leporids to dig their own burrows. The scent of flowering sagebrush cut the dust and twanged in the nose. Old sage shrubs, the kind favored by the rabbits, had been battered by cattle, the grass they use in spring depleted. I asked the DNR man about the powerful rancher who leases most of the acreage from you, me, and the pygmy rabbits. I wanted to know if he distinguished between public land and private land. "Heck, no," the DNR man said. "It might as well be his."

To some users of state and federal lands, those acres are theirs, and the other owners, especially if they come from western Washington, had best keep out and shut up. When someone else at Sagebrush Flat suggested that canceling this rancher's grazing land might be seen as a "taking" of private property, I felt I'd heard the last word in denial of the common weal. In fact, state law allows such leases to be canceled for a "higher and better use." If ever a phrase were concocted to bring out our polarized values, this is it.

The schism in values does not neatly fall, as some assume, along lines of left and right, Republican and Democrat, urban and rural, rich and poor. Although the stereotypical antienvironmentalist is seen as a right-winger (and not without cause), many a Marxist couldn't give a hoot about owls or the species dialectic. It is true that some of the sharpest critics of "federal set-asides" in the Congress are western Republicans and that most environmental legislation of consequence has been sponsored by Democrats. But many a Democrat does little for his home habitat, and Nixon did more for the land than Clinton and Gore have managed together so far, despite their good intentions. When Secretary of the Interior Bruce Babbit went forth to seek substantive reforms in grazing and mining practices on the public lands, he ran into a wall of rural resistance. He thought he had his ducks lined up, but the ducks saw things differently.

It's not that country folk are anti-nature. What sense would that make? They do see city people as romanticizing the out-of-doors, sometimes shutting down traditional livelihoods in the process. City Sierra Clubbers sometimes view small towns as nests of redneck woods wreckers. But the countryside contains many a quiet bird lover and slug hugger. Not nearly as simple as rural versus urban, the gap we seek to pin down zigzags all over, across all lines and muddy borders, dividing classes, towns, families, and even individuals in their prickly ambivalence like some crazy fault line. And of fault, there is plenty to go around.

So where are we to go with this unhappy knowledge of a plenitude of deeply unshared values? It is certain that no number of "scoping" sessions, town hall meetings, talk shows, or public hearings will begin to ameliorate the problem. Mediation, arbitration, referenda, initiatives, and legislation only serve to force closure that will rend again at the earliest opportunity. The courts may provide a stronger suture, but the opposing tissues, rejecting one another, will pull back until the next litigation. Compliance is one thing, true cooperation quite another, and compromise usually means just that: someone, or something, of value is compromised. And as the agricultural chemical industry so doggedly demonstrates, real and lasting reform is too often like tomorrow according to Janis Joplin: "Tomorrow never comes, man."

It would be uncommonly naive to think that consensus in all things that matter will ever be achieved. Yet something in my biologist's heart makes me unwilling to accept the possibility that our raging differences in matters of life and death are inevitable and insoluble. It simply isn't adaptive that a species laden with values should be so riven in their expression. Of course, much of what we do is patently and strikingly maladaptive, so why should attitudes about nature be any different? Because it has come to this: change, or perish. And one of the changes had better be in the direction of greater common purpose.

It is in that word *purpose* where I believe a watt or two of light may be found, if anywhere. The ideological bogs we slip happily into have at least one thing in common—some assumption of purposefulness to justify the actions we condone or condemn. I am not implying that the jet-skier, out for mindless fun, acts out of any profound self-awareness. And Tom's friend Bill was no ideologue when he asked about snail sniffers. But if there were no underlying homocentric ethic, rabbits and roaches would ride high, wildland rivers would wend uninvaded. The countervailing view is driven by a biocentric ethic that takes all species into consideration. Small wonder that values hatched by such differing senses of purpose seldom meet.

Intriguingly, many of the harshest critics of saving this or that "silly" species consider themselves religious. For example, the Christian Coalition backs candidates whose voting records on environmental issues are rated near the bottom by the League of Conservation Voters, and one of the coalition's highest priorities in the 104th Congress is gutting the Endangered Species Act. "Useless" critters that get in the way of economics, as in "that damn owl" or "those goddamn little rabbits," stick in their collective craw. Yet it seems to me that people who believe in direct, divine creation of each living thing should consider every life form to be blessed, not damned, devoutly to be protected, or at least not actively destroyed.

When I hear professed Christians denigrate owls and murrelets, as I often do, I want to ask them this: If you believe in a God who is supposed to have created these creatures, shouldn't He be the only one to decide the time of their demise? This matters, because the casual damning of nuisance rarities can spawn attitudes and actions that lead to the ultimate equivalent of actual biological damnation for species—extinction before their time.

On the other side, many conservationists belong to liberal denominations or none; others adopt some sort of muddy pantheist-animist noncreed. They rightly conclude that maintenance of biological diversity carries the seeds of our own survival. But sometimes they miss the part that human communities play in nature. They need to accept our own species in the natural equation.

Signs are appearing that at least some people are working toward a shared new sense of purpose. Much of the conservation community has invested itself in sustainable agriculture and other means of finding a fit for humans in the scheme of things. Meanwhile, a "green spirituality movement" has arisen to spark spiritual respect for the physical world. The broad range of outlooks, from the liberal Episcopalians' Creation Ministry to the conservative Evangelicals' Green Cross— all dedicated to conserving the rich gift of the world—demonstrates that what they jointly call the Creation can indeed be an ideological bridge. The nonreligious too have an equal stake in declaring interdependence.

The one glimmer that I see radiates from the slim chance of a common commitment to this thing, this everything, called "the creation." Whether we see the world as made or arisen, its sacredness can no longer be in question. We must stop damning the sacrosanct, whether with casual curses or with giant dams.

To paraphrase Aldo Leopold: a thing is right when it tends to preserve the integrity, stability, and beauty of the creation; it is wrong when it tends otherwise. If only one torn value could be annealed and held closely in common, it should be this one.

Ditch, Creek, River

(*Illahee*, 1995)

I've written a lot about the High Line Canal (it pops up throughout this book)
and about various other brooks, streams, cricks, and rivers. But having a col-
umn focused on my own river of home, "Gray's River Almanac," gave me
a chance to weave all my beloved watercourses—and those of all the other
water-lovers—together into one big, braided flow.

A recent visitor, having read my essay "Robert Gray's River" in *Wintergreen*,
wrote later that he was surprised to find my study window facing away from the
river. "I'd pictured you looking up from your desk to the river," he wrote. And
so he might. Gray's River is so central to my life that I might well be expected to
orient my daily workspace toward its lulling sinuosity.

Actually, I hadn't any choice in the matter. Our bedroom occupies the front
gable of an old Swedish farmhouse. The room available for my study is the tiny
nursery off that bedroom on the west side of the house. Its sash window opens
onto a mixed woodland of red and white oak, hornbeam, birch, and sugar
maple—all planted by H. P. Ahlberg, the Swede of Swede Park—and the path to
his former ornamental pond that is now our richly mounded compost heap. We've
made a heather garden below the window in an acidic spot that was formerly the
boneyard for dismantling great oak branches. I can see another path curving up
between ivy and huckleberry to the strawberry and garlic patches behind Thea's
studio. The branches of Washington's greatest red oak, planted from an acorn in
1875, reach within inches of the panes and, in heavy summer foliage, moderate
the afternoon sun. I can stretch to see this oak's massive, friendly trunk. But of
the river, no glint, no ripple or eddy is visible from the space where I write these
words.

Not that it greatly matters. I see the river from the front porch, the living
room, the dining room, and the bedroom, which on cool, misty days often serves
as my satellite office in any case. Our bed, with its grandstand view of the river, its
eagles and ospreys, mergansers and herons, morning mists and sunset glimmers,

stands just six paces from my desk. Besides, it's probably just as well I can't see the river when I'm trying to write. It's one thing to cast my eyes over the variegated green backcloth of the woods for relief from the dancing pixels; it's another to give in to the visual seduction of a watercourse—any watercourse. For there lies a mental and sensual voyage, a vicarious partnership with moving water from which I might never make it back to the task at hand.

I have always found the flowing routes of water irresistible. A brook just like the ones in my picture books crossed the Dusty Road by a dairy, just a block or two from the north Denver home where I spent my first five years. Trips across town to my grandmother's house, or to our new house site on the edge of the plains, meant crossing a series of creeks and gulches that drained Denver's hinterlands into the Platte River via Sand Creek, Clear Creek, or Cherry Creek. There were certain grassy glens alongside these urban streams that attracted me urgently, no matter how close to the road, and I always begged to go "camping" beside them. My father took us to the mountains instead, where I encountered real streams that you could really camp beside. But they were hard to follow, with their boulders and bushes and steep gradients. So when we came to live near a prairie irrigation ditch that seemed to run forever and invited me to walk alongside or float as far as I wanted, I knew I'd found my Mississippi. Since the High Line Canal, there have been dozens of watercourses streaming through my life.

I have lived near Ravenna Creek, the stream in the bottom of a deep ravine beside which my mother spent her Seattle childhood; in a houseboat on Seattle's Lake Washington Ship Canal, where I canoed to my university classes; under a thatched cottage roof beside the River Great Ouse in East Anglia, a canalized river that I could have traveled lock by lock through the endless Fens. I've walked up Highlands streams in Papua New Guinea to see endemic swallowtails and giant stick insects; along Highland burns in Scotland where the Scotch argus and the red grouse fly; beside high country meltwater in the Rockies, the Sierra, the North Cascades, and the Olympics. And I have finally settled beside this river named for Robert Gray, between two roads and a creek.

The creek has no name now. The Swede might have had a name for it, or the Wahkiakums before him, but I haven't learned it. It's not a long creek, only a mile or two. It arises in the lap of a small mountain, one of the lower Willapa Hills, due north of the Gray's River Covered Bridge. Dodging through second-growth firs and hemlocks, it skirts a couple of houses before plunging under State Route 4 in a culvert. That's where it reaches Swede Park. As the old farmstead known by that name was carved up, the creek became the western boundary of the land that would become "mine," otherwise defined by a V between the junction of SR 4 and Loop Road.

As it emerges from the culvert, the stream enters a flat that was once a trout pond dammed off by the Swede. The town waterline breached the dam, but still holds back enough flow to make a moderate salamander pond in winter and spring. Another culvert beneath that pipe, then a drop into a steep ravine of friable sides. Alders, willows, salmonberry, and a few great spruces line the creek here, along with the sycamore maples and English ivy that are the outliers of H. P. Ahlberg's exotic influence on the place. The vestiges of his grand landscape plan can still be seen in the rotting frames of cedar flumes he built to divert the water here and there. (When the rigors of the rainworld overtook his resolve, Ahlberg returned to Sweden in 1911. The next two generations continued the landscaping with growing desultoriness until the 1960s or 1970s. When I came in 1979, the salmonberries were poised to take it all back, and I've offered only token resistance.) In its bottoms, the ravine receives a waterfall from another small stream to the west. "Our" creek makes a little waterfall on my side of the line, now dammed by a fallen willow; irrigates a skunk cabbage swamp; and disappears into blackberries before entering a big new culvert beneath Loop Road and leaving my jurisdiction. (Its considerable winter flow—under the influence of the 120-plus annual inches of rainfall, most falling between November and February—rotted out the old culvert and threatened to take the county road.)

The next drop takes the stream past the site of a former great barn that it once watered. The Swede's grandson pulled down the barn, and his sons have scraped the brambles off the vacant site. Stately hornbeams still shade its far side. The flow reaches the bottomland in a marsh of tree frogs and rush tussocks, drained to the west by still another culvert beneath Covered Bridge Road. By now the flow is very slow and swampy. As it seeps below our mailbox, under the rim of Loop Road, it makes a place every spring for yellowthroats and their witchety song. There were teal, redwings, and beavers too, until the widow of the Swede's grandson had the beavers trapped out, fearing that they were flooding the field that no one uses anymore.

When Gray's River floods in the winter—five times last year after three years with none—the last stretch of the stream disappears beneath the valleywide beast that the river becomes at its brownest and biggest. The rest of the year it dawdles in a small channel to its final culvert beneath a silted-over gravel-hauling track, pools nearly still beneath it, then finally dribbles into a wide-swinging pebble shoal of the river. And that's all there is. Too obstructed for salmon, too short for much volume, too insignificant for a name.

Yet this stream has issue. The frogs, the yellowthroats, the 'manders; the skunk cabbage and the insects that come for its pollen or its jungly leaves; the pleasure in a morning extension of my mail walk to visit its pond before returning to work a hundred meters east—these and a thousand episodes and organisms unobserved by me or anyone give meaning to this tiny channel. Above the western slope of its ravine, a prolific patch of trilliums has yearly bloomed among a salad of lush *Mianthemum* leaves. This spring the site was logged by my neighbor, a fisherman hurt by the salmon breakdown. I'd asked him to let me know if he ever planned to cut the big spruces just over the property line on his side, and he left them. The ravine has been denuded at least twice before. Enough time and a gentle, restorative hand could bring the fish back to a stream that once knew the flashing backs of spawners. And maybe then it would find its name.

Wherever water flows, it carries the possibility—and the considerable power—of making connections, for life is concentrated there. This is why my ditch in eastern Colorado furnished such a powerful window on the world, for it served as a green umbilicus from the mountains to the plains and back again. This is why Ravenna Creek was the life-flow of my mother's girlhood, why, when she took me to Seattle in 1964, what she first wanted to show me was "The Ravine," why I later took her ashes there. And it is why the lower reaches of Ravenna Creek are now to be "daylighted," brought up from the stream purgatory of the storm drains to enliven the surface once again, from park to neighborhood to shopping center to nature reserve to marsh, finally to refresh Union Bay.

Urban naturescapers everywhere are discovering the alchemy that water can accomplish in the form of a living stream on the surface, where it can be enjoyed. From Stephen Foster's Suwannee to Bruce Springsteen's Jersey rivers, our culture has always venerated the streamside. When Bob Dylan wrote about watching the river flow on by, his impulse did not fundamentally differ from Johann Strauss's "Blue Danube" or Roy Orbison's "Blue Bayou." Thoreau's *A Week on the Concord and Merrimack Rivers* tells of a different place and time, but as a love song to a river, it does not differ in kind from Ann Zwinger's *Run, River, Run* or Ellen Meloy's *Raven's Exile*, Hemingway's "Big Two-Hearted River," or the Colorado and Escalante writings of John Wesley Powell, Everett Ruess, or Edward Abbey. John Hillaby's Yukon, Robin Cody's Columbia, Robert Perkins's Back River route to the Arctic Ocean—these heroic solo expeditions embrace the same river-love as *Wind in the Willows* and *Lovely Is the Lee*. When Springsteen sings of going "down to the river," he sings for everyone who has ever known the pull of gravity on water between two banks . . . for all of us who would go with that flow, wherever it leads. For it is the power of that universal flowing to control, to limit, to inspire, to empower, to validate, to thrill, and to take our lives. Nothing affects all things more, except the sun and ourselves . . . and we are merely upright streams. We like to think of ourselves as closed systems, independent. The brevity of survival in the absence of inflow puts pay to that conceit, while that poor man recently stranded in Oregon's Coast Range lived for nine weeks on melted snow. Yet anyone whose bladder has been held beyond comfortable limits knows the immediate need for outflow. A few years ago I was on a plane bound for Denver. Crosswinds prevented landing for many minutes. I'd neglected to get up when I'd had a chance, and now I was bursting. When we finally landed, the attendant approached and said I looked pale. She asked, "Would you like a glass of water?" I almost lost it then and there. And when, that autumn, I was dehydrated while backpacking and would have given one boot for that same glass of water, I understood the sense of being dammed at either inlet or outlet.

Now each day, when I carry the sacred chamber pot down that path visible from my study window, out to the compost heap, and add the night's water to the good black growing humus where the worms live and the possums forage, I am participating in the great cycle of hydrogen and oxygen, caught up in the gyre of all life. Sometimes there is crab shell on the pile, and it reminds me of the crayfish shells I found along the High Line Canal in the old days, along the agate-strewn beaches of Gray's River last summer, on the creekbank last week. Crawdads in the ditch, crawdads in the creek, crawdads in the river. In this time when boundaries are shifting from straight lines to watersheds, perhaps we are coming close to knowing the true importance of water. We know that if we treat this substance well, it will sustain us. But we should also remember the watercourses that have carved our lives, for they flow through us yet, and ever shall.

Elegy Written in a Country Farmyard

(*Illahee*, 1995)

Today is one of those days that makes you pretty sure there's no better place to live than Gray's River Valley: leap day, at the tag end of one of those February weeks when Venus rages in the night like a supernova, and the days give brilliant a whole new sense. Purple crocuses spatter the tousled lawn; skunk cabbages and daffodils daub the drabness out of winter with yellow excess. Ravens and bald eagles play outrageous stunts in randy bonding, and the mew gulls and dunlins make their last sweeps of the valley floor before drifting down the Columbia toward the coast, like some tardy foamtide following the freshets out to sea.

The sanguine prospect from my porch follows weeks, months of stuff that made you pretty certain that this is a ridiculous place to live. High tides in league with wild downpours and the east wind brought floods, followed by snow and ice and yards of rain, then still higher tides, greater rains, and more floods, with yet another promised by the *Farmer's Almanac*. If not quite a Midwest winter, this has been a hard one in Willapa. Still, as I bask on the sunstruck porch with the baking pussycat, it is difficult to imagine that all is not aright with the world. Hard to believe, for example, that many of my neighbors are struggling their way out of floodwater mud. Strange to realize that this is the last essay I shall be writing for *Illahee*—whose very name means home—since the magazine and its own home, the Institute for Environmental Studies (IES) at the University of Washington, have been inexplicably abolished by shortsighted administrative fiat. These facts might seem more real after dark, in Venus's chilly glare.

By now the valley should be gearing up for the great greening that March and April will bring. But there is so much silt covering the postflood fields—windrows, furrows, mudflows, windthrows of the Willapa Hills' good soil—that the wintergreen grass cannot be seen, and it's hard to imagine much coming up through the new alluvium for a long time. By now, too, there should be near-deafening frog song. Unlike so many amphibians everywhere, Pacific tree frogs are still numerous hereabouts. Their chorus began unseasonably in December, paused, then halted with an arctic front. It resumed on cue, but these evenings merely hint at the choristers' presence. The diffidence of the frogs might mean that the bulk of them simply washed out of the tussock marsh near the covered bridge when the valley became an Amazon; or maybe they were buried in so much mud that they haven't yet surfaced.

Most of the houses prone to flooding (for it floods almost every year here) have long since been abandoned, and you see their prows poking through the reclaiming brambles along the banks of what must have struck their builders as a bucolic stream. But this year many families stood in disbelief, knee-deep in cold river flow in their living rooms. It was prescient of a wry-witted friend of mine from Berkeley to quip, upon greeting me at a meeting, "So how are things in Gray Water, Washington?"

Surely this was the winter of the gray water. And if, in eighteen winters here, I have seen something like thirty floods, I had never seen it like this, when the flow nearly reached the floor of the covered bridge as it licked the withers of horses with nowhere to go, and someone's ostriches paced surreally through the alien element. When the highway was put through here in the 1930s, it disrupted the springs, so that even our river-bench farmhouse suffers a flooded cellar as the stony loam saturates and the yard becomes a lake. For the second year in a row, our furnace motor was submerged, the sump pump screaming valiantly underwater. And now that same highway, plagued by dozens of slides and massive slopes ready to dump, is closed indefinitely.

The shifting earth and water remind me again of the institute and its deepsixing. IFS has always been a nursery for effective dialogue, research, and change in land use concerns. *Illahee* has provided an elegant and reliable venue for informed discussion of Northwest environmental issues. You can't expect the commercial or advocacy press to do the same. For example, the ordinary media have largely been blindered to the link between erosion and poor forest practices for decades. Simply by driving around the logging roads in the Willapa Hills, you can see many small tributaries whose headwalls have failed when their tree cover was removed, exposing them to saturation and certain slump. The connection does not seem subtle. Sure, natural slides occur; erosion is part of the process of landscape formation. But the frequency, severity, and aftermath of floods in the timbered West have clearly been exacerbated by removal of the absorbent, soil-holding blanket of the forest. *High Country News* recently reported on massive erosion on the heavily logged Clearwater National Forest of Montana. Apologists blamed Mother Nature; but only since recent road-'dozing and logging on steep slopes have the Clearwater's salmon beds silted, its once eponymous flow grown mudlorn. *Illahee* might have been the place where this sticky issue was examined in suitable depth.

Few in this timber-dependent region want to believe it, but steep-slope clear-cutting and road building seem unavoidably implicated in the enormous movement of saturated soils during floods in the forested Northwest. Those gullied deposits of soil basting the valley floor came from somewhere. The sheer scale of erosion is remarkable. But what I find truly impressive is the depth of denial that has for so long kept this recognition from surfacing generally—denial, in fact, on a truly heroic scale.

State Route 4, the same local highway now closed, was cut off several years ago for more than five hundred days by a huge slide that took out more than a thousand feet of its bed. The local economy reeled under the reluctance of tourists, truckers, and others to use the detour on curvy little logging roads, and some believe it has never quite recovered. Certainly Gray's River sank even deeper into senescence during that isolated time. Repair costs to the taxpayers rose into the millions. The fact that the slide occurred beneath root-dead, logged-off hillsides barely attracted mention, and when it did, denial came fast, hard, and sharp.

Finally, this spring, the obvious became unavoidable. After unprecedented, widespread slides, the press began to connect soil movement and steep-slope clear-cuts. Cautious attributions of cause and effect began to creep into the papers and radio a few days after I-5 and I-84 (also closed by slides of unstable slopes) were reopened. "Clear-Cuts Paved a Path for Mudslides, Forest Service Says," heralded one AP headline. Another story estimated that fewer than 10 percent of the slides had been unassisted by roads or logging. A welcome change in attitude came home clearly to me at a recent meeting of Gray's River Grange #124.

I have been a Granger for seventeen years, both to meet folks and hear stories before they are gone, and also to take part in the best local venue for positive change in the community. On this occasion, one of the county commissioners was announcing his candidacy for the state legislature. Mark Doumit is a fisherman and a farmer with generations behind him of resource-based family in Willapa. When Bobby Larson, longtime Grange master, asked what could be done to rebuild the watershed after the floods, Mark agreed that doing so was a high priority; and when Bobby mentioned a timber official who disclaimed any industry responsibility for the damage, the audience—all local people—audibly groaned. Ten years ago, in contrast, a former county commissioner and logger had looked me in the eye and said earnestly, "Why, there's no erosion in these hills!"

I Was a Teenage Lepidopterist
(*Portland*, 1996)

Another editor who from time to time has given me my head to run where I will has been Brian Doyle, redoubtable voice and vision-maker of Portland— *probably the best university magazine in the country. In this case he let me write about just what it is that I've seen in butterflies all these years, that they have kept me such good company.*

Last weekend I went forth once again with a group of initiates, seeking the balm and benisons that only butterflies can bring. We wafted instruments of cottonwood and gauze and wielded silvery steel stamp-tongs in gentle gestures of capture, observation, and release. Wings the color of a puma settled in the tawny road dust and became invisible, again and again: arctics. Chocolate wings bobbed up from roadside grasses as we passed, then settled among the meadow flowers: alpines. I netted a fallen flax petal that got up and flew, becoming a blue butterfly. Like that noted lepidopterist Vladimir Nabokov, we examined its scintillant lunules and aurorae, teased out the pattern of spots in its wings, and deduced its name, as given by some earlier scientist. As the blue flew off unharmed, a tiger swallowtail drifted in to nectar on a scarlet columbine. We watched his coiled straws unfurl into an efficient proboscis, spread his claspers with a soft squeeze, observed the aedeagus whence the spermatophore flowed to his mate's *bursa copulatrix,* and these words and visions were poetry to us. The swallowtail too flew away free, as we spotted a checkerspot fluttering around a purple penstemon.

The summer I turned thirteen, in 1960, I decided to teach a butterfly class. I had filled my room with cigar boxes bottomed in Cellotex, leaking fumes of moth balls, and pinned with glorious rows of all the local butterflies. My bookcase contained the standard tomes on Lepidoptera by Holland, Klots, and Brown. I'd reached the point of diminishing returns with the local fauna, seldom finding species new to my cabinet in my habitat of first and last resort, Colorado's High Line Canal. Trips to the mountains, where arctics and alpines flew, were too few to sanctify the summer. I thought I knew a lot, and I had a passion for sharing my knowledge and my burning enthusiasm for butterflies.

I also wanted to make a few bucks toward the Vespa I planned to buy when I turned fourteen. So I undertook to teach a butterfly class. Of course, nobody came. My best friend, Jack, who had been swinging a net with me for two years, wasn't going to pay to do what we did anyway. My only acolyte, Eddie, couldn't afford it because he'd already exhausted his allowance buying butterflies from me. The other kids preferred Little League or the pool; certainly not taking a class, in *summer,* from some other kid. So I put away my charts, lesson plans, and assignments, and went back to the good old irrigation ditch, its wood nymphs and admirals, with my net and a border collie named Fashion, borrowed from my stepsister JoAnn, a model.

The next time I tried to teach a butterfly class was in 1967, my last summer as a teen. I was an undergraduate at the University of Washington, hoping to stay in Seattle instead of going back to Denver to work as a mailman, as I had the previous summer. I hatched a class and worked hard to plan and promote it. This time I got one student, a precocious high school lepidopterist named Jon Pelham. But he knew as much as I did, so we soon dropped the pretense of the class in favor of an extended field trip. I went to work for the Sierra Club, and Jon and I set out on a collegial butterfly romp that has now lasted thirty years. We're summing up what we've learned in *The Butterflies of Cascadia,* and finding it's not nearly as much as we thought we knew back then.

Now, when I can teach as many butterfly classes as I want and they are nearly always filled, I realize that I was merely ahead of my time. Public fascination with natural history has grown dramatically, and field seminar programs, such as the North Cascades and Olympic Park Institutes, have proliferated across the countryside. The ecological awareness that was just a'borning in 1967 has matured, leading many people (especially urban internees) to seek a personal acquaintance with a side of nature they fear they might be losing without ever having known. This gives me the rare chance to play their innocent enthusiasm like an instrument, to open their eyes, minds, and hearts with a rainbow resource that glitters in their fearful fingers like so many fragile gems they never knew existed.

When I place a butterfly, unharmed, on a child's nose, the tickle is a kind of transcendence. When I do the same for adults, who struggle to fix the scintillant object in their jaded, presbyopic vision, and the magic happens, that letting-down of all defense and letting-in of all delight, I realize what it was I really wanted as a teenage lepidopterist in search of a class: not just the money for a scooter or an excuse for a summer job, but a chance to spread the unalloyed pleasure I'd found in this particular stained-glass window on the world.

Eventually I bought my Vespa through a Faustian bargain: collecting specimens professionally for an Eastern dealer, whose checks allowed me to buy gas and replace the constantly fraying throttle cables so that I could collect farther afield, amassing bags of specimens to send to the dealer. In the process, I lost much of my own innocent joy in the chase.

I didn't work again as a professional lepidopterist until after graduate school. Then it wasn't bagging a big catch for a dealer, but consulting with the government of Papua New Guinea on the conservation management of their giant birdwing butterflies—chartreuse and sapphire beauties the size of dinner plates.

Over the intervening years, conservation research, distributional studies, and butterfly teaching have replaced my old cigar boxes as repositories of love and lore. In my prior vocation as a conservation biologist, butterflies always played a central role. Now I am chiefly a writer, doing just a dab of science on the side. And I find that my aim is to restore butterflies not only to the countryside, but to their onetime role as my delightful avocation.

When I teach about butterflies every summer, I see my students fly away with a fresh appreciation of the world, a renewed or discovered dedication to conservation, and a will to get outside: all gifts from these elegant but easily overlooked creatures. And what I want always, still, is someone to teach *me* how to look at my surroundings, to look at the world as I did when I was a teenage lepidopterist. I guess it will have to be, always, still, the butterflies.

On the Outside

(*Society for Conservation Biology Newsletter*, 1998)

After kindly giving me an award, the Society for Conservation Biology requested an essay for their house organ. So many conservationists with a job had openly envied my freelance situation that it occurred to me to give them something of what that's like in real life. Writing this made me realize the odds I'd been working against for fifteen years. Now, having survived more than that long again and still going, I feel more than ever that I made the right choice when I cut loose.

When I received the Society's Distinguished Service Award in Victoria, it was presented to "An Individual Outside of Academia and Government." Outgoing President Dennis Murphy kindly noted that the award recognized work and writing in the field of invertebrate conservation. Given this pulpit, I would like to speak to the conservation of small-scale life, from a posture outside institutions—and tie the two together if I can.

When you are a conservation biologist in government, academia, or an NGO, there are certain things you can do, and certain things you cannot. You have the power levers, influence, prestige, backup, and authority vested by your position. You also have the special set of restrictions, constraints, and degree of muzzling that go with that job.

Not infrequently, bureaucrats and institutional activists express envy of my independence. From time to time one of them makes the break to the freelance life, but most go back. For when the anchor of the job is cast loose, a whole new set of opportunities and limitations takes over. Hopefuls tend to forget the latter until they have to confront them in real life.

One does indeed gain a measure of independence. But the first, or bridging, step often consists of taking on consultancies and EIS-type work. This attaches its own species of thrall. Scientists who go to work for developers, certain they can maintain their objectivity and clean hands, may find themselves compromised before long, and listening hard for whispers of "biostitute" behind their backs. Working for the other side, or for the "stakeholders," in pursuit of that elusive "win-win," can make similar demands on intellectual and ethical freedom. I have known splendid and admired academics to lose credibility for endorsing unfounded or hyperbolic eco-rhetoric, as well as the other way around. In short, freelancing does not always guarantee, or equate with, real independence.

If you truly retain your separation from defining and compromising allegiances, it probably means you are not being paid for your contribution—at least not regularly: you do it out of love, fear, and rage, and they don't pay for rent or beer. That's the part that many wannabes, with office frustrations soothed by a biweekly paycheck, benefits, and support base, willfully tend to forget.

It is such a route that I (perhaps foolishly) have followed. After leaving stewardship work with The Nature Conservancy, I consulted with IUCN/WWF long enough to get the *Invertebrate Red Data Book* published (with Sue Wells and Mark Collins). But an inglorious period in WWF-International's life (the CEO was on leave from a South African tobacco company, for example) conspired with desires to write and leave the city to send me permanently among the ranks of the un- (or, charitably, self-) employed. The great nature writer Edwin Way Teale favored me with one superb piece of advice: don't go freelance until your career warrants it. This I flagrantly ignored.

For fifteen years I have supported my conservation habit with writing books, speaking, and Paladin-style teaching. In that time I have suffered no control whatever over how I might exert my opinion, how I spend my time, or where I may live. I have, in fact, lived and worked out of an old Swedish farmstead a hundred miles downstream from my old office in Portland.

I have also done without a paycheck, benefits, and Social Security contribution (the real killer for freelancers, along with health insurance). I have had no travel budget, communications allowance, or photocopy facility, and no one to pay conference or journal fees, page or reprint charges, no agency backup or institutional imprimatur. This support, often taken for granted, tends to be forgotten by professionals when they survey the green pastures "outside of academia and government." Yep, you can cast off the reins and live where you choose: IF you can pay your bills.

This condition affects what one can do. When I attend a conference as a keynote or guest participant, and take part fully and with enthusiasm, members wonder why I do not join the organization. But as I probably attend twenty conferences and annual meetings a year on average, the dues and registration fees alone would beggar me. So the meetings I can attend just because I want to, and the subscriptions I can maintain, are very limited. I have belonged to the Lepidopterists' Society since 1959, and there have been periods when it was the only dues statement I could meet.

One of the greatest challenges for independent scholar/conservationists is convincing agency people that this is NOT our job. Wildlife and parks agency people, TNC folk, journalists, and others seeking expertise often have a hard time understanding that no one pays independents to do what they do, and there is a living to be made too. For example, the leading earthworm biologists on the West Coast are amateurs; the chief spider biologist in the region ekes a modest living on survey contracts and such, but has no paid position; and three of the most knowledgeable Northwest lepidopterists are, respectively, an unpaid curator-of-convenience, a truck driver, and a well-paid but extremely harried physician. Yet all of them find their knowledge in (sometimes unreasonable) demand by people whose days are spent on a payroll.

More and more, specialists in systematics and the natural history of organisms of concern are unemployed, at least as such. And if these resource people also happen to be dedicated to conserving the resource, as many of them are, their usefulness and their overcommitment at least double. It means that independents cannot always perform as their colleagues in government, the advocacy community, and industry would like them to. Sometimes they withdraw to their lairs, or the field or lab, out of sheer self-defense. It also means we must pick our battles carefully. I have concentrated on certain modest old-growth stands in the Willapa Hills, keeping my county roadsides unsprayed, the Washington Natural Heritage Advisory Council, and an array of invertebrate conservation activities, including biogeography and habitat protection of Northwest butterflies, the migratory monarch phenomenon, and support of the Xerces Society.

When I first wrote on the subject of Lepidoptera conservation, thirty years ago, my paper was rejected from the relevant journal—probably for its editorial shortcomings, but also the topic was considered arcane. Not so in Britain, where I studied for a year at the Monks Wood Experimental Station with John Heath, Eric Duffey, Jack Dempster, Mike Morris, Norman Moore, Jeremy Thomas, Ernie Pollard, and others: all working on rare insect biology and conservation for the British Nature Conservancy (later the Institute for Terrestrial Ecology). From that experience came the Xerces Society in 1971, named for the extinct Xerces blue, which was lost from the San Francisco Peninsula in 1943.

In the quarter century of the Xerces Society's life—by no means wholly or even largely on its account, but measured by its existence—invertebrates have become big business in conservation biology. Literally, too—many forget that the Habitat Conservation Plan, now the darling of Bruce Babbitt and the very fulcrum of public discourse on endangered species, had its beginning with accommodations made on California's San Bruno Mountain for developers versus the federally endangered Mission blue. Some believe that the butterfly, and perhaps the ESA, would have followed the Xerces blue to extinction without the HCP; others feel the outcome is still debatable. What is certain is that insect conservation has become not only historically important, but commonplace. The same journals that considered the subject esoteric in 1967 now seldom publish an issue without conservation papers.

Insect conservation has also shown me the greatest danger to conservation biology, within *and* without institutions. That is the potential for enmity, rancor, and counterproductive cannibalism within the ranks of believers. For we are all that, or we wouldn't be doing what we are doing, for love *or* money. It's too hard. When we dismiss, dis, or rumble with one another destructively, we deliver the biota into the eager and willing hands of its enemies. Of this, I am convinced.

Of course, there will always be debate, and should be, over issues: we shall never find total consensus over reintroductions, species versus systems approaches, and many other points of philosophy or practice. Naturally. But when I see competing consultants becoming mortal enemies, or whole bodies of opinion demonized, I worry. Lately, I have been concerned to hear some botanically driven fire ecologists attempting to marginalize independent lepidopterists who clearly have the goods (and data, and numbers) on certain overenergetic burns that are hard on insects of concern—hard to the point of local extirpation with little potential for recolonization, in some instances. Debate is good; discrediting those who dissent is unhelpful. The messengers are not the enemy, even when the tale they bring is inconvenient.

I accepted my award with great pleasure and joy, for all those who have toiled on behalf of E. O. Wilson's "little things that run the world," and for all who have worked from the outside, with all the satisfactions and challenges it brings. For in the end, there are no independents; we are all interdependent. And among those who struggle to keep what's good in the world, there is no outside—or better yet, it is *all* outside.

The Earth Turns, and We Go On

(Daily Astorian Millennium Edition, 2000)

Steve Forrester, the progressive, impressive, and persistent publisher and editor of the Daily Astorian, *published at the mouth of the mighty Columbia, importuned me year after year to write something for his paper. At last, when a special section was planned to address the coming millennium, I felt my time had come. I'd like to say it was for Steve, but it was really that solid silver heron in the millennial moonglade that did it.*

In this last December of the hundredyear, the moon has been bigger and brighter than any of us have ever seen it before or ever will again—and the skies cleared for it. That fact alone might cause some to pronounce the solstice a miracle.

But there is more: as my wife Thea and I walked down the road to watch giant Luna's moonglade on Gray's River beneath the pewtered outline of the Covered Bridge, a warm breeze blew from the east. In the morning, summer yellow poppies bloomed by the garage, and marah—what many of us call wild cucumber—was starting in again to sprout and twine and bud, months ahead of schedule.

The first of the varied thrushes, those birds of the deepwood like robins with orange eyeliners and black necklaces, had come down from the higher forests, but they lacked conviction. Most years, a succession of frosts drives them downhill in their dozens, in search of seeds and insects and the milder nights of the floodplain.

Ah, the floodplain—that river's hemline that bounces up and down with the fashion and was indeed in flood just days ago. One night, one hundred people gather for the potluck, Yuletime songs and stories, and Santa's visit at the Grange Christmas party; the next night, a foot of river flows through the Grange hall.

Then the river rolls over in its bed, as it has thousands of times through the ages, homesteads become islands, big red helicopters from the US Coast Guard in Warrenton evacuate a family, and the water system washes out.

Now we boil water, as workers and officials seize the unseasonal days to make things work again. In the potholes left over from high water bob mergansers, coots, and ring-necked ducks. And as the moon rises for the second night of its great show, a single great blue heron stands on the shingle below the bridge, set in solid silver.

In these times of changing days, seasons, eras, we look for signs. Some seek signals of prophesy come true, convinced that our fixation on arbitrary numbers somehow matters to the universe. Others, bored with the regularity of life, look for something—*anything*—to happen to liven things up. And signs there are; but they may not be what we are looking for. Bracketing the change of century two times ago were the comings of Robert Gray in 1792 and Lewis and Clark in 1805. They too were looking for signs—fresh water in Gray's case, salt water in Lewis and Clark's. Between them they unzipped the continent. For his trouble, Gray got a harbor, a river, and the Grange hall it recently ran through, all named for him, as well as a load of sea otter pelts, cheap. Lewis and Clark gained undying fame, the gratitude of their president and people, and a load of celebrations about to explode in our midst. The sublime isolation of the American West was about over, and they made sure of it. But there was something, someone, here before them. Had the Native Americans of the Lower Columbia possessed a tradition of apocalyptic revelation, they would have been entirely warranted in seeing dark signs in the arrival of Gray and Vancouver's sails, Lewis and Clark's canoes. Their lives would never be the same; for their cultures, it was all downhill from there.

Ours, on the other hand, rose and soared for a while. First trapping and trade, then fishing, followed by farming, and finally logging, all grew, flourished, and fell, over the two centuries of European occupation of the Columbia Pacific delta and its watershed. Not that they have entirely passed from the scene. Trapping is down to a few muskrats and nutria, but fishing is still vital—even if the catch is crab and hake and the occasional current-driven glut of tuna, instead of the supernova of salmon it once was.

Farming, once diverse along the river until damp, disease, and markets drove most of it out, has passed through dairy (surviving in pockets here and there) and on to beef cattle and hybrid cottonwoods. Logging has shifted from what once seemed a cornucopia of timber and fiber filled by rank upon rank of Very Big Trees, to a fluctuating trickle of pulp from conifers that could be mistaken for slightly overgrown Christmas trees. No question that these industries under-girded an economy that is now sliding lackadaisically into tourism and recreation. No question either that the changes we have both wrought and suffered over the past half century have ensured that the resource picture here will never be the same, nor the opportunities.

But all is not elegiacal in the Lower Columbia realm. "Change" can he a syn-onym for "fresh." Many have come to value our beaches, our rivers, our tattered remnants of forest as never before. Are we not more attuned to the richness of our people's history than most, so steeped in it are we, here in the orbit of the oldest city on the West Coast outside the Spanish colonies? These degrees of awareness make us more dedicated, it seems to me, to protecting what's left, both of our built environment, and that which was built without us.

The people who were here before us did not survive our successes in any numbers, so the Indian renaissance may be subtler here than in some other places where the ravages of displacement and disease were less complete. Yet the Chinookan and coastal people that remain are finding their feet and their foot-ing, and another century may see a populace in which diversity does not merely mean different flavors of Scandinavian.

And the people who were here before the Indians have survived, if dimin-ished. The canvasbacks may still be seen in certain months in Baker Bay. The elk still mouth the grass at Jewel and across our valley. If the Fred Meyer Mitigation Wetlands should properly be called the Fred Meyer Bramble Patch and Parking Lot Runoff Basin, the dunes of Fort Stevens still host peregrine falcons in steep, fleet stoops, and the rare wildflowers still open in May on Saddle Mountain. Do the humans who live here tend to notice such things, and to care about them? If not, why live here, away from the easy charms of the city? I'd like to think that the dwellers of the Lower Columbia care what the region amounts to after all these years, and what it shall be like after many more.

For my part, I'll be watching for signs. I'll watch for the return of the rain with the waning of the millennial moon, the freezes that will still come to shrivel the marah and send the slugs back into hiding; then the breaking of the salmonberry buds in the scrubby brakes between the towns and the forests. The turn of the year for some means gummed-up computers, for others vague disappointment over the fact that despite whatever modest disruption actually has occurred, nothing fundamental has changed.

For me, that is exactly what I'm counting on to mark another new blank page on the calendar: the skunk cabbage unfurling in the sodden marshes, the people going about their business in the sodden towns, the sun climbing and sinking just the same.

The earth turns, and we go on.

Resurrection Ecology
Bring Back the Xerces Blue!
(*Wild Earth*, 2000)

With the Xerces blue's last stand, the Presidio, now restored to something like original habitat, the idea put forth in this essay struck me as too good to miss. Others apparently agree: it's been reprinted all over. As far as I know, no one has yet undertaken the experiment.

In 1875, San Francisco lepidopterist Herman Behr wrote to his Chicago colleague Herman Strecker, lamenting that the Xerces blue butterfly was "now extinct, as regards the neighborhood of San Francisco. The locality where it used to be found is converted into building lots, and between German chickens and Irish hogs no insect can exist besides louse and flea." Eventually, Behr's prophecy panned out, and the Xerces blue ceased flying altogether.

Contrary to the popular conservation aphorism, extinction may not always have to be forever. Occasionally, the thoughtful reintroduction of an organism closely related to an extinct type can result in the functional reconstruction of the animal or plant thought to be lost in toto. The conditions permitting such a Lazarus act are rare, and their employment raises all sorts of philosophical questions. Still, reestablishment of near relatives in restored habitats may be an act worth considering in some cases. I would like to nominate the Xerces blue as a candidate for such radical reconstitution.

Often, when a taxon (a kind of plant or animal) becomes extinct, it leaves behind related taxa that might or might not have fully speciated (become separate species) since their isolation from one another. The surviving taxon, if all the facts were known, might be considered a different subspecies from the extinct type, or a different (but very close) species. This can be a difficult distinction to make with certainty, even with both members alive. But the Endangered Species Act allows for the listing of subspecies, recognizing that these are the active units of evolution, where differentiation is in the process of occurring. Far from irrelevant side issues, subspecies are where the action is in evolutionary terms. So when a creature drops out due to environmental change, surviving related taxa in not-too-distant localities may contain much the same genetic complement as the lost ones. Transported to the site of the extinction (assuming its supportive conditions have been restored), the survivor may re-\inoculate the place with organisms similar to those lost; and in time, under those conditions, may evolve traits that make them virtually indistinguishable from the original occupants. This has occurred in nature, as when extinct Floridian butterflies were replenished by wind-assisted arrivals from the Bahamas and Cuba.

As denizens of stressed habitats decline, the number of instances where purposeful reintroduction may prove a useful tool will increase. For example, in 1975 I rediscovered a federally threatened butterfly, the Oregon silverspot *(Speyeria zerene hippolyta)*, in coastal Washington. Subsequently, development and a series of harsh summers seem to have wiped out the insect. State funds purchased critical habitat and managers aggressively planted violets for the larvae, but no adults could be found. Now the recovery plan envisions introducing related fritillaries from Oregon coastal colonies that are doing better. The genetic similarity is probably close enough for success, now that prime habitat is protected and improved for the species. But in this case, both the extinct and the donor populations belong to the same subspecies. Such an outplant recently bolstered an Oregon site with individuals bred in captivity from local parents.

Two celebrated experiments in more disparate reconstructive introduction have taken place with British butterflies, one an effective failure, the other an apparent success. In the first case, the English large copper *(Lycaena dispar dispar)* died out in the great fens of East Anglia when they were drained in earnest in the eighteenth and nineteenth centuries. The last individuals of this inch-and-a-half brilliancy, flaming metallic orange like a living ingot, flew in 1847. English entomologists, among them Lord Walter Rothschild, much disturbed by this and other losses, instituted the first committee for insect conservation in the 1920s. Among other measures, they set aside Woodwalton Fen, an extant, undrained remnant of the vast marshes sacrificed to agriculture. Committee members introduced the German large copper *(L. d. rutila)*, hoping to replace the original. But the butterfly did not take. Later, they tried again with coppers from Dutch coastal fens *(L. d. batava)*. And after a fashion, this effort worked: you can go to Woodwalton today and you might see large coppers. However, their survival has depended on extraordinary management measures, including planting out the host plant, great water dock; manipulation of aquatic-edge habitats; taking the larvae indoors for the winter; and building an enormous (and expensive) clay apron all around the perimeter of the reserve, as the surrounding fenlands have shrunk by many feet through desiccation and blowing soil.

While studying this and other practices in British butterfly conservation in the 1970s, I heard it said by biologists involved in the project that, by some morphometric figures, the descendants of the introduced butterflies statistically resembled the extinct British coppers more closely than the Dutch founder stock. I have never seen any data published in support of this instance of microevolution, but this is, after all, what one would expect in time. In 1999, however, at an international symposium on Lepidoptera conservation held in Oxford, I was told that inbreeding depression had reduced the surviving Woodwalton population to virtual homozygotes, with little genetic variability or elasticity, and an effective inability to adapt to environmental change. The effort has not been without benefit, since Woodwalton is an important refuge for many other wetland species. But the "English large copper" is now, essentially, more a coddled clone than a viable resurrection.

The second instance involves another popular English insect, the large blue *(Maculinea arion)*. About the size of the copper, it was a brilliant pale blue emblazoned with prominent coal spots. In the nineteenth century it inhabited certain meadows and downlands across southern England. But not long into the twentieth, the large blue began dropping out of one habitat after another, and its own committee was formed. Reserves were established and potentially harmful activities prevented, including collecting, grazing, and burning. The blue's larvae feed initially on wild thyme, not a rare plant. But its life history then becomes almost surreally baroque. The partly grown caterpillars drop onto the ground, where they are picked up by foraging ants. Placed in the ants' brood chamber underground, the butterfly larvae become carnivorous on the ant larvae; this is tolerated, and the ants milk the caterpillars for honeydew produced by specialized glands possessed by the larvae of many blues. Pupation takes place in the ant nest. In the spring the butterfly crawls up and out, spreads its wings, and begins anew.

Whenever an organism possesses such a degree of specialization, it is elegantly adapted to a certain narrow range of conditions, but extra vulnerable to their disruption. In fact, several of the listed endangered species in the United States are other species of blues possessing complex commensal relationships with ants (though none so bizarre as *Maculinea!*) and fine-tuned habitat needs often involving fire and overstory—the Mission blue, the El Segundo blue, the Palos Verdes blue, and Smith's blue, all of California, and the famous Karner blue of the Northeast, named by novelist/lepidopterist Vladimir Nabokov. Because the specific needs of the large blue were imperfectly understood, losses continued in spite of protective efforts. Finally, in 1979, the final individuals, removed from the last site to the laboratory, flickered out without issue—and the English large blue became extinct.

Dr. Jeremy Thomas of the Institute of Terrestrial Ecology had studied the detailed life histories and mortality factors of several English rarities, and his findings often guided reserve management that led to their recovery. Just about the time the large blue crashed, he cracked its management mystery. It turned out that the early conservationists had it wrong—the large blue had coevolved with fire and sheep, and actually required their effects. In the absence of burning and of grazing by sheep and rabbits, the nature of the turf altered; thyme was reduced through competition with gorse and coarse grasses, and most importantly, the dominant species of ant changed. The newly dominant ant picked up the blues' larvae all right—then ate them! At last Thomas had the formula for large blue management, and the butterfly's large constituency in Britain guaranteed funds to put the reserves back in shape. But the blues were all gone.

In 1981, Dr. Rudi Mattoni, editor of *The Journal of Research on the Lepidoptera,* published a memorial issue with a black cover bearing the following epitaph:

In Memoriam: *Maculinea arion eutyphron,* c. 10,000 BC–1979 AD

"the wide open spaces

are closing in quickly

from the weight

of the whole human race."

— Waylon Jennings

Yet in the wings, so to speak, awaited relatively robust populations of large blues only ten thousand years or so removed from the British cohort. This subspecies, the Swedish *M. a. arion,* was to become the founding stock for new large blue colonies in western British habitats that had been energetically and precisely managed to restore optimal conditions for the butterfly, the thyme, and the correct ant. And such has been done, with the support of Butterfly Conservation and other organizations, agencies, and companies. At the Oxford symposium, Dr. Thomas reported impressive indications of success thus far. Care has been taken to maximize genetic diversity, and to avoid other pitfalls experienced by the century of experience with the large copper.

Many more subspecies than really exist have been named for the large blue, as for many European butterflies, where practically every valley's "race" bears its own name regardless of biology. These local ecotypes may have genetic bases and therefore evolutionary and conservation significance. But the currently accepted model recognizes three major European subspecies, with both the Swedish and UK forms belonging to *M. arion arion,* the original type named by Linnaeus.

However, Thomas points out that there are detectable (and mainly unpublished) differences that he believes most taxonomists would consider great enough for classification as two true subspecies. The Swedish individuals that he and his colleagues used for reintroduction were, on average, significantly larger and more heavily marked with black than any of the original UK populations. More importantly, they were adapted to a warmer summer climate (one to two degrees C) than any UK site, which affects their emergence dates. This is crucial, because it determines whether adult emergence coincides with thyme flowering for optimal egg laying. "They have been able to 'shift time zones' fine on most UK sites," says Thomas, "but interestingly, in the Cotswolds—much the coldest of the former regions inhabited by subspecies *M. a. eutyphron*—they haven't, and Swedish adults emerge two–three weeks late there, condemning the females to oviposit in the coolest parts of sites where thyme flowers later but where the host ant is most scarce. Needless to say these are the only introductions that have failed." He reports record numbers elsewhere this year, with extraordinary (and unsustainable) densities in Somerset, and large blues flying in twelve sites total, including some newly colonized nature reserves.

Which brings us back to the Xerces blue. One century after the large copper last shimmered over the black fens of England, the Xerces blue disappeared from California. Even after Behr's lament to Strecker about its decline, the butterfly remained common in places. William Hovanitz, a prominent California lepidopterist, used to bicycle out to the Presidio and collect as many as he liked without making a dent in their numbers, as he worked out their life history. He made a point of speaking about the area with the Presidio commander, who left it undisturbed for the time being. The renowned insect photographer Dr. Edward Ross and Harry Davis of UC-Davis were the last entomologists to see Xerces blues on the wing. They observed them around a blue-flowered lupine near the Marine Hospital above Lobos Creek, on a slope at the head of a natural amphitheater. There, Ross told San Francisco butterfly authority Barbara Deutsch, one could see many individuals together on a fine spring day. That upland was subsequently flattened, graveled, and built upon by the army's ordnance department. Drs. Hovanitz and Mattoni photographed a small patch of deerweed persisting into the 1960s at the Presidio on a baseball diamond, and presented a one-page article in the *Journal of Research on the Lepidoptera*, showing the habitat. But the last known Xerces blues flew over dunes at the Presidio in 1943. In 1956, Dr. John Downey, successor to Nabokov's blue-butterfly studies, documented the biology and extinction of *Glaucopsyche xerces*.

It was the decline of the British large blue that brought modern attention to *G. xerces*. On December 9, 1971, T. G. Howarth of the British Museum (Natural History) gave a talk in London cautioning that the large blue might soon be lost;

and that if it were, we should take it as a symbol and resolve to lose no more British butterflies, of which there are, after all, only sixty-some species. In the end, the large blue was indeed lost (then found again, in Sweden). But Howarth's injunction had a further-ranging impact. Having heard his lecture, I decided that night that a group should be formed to remember the Xerces blue and to work for butterfly conservation in North America. The Xerces Society has since become an international voice for all small-scale life and its habitats.

The Xerces Society will soon be thirty years old; the Xerces blue has been gone for nearly twice that long. The very changes that brought about Golden Gate Park, the Embarcadero, the Marina, and the neighborhoods of San Francisco replaced coastal dunes, hills, and swales with pavement, buildings, and parks. The same kinds of changes led to the endangerment of the Mission blue, and as commercial use of the city densities today, even the once-common butterflies of vacant lots and alleyways are becoming scarce. However, an opportunity looms that could exemplify a whole new era of butterfly (and habitat) sensitivity and imagination in San Francisco and elsewhere. Three conditions have converged to create this possibility.

First, since Xerces' demise, the military reservation known as the Presidio, where the butterfly last flew, has become part of the Golden Gate National Recreation Area. Extensive wetland restoration is taking place on part of the Presidio along San Francisco Bay, and in the western section of the old fort, restoration of native San Francisco duneland habitat is under way.

Second, a California recovery tantamount to the restoration of the large blue in England is under way. A Los Angeles cousin of the Xerces blue, the Palos Verdes blue (*Glaucopsyche lygdamus palosverdesensis*) was thought to be the first federally listed taxon to become extinct on the government's watch. But it was later rediscovered at a US Navy fuel depot by Dr. Rudi Mattoni of UCLA, a prominent authority on the biology of blues and a veteran of conservation efforts on behalf of the endangered El Segundo blue. The Palos Verdes blue has since become the target of a major lab-rearing and restoration effort by Mattoni and colleagues, and the early results are promising.

Third, some fairly near relatives of Xerces may be extant today. A paper by Thomas C. and John F. Emmel in the recent tome *Systematics of Western North American Butterflies* (Mariposa Press, 1998) describes a new *xerces*-like subspecies of the silvery blue (*Glaucopsyche lygdamus*) from Santa Rosa Island, one of the California offshore islands and part of Channel Islands National Park. Although the males are a paler, more violet blue than those of *G. xerces*, and the females browner, the underside hindwings bear prominent white halos around the black spots, and sometimes only the white spots as in "the true *Xerces* of San Francisco." As the Emmels put it, the name they gave the new subspecies, *G. l. pseudoxerces*, "reflects its phenotypic similarity to the extinct Xerces blue, and recalls the opportunities for evolutionary biologists and geneticists that were lost with the passing of the highly variable Xerces blue in 1943."

The discovery of an animal bearing a striking similarity and reasonable relationship to Xerces, contemporary with a vigorous attempt to restore suitable habitat in the last place Xerces existed, suggests a symbiotic possibility too obvious and appealing to ignore.

Some lepidopterists, such as Dr. James A. Scott, author of *The Butterflies of North America,* believe that the Xerces blue was, in any case, conspecific with (i.e., the same species as) the silvery blue. Whether this is indeed the case or they are simply closely related, it is unlikely that *G. lygdamus* and *G. xerces* differentiated very long ago in the evolutionary past. The Emmels found *G. l. pseudoxerces* females ovipositing on California broom (or deerweed, *Lotus scoparius),* a legume that was the Xerces blue's primary, if not sole, caterpillar host plant in San Francisco. It is a plant that, if it is not already being incorporated in the Presidio habitat restoration, should be.

But the Xerces blue was not restricted to seaside habitats, and some believe it was not strictly a lotus-eater. Tree lupine has been reported as a host for it, and the larvae consumed Nuttall's pea in the laboratory. Nor was it always white-spotted; there was both a form with small black irises called "polyphemus," and one with larger dark centers called "antiacus" that quite resembled the silvery blue. It was just this extreme polymorphy that made Xerces so interesting from a population genetics standpoint. So the fact that the new island subspecies is the closest in appearance to the usual form of the old Xerces blue might not be the most relevant factor in deciding whether *G. l. pseudoxerces* would be the best founder population for a reintroduction. In fact, Rudi Mattoni, to whom the idea of restoring Xerces occurred years ago, thinks it might not. After all, a silvery blue population that had evolved closer to the San Francisco Peninsula might well prove more suitable for local conditions than one from southern California, just as the Swedish large blues suited Somerset more than the Cotwolds. And geographically closer silveries might also be more recently related to Xerces than the Channel Islands population. Besides, it would likely prove much easier to obtain and transport living material from outside a national park than from within.

The likely candidate would be *G. l. incognitus* (formerly called *G. l. behrii*) from Marin County, Santa Clara, and elsewhere on the north and central California coast. Mattoni suggests that this subspecies could be laboratory reared en masse (by methods he has perfected for the Palos Verdes blue) and interbred to achieve something of the polymorphy of Xerces, while strengthening genetic variability. In order to further broaden the gene pool, founders should be drawn from several sites, a measure that Yale professor and eminent Lepidoptera geneticist Charles L. Remington suggests for any insect introduction that hopes to succeed.

Regardless of the subspecies employed, the reintroduction of blues to the Xerces' last habitat seems an idea whose time has come. There would be nothing to lose by introducing Xerces-like silvery blues to the Presidio but a modest number of founder individuals; and there might be a great deal to gain in terms of expanded support for the restoration and refined management practice. I feel the attempt would be worth it, if only for the vigorous debate and solid experience it would promote in the young practice I am bound to term Resurrection Ecology.

Reintroduction is a last resort that should never be undertaken until the original extinction is virtually certain, and this can be difficult to prove. For example, the Palos Verdes blue had been thought extinct for years before Rudi Mattoni rediscovered it. But with so many people searching for the Xerces blue over so many years, its extinction is virtually certain. Furthermore, reintroduction is pointless unless the original causes of extinction have been reversed. Restoration of damaged habitats is an imperfect science at best, and the hope that the resulting simulacrum will have much in the way of functional equivalency for its denizens is a long shot. For example, when I read the following statement by a Chinese official responding to criticism of a railroad spur through sensitive landscapes in the Hong Kong New Territories, my heart dropped: "The report recommends both temporary and permanent mitigation measures to meet the environmental standards and requirements, including the creation or reprovisioning of wetland at the Long Valley area." "Reprovisioning wetlands" seldom approximates the complexity, diversity, or reality of the original. Many habitat conservation plans fail for the same reason: it is easy to talk about replacing taken species, but very hard to do it.

Nonetheless, perhaps the Presidio restoration will succeed in bringing back a patch of habitat bearing some resemblance to the city's lost landscape. This patch could grow. If all went well, and if local conditions acted upon a similar genome to fix the white-spotted blue butterfly and attune it to the rebuilt habitat, who knows? At some future date, we might even be able to say, as the British can rightly crow about their large blue: Xerces flies again!

Reflections in a Golden Eye

(Prologue for *The Fading Chorus*, Island Press, 2000)

This essay almost didn't happen. An editor at Island Press asked both Ann Zwinger and me whether we would write the introduction to The Fading Chorus, *hoping that one of us might accept—sort of the reverse of multiple submission. In the event, both Ann and I accepted, placing that editor in a pickle. Ann offered to drop out, but I knew she really wanted to do it and felt bad. Besides, she had been an idol, then a mentor, finally a dear friend of mine, and I didn't feel I could bump her. But I really wanted to write it also. Finally a solution occurred: one of us would write the prologue, the other an afterword; and that's how it went. We flipped for it, and were both happy with the outcome, the two of us bookending all the frogs and toads, as it were. I was even happier when, a few years ago, Thea discovered hundreds of toadlets on a flood-zone beach of Gray's River, a mile from our home. A good population of northern toads has thrived there ever since.*

> Who knows whether these broken heavens
> Could exist tonight separate from trills and toad ringings
> —Pattiann Rogers, *The Power of Toads*

Last summer, my wife, Thea, and I were looking for border butterflies along the shores of Clear Lake, in the foothills of the North Cascades in Washington State, just below British Columbia. I was following an unseasonably late Sara's orange-tip to make sure of its identity. Thea had just spotted the first dun skipper ever recorded in Whatcom County.

I heard her call. "Oh!" she cried. "Come quick!" I ran back to find her staring into a ditch, incredulity like the hot sun on her face. I looked, too, and saw what she saw—thousands of big bugs crawling out of the dry ditch and heading in all directions.

At least, I took them for insects at first. "Geez! Crickets!" I said. The whole ditch and roadside were alive with the creatures. But then we both looked at them more closely, and when our shock gave way to clear eyes, we saw what they really were: toads!

Toadlets, actually—each one an inch in length or half that, not long from the tadpole. In fact, and now we remembered, we had recently seen the nearby lakeshore brimming with polliwogs, but at the time, we hadn't known they were toads. Now, to stand there and behold tiny, scurrying, squirming hoppy-toads by the many, many hundreds—well, we were thrilled.

Time was, one could go for a walk in the Cascades and be reasonably sure of encountering a few northern toads. *Bufo boreas* was a regular, even common resident of most of the moist and montane Maritime Northwest. But not any more. Now, the rest of Washington State seems much like the Willapa Hills, where my wife and I live, which seem always to have been essentially absent of toads. With the exception of a few little ones hanging around the lights of the comfort station at Keller Ferry on the Columbia River a couple of years ago, this mass emergence was the first sign of them I'd seen in years. And when I'd attended a meeting of the Northwestern Vertebrate Society in Astoria, Oregon, not long back, one of the presented papers had carried this shocking subtitle: "One More Nail in the Coffin of the Northern Toad."

Toads. I had always been fond of them. My first acquaintance with them had probably been through the Thornton Burgess Bedtime Stories, which doubled for me as storybooks and natural history texts all through my early youth. Burgess's animals may have worn waistcoats and top hats, but they also did the things those animals really do. Old Mr. Toad, for example, shoots out his tongue for fat, green flies; goes hop, hop, hipperty-hop down to the Smiling Pool to take part in the spring chorus; and shows Peter Rabbit how he can disappear by digging his way into the sand for the winter. Harrison Cady's broad-mouthed and bumpy portrait still defines the species for me more than any field guide mug shot. The adventures of Mr. Toad, along with those of Paddy the Beaver, Billy Otter, Mr. Blacksnake, and Chatterer the Red Squirrel, constituted my sole experience with toads in the wild for some years, as they were missing from our dry, new gardens on the unmade edges of the Denver suburbs.

Then there came that other Mr. Toad, the one with the motorcar that went Poop! Poop! Admittedly, I saw the Disney version of *The Wind in the Willows* before I ever read Kenneth Grahame's enchanting book. Perhaps Toad's misadventures on the open road do not exactly mirror natural history. But when I read of Mole and Ratty finding the baby otter safe on the reedy island in the river, in the protective care of the Piper at the Gates of Dawn, it surely lured me out to my own local watercourse to seek such things for myself. In the intermittent ditch that was my Valhalla, amphibians proved as elusive as otters or the land snails I so keenly coveted. Yet even if I never found a toad on the High Line Canal, one would nevertheless play a role in telling the story of that prairie "crick" many years later. In my book *The Thunder Tree*, I brought a *Bufo* to the High Line in the form of an inadvertent passenger and observer. There, a semifictional narrative describes the entire length of the canal through the eyes of this vagrant toad, who hopped onto a mat of moss in the high country and then washed down the Platte River and into the canal in the spring runoff.

The idea for the toad's journey arose from my first real encounter with *Bufo boreas*. In the summer of 1964, most of my friends were working at dreadful jobs in Denver for six bits per hour. To escape into the mountains, several of us took an even more dreadful job that my older brother Tom had found, clearing trees for power line right-of-way at an elevation of ten thousand feet in the Rocky Mountains, way up above Georgetown, for $1.25 per hour. Because we had to show up for the backbreaking work at six in the morning, we just camped nearby, on the edge of an alpine bog. One day, after the grinding work, I was prowling the willow-fragrant sphagnum moss when I spotted a small western toad. Two weeks later (when we'd had all of that job we could stand), we left for home, and I took the toad with me. I named it Todd, after one of my workmates, kept it for some weeks in a mossy terrarium, and then released it in its home habitat before the frost settled in. Todd served as Herpetology 101 for me and initiated a lifelong love affair with the real thing.

When I went off to college, I very much hoped to learn about "herps" in an academic context. There was still a rich array of naturalists on the faculty, and I managed through stealth and guile to take many of their courses. But I never got a herpetology class; my education in amphibians, such as it is, was self-won. I'll not forget the first time I went to hear an evening chorus at Carkeek Park, where a ravine runs down to Puget Sound in north Seattle. The raised voices of Pacific tree frogs erased all else in the night, even the sound of a passing train. (The creatures' sweet cacophony still graces the valley in which I live, from late February into April each spring.)

My younger brother, Howard Whetstone Pyle, whom we call Bud, took the nickname Toad in high school. Trying to remember why, as I first wrote this, I figured the name came about because he was a creative, nonconforming kid who identified with the self-contained individuality of toads, unconcerned with popularity. But when I ran this theory by him recently, Bud erupted with mirth and a definitive "Balderdash!"

"Why was it, then?" I asked.

"Too many Gomerisms!" he replied, laughing. Having also grown up with the name Pyle, I knew just what he meant. "Besides," he went on, "toads are cool beasts."

Back then, Bud made a sign for his room that read "Toad Abode," and we began exchanging toad amulets and figurines. (He made a classic for me in a high school art class: "Toad in a Stained-Glass Bog.") This led somehow to my collecting toad effigies—a hobby I've tried earnestly to limit ever since, with very little help from my friends. As an undergraduate struggling with chemistry when I wanted to be birding instead (usually succumbing, and consequently flunking chemistry), I developed a positive mania for toad collecting. Only now do I recognize it as a displacement activity. I wanted to be a naturalist, and the university wanted something else for me. One way to defuse the uncertainty and frustration was to put it all aside and go hunting for toads in strange places.

I would haunt junk shops, import stores, and Goodwill stores in search of toads of glass or porcelain, stone or metal, plastic, plaster, or wood. In those days, there was a St. Vincent de Paul thrift store down at the end of a dock on Lake Union, where rare artifacts might be unearthed from beneath heaps of stale discards and mounds of free shoes. Staffed by Dickensian figures in long, dirty coats, this warren was a vestige of an earlier age. Of course, we clothed and furnished our lives from these places, too, but I was always on the lookout for toads. I was not very discriminating. My sole criteria were diversity and that the objects be more toadlike than froglike (many finds, of course, showed hybrid characteristics). St. Vinnie's often came through.

Occasionally, I found a real prize: a big, fat sandy-backed Japanese toad with a toadlet on board, which still abides next to our stove; a glass *Rana amethysta* blown especially for me after I demonstrated the appropriate gestures and calls, on the isle of Murano, near Venice; a very old Chinese virility amulet prized from the depths of a true junk trove in the bowels of the Pike Place Market before its gentrification. This heavy brass toad crouches in a smooth form easily concealed in the folds of a gentleman's robe and bears on its ventral surface an immense erection. But the apotheosis of the toad collection was Dudley. Named for my robust high school discus-throwing partner, Dudley was a huge papier-mâché toad, correctly colored and proportioned, built by a friend named Marsha. Dudley occupied a significant part of several apartments and small houses until, during an extended trip of mine abroad, he hopped away into an unknown oblivion.

This peculiar compulsion aside, my life has been a vessel for many a flesh-and-blood toad since. There were the classic toads of English gardens, *Bufo bufo*, of which George Orwell writes so wonderfully, out among the snails (finally), the hedgehogs, and the gnomes. There was a tiny red-spotted toad negotiating the damp edge of a concrete cistern in the Chiricahua Mountains. Most recently, there came a toad of such stolid mass and magnitude that it reminded me of Dudley. We had just parked at a motel on the fringe of Tucson, Arizona, when observant Thea spotted a big lump beneath another car. "That's a toad!" she announced, "or else a big rock."

Toad it was. With imposing glands on its legs as well as viscid parotids, it did not invite handling, but we watched for some time as it hunted and snuffed crickets in the glow of the lamp standards. So large was this toad that we wondered whether it might be an introduced marine toad (*Bufo marinus*) from Brazil. Just days later, though, I read galleys of Ken Lamberton's *Wilderness and Razor Wire*, a remarkable account of a naturalist's life in prison and the weeds and creatures that kept him sane. One chapter eloquently tells the tales of the toads that haunt the edges of the prison yard—the spadefoots, after rain, and the Sonoran Desert toad (also called the Colorado River toad, *Bufo alvarius)*. The latter is a lunker, and we had found this parking-lot monster on the very hems of the Sonoran Desert. I realized then that our dramatic encounter in the night had been with a native species—a true desert toad, surviving so far in spite of the worst Tucson could do. This lone toad, an asphalt epiphany, had called a single note in the night air—a note of hope for toads and their kin everywhere.

Las Monarcas
Butterflies on Thin Ice
(*Orion*, 2001)

I'd been involved in monarch study and conservation since the seventies, first visiting the great Mexican wintering grounds in 1981. The issue of Orion *in which it appeared was devoted to monarchs, featuring a piece by the great monarch guru, Lincoln P. Brower, on the perils they face from GMO crops. I had spent the autumn of 1996 in their company, resulting in* Chasing Monarchs: Migrating with the Butterflies of Passage. *Nowadays monarchs are an even bigger deal, proposed for listing under the Endangered Species Act. Details have changed, but this essay still gives a good overview. Thanks to Professor Brower, monarch conservation was on the agenda for recent summits of "The Three Amigos"—Mexican President Enrique Peña Nieto, Canadian Prime Minister Justin Trudeau, and US President Barack Obama.*

In the morning, the Mexican alpine sun hit hard and bright and the snow melted fast. We walked down into the center of the colony, where a foot or more of frozen monarchs lay in sheets and windrows, a gray-and-ochre sediment on the forest floor. It was a disaster scene: pathetic, when you thought of all those long, improbable journeys wasted, yet magnificent in its sheer magnitude. Once I got over the shock of walking on butterflies ("They're just like dead leaves," I told myself), they beckoned me into their serried, fallen number. Hacking, hurting, eyes burning from the reflected brilliance of the snow and the wings, I lay down in a soft blanket of perished migrants.

This was the first time I'd ever visited the winter-massed monarchs in Mexico, also the first time the scientists studying the phenomenon had experienced a heavy blizzard on the ten-thousand-foot Sierra Chincua. Unprepared, their camp in disarray, they struggled to keep fires alight and stay warm.

My luggage hadn't made it to the mountains with me, but a wicked bronchitis had, thanks to the mustard-colored air of Mexico City. I bunked in a spare tent with Tom Lovejoy, chief scientist for World Wildlife Fund-US. A borrowed sleeping bag and Tom's long underwear, which I have never returned, saved my life.

Now I was cocooned in that pile of soft orange wings. I felt received, at the same time thinking *all that way, just for this.* I think I slept. And when I opened my eyes, the ice-blue sky was filled with bright spinners and floaters and gliders, like doubloons falling in and out of focus through seawater. Sunwarming monarchs launched and rose, even more, it seemed, than all the ones struck to the ground by the now-forgotten storm. Behind me, the shaded trunks rose into their own treetops, thickly furred in fox-colored clingers, and the canopy of the oyamel firs themselves spread an immense tent of solid gold filigree overhead. I lay there, millions of monarchs above and below, and I was healed.

We think of animals migrating from cold places to warmer ones for the winter, not from a temperate site to a potentially arctic one. The reasons for migration usually have more to do with food supply than they do with temperature, though for cold-blooded monarchs, both factors count. Still, who would have guessed that the winter hideaway of the wanderers would confront them with lethal blizzards? As if they hadn't enough to deal with already. Local farmers literally grazed their cattle on living monarchs in those days, and nearby, logs lay stacked in the snow, awaiting transport to mills below. Oyamel fir: *Abies religiosa*, holy incense of the Toltec, warmth and shelter for the Tarascan Indians, the canopy of Sierra Chincua—and the winter sanctum of *las monarcas.*

When Lincoln Brower's field expedition awoke to snow on the mountain, the precise location of the eastern monarchs' wintering grounds had only been known for a few years. Not that the migration had gone unnoticed: even when Georgia naturalist John Abbott published the first known color portrait of the monarch in 1797, he knew that this was no stationary species. Over the years, people spied fresh butterflies southing in the fall and tatty ones northing come spring. By 1878, the versatile government entomologist C. V. Riley proposed a north–south migration to account for the insect's here-today, gone-tomorrow reputation. In the late 1930s, Dr. Fred Urquhart first graced monarchs with sticky, numbered tags, an enterprise that occupied the Ontario naturalist, his wife Norah, and thousands of volunteers for the next half century. Now and then a tagged monarch was recovered en route, allowing lines to be drawn on a map.

By the 1970s, many assumed that the eastern monarchs went to Mexico, but no one knew where. Finally, in the first days of 1975, Urquhart collaborators Kenneth and Kathy Brugger found the eye-popping masses on Sierra Pelon and Sierra Chincua, deep in the Transverse Neo-volcanic Belt in the state of Michoacán. The "discovery" really meant revelation to the outside world, since the local Indians had always known the orange butterflies that arrived around the Day of the Dead, bringing back the souls of the departed children. But how could they know that these butterflies they call *las palomas*—the doves—were utterly unique in the world, or that they would soon bring the eyes of the world into their shared home?

Urquhart reported the find—one of the greatest in modern natural history—in *National Geographic*, but tried to keep the location secret. Monarch researchers William Calvert and Lincoln Brower found it on their own within the year. At the time, I chaired the Lepidoptera Specialist Group of IUCN (the World Conservation Union), which met in Washington, DC, in June 1976. The air was electric with the news from Michoacán. By acclamation, we designated the migratory monarch our top priority in world butterfly conservation. Brower and I had arrived at the same notion: the migratory monarchs were an endangered phenomenon. I included the Mexican and California winter colonies in IUCN's *Invertebrate Red Data Book* as Threatened Phenomena, a new category in the listing of species in jeopardy. Dr. Brower's field research aimed at understanding and conserving that phenomenon was five years under way when serious winter and I visited for the first time.

The monarch is far from endangered as a species. It was the first butterfly I saw upon deplaning in Papua New Guinea, Costa Rica, and Hawai'i, and it is common in Australia and New Zealand, but native only to the American tropics. Monarchs belong to the butterfly subfamily Danaiinae, called milkweed butterflies because they feed on members of the plant family Asclepiadaceae as caterpillars. Lacking a winter hibernation in any stage, danaiines are truly tropical. The availability of abundant milkweed in the North, together with the need to avoid prolonged frost, drove the evolution of the monarch migration. Once milkweeds reached places like Hawai'i monarchs soon followed, whether as off-course migrants or human introductions. Now the monarch, like the painted lady, is one of the most widespread butterflies in the world. Their alternate names, after all, are respectively the wanderer and the cosmopolitan butterfly.

So it is not the species, a wonderfully adaptable generalist in its nonmigratory mode, that is jeopardized. It is the grandest butterfly spectacle on the planet that stands at risk, and one of the most dramatic and elegantly evolved animal migrations of all. And that doesn't mean just the Mexican winterers, for monarchs also concentrate on the California coast. The Butterfly Trees of Pacific Grove, "Butterfly Town, USA," were known and visited well before Lucia Shepardson began to popularize them in 1898. Variable colonies are now known from Mendocino to Baja, with the largest clusters forming in Santa Cruz and Santa Barbara.

Celebrated by artists from John Steinbeck to the Beach Boys, and visited by millions, the California monarchs arguably make up one of the most cherished elements of the state's natural heritage. Likewise, the eastern monarchs enjoy enormous popularity and affection from all sorts of people. In recent years, the Entomological Society of America and other groups lobbied hard to have the monarch named National Butterfly by Congress, and nearly succeeded. It seems incredible that our most familiar butterfly could drop out altogether. But if the migration fails, it will, for the abundant monarchs of our American summer depend upon their winter refuges for replenishment. To ensure their future we need a clear understanding of how migration works. And one of the biggest questions is this: How do monarchs in the East and the West actually divvy up the North American continent?

I remember a day in western Colorado, motoring to a noted habitat with my graduate advisor, Charles Remington. A lone monarch perched among a throng of Charlotte's fritillaries, fiery orange males, chocolatey females, nectaring on big purple bull thistles. I asked my professor where he thought that monarch would end up. The reigning idea was that all of the fall monarchs from west of the Continental Divide wintered on the California coast. We were on the western slope, all right, if by less than a hundred miles; but it was a long, hot, arid way due west to California, across the Great Basin. Could it not be just as likely that a monarch in the intermountain West might follow the major drainages southward—the Green, the Colorado—and wind up in Mexico? Besides, as a former kid collector who'd haunted the Colorado high country whenever possible, I had seen monarchs crossing the Rockies crest in both directions, and doubted its effectiveness as an ultimate barrier. Remington, a Yale biologist who had founded the Lepidopterists' Society in the year I was born, knew as much about North American butterflies as anyone. He suggested that the number of monarchs breeding in the Basin and Range region might be insignificantly small. But neither of us knew where this one was really bound when it sailed off on the wind.

Twenty years later, I decided to look into this question. I found that the "Berlin Wall" model of monarch migration was based on assumption and repetition rather than fact. Most of the monarchs tagged, recovered, and mapped in the

West had actually been caught in California or Ontario and shipped elsewhere prior to release. These transfer exercises proved nothing about the paths or destinations of wild monarchs, yet they ruled the popular concept of western migration for decades. To find out what was really going on, I thought, one could do no better than migrate with the monarchs. So I followed the western migration, chasing monarchs, throughout the autumn of 1996.

I began at the northwesternmost breeding grounds, in the Okanagan Valley of British Columbia. My plan was to locate monarchs at their nectar sources and overnight roosts, then follow them as far as I was able on foot. I'd catch and tag them when I could. And when they rose and flew away, as they always would, I'd take their vanishing bearings—the direction in which they disappeared—as my running orders. I'd follow in the same direction, as much as the topography allowed, until I found more habitat, more monarchs . . . and then do it all again, as far as I could. In this manner I believed I could follow the general trend of the migration, wherever it took me.

The monarchs I found in the early autumn sprang from the milkweed fields of the borderlands. Their mothers had laid pale green goosebumps of eggs on the fleshy, furry foliage. Tiny caterpillars ate their eggshells, then tender leaves. They grazed and molted four times as they grew into two-inch cream, yellow, and black banded caterpillars dangling black filaments fore and aft, perhaps to intimidate predators. Roaming the milkweeds at will, the larvae gained further protection from educated birds by advertising their vile taste—a gift of the milkweeds and their poison-laced latex.

One more skin change, and what came out was an inchoate pre-pupa that soon crystallized, as it were, into one of the loveliest of butterfly chrysalides: clear pale jade, studded with the uncanny molten gold that gave butterfly pupae their Greek name, chrysalis: gold box. Inside, the melted tissues of the worm-like, chewing larva reassembled into the workings of a flying, sucking butterfly. One morning in early September, the wadded creature emerged, pumped blood, spread soft, silky wings, hung, hardened, and flew. Then I would follow, until my unbreakable contract with gravity compelled me to fall behind.

Most butterflies, fresh from the chrysalis, quickly mate. But the autumn-emergent monarchs still make juvenile hormones that keep them sexless. Instead, their whole energy and purpose go in service of an irresistible urge to propel themselves to somewhere else. These very individuals will complete the entire journey deep into Mexico or out to coastal California. Again and again I saw them rise on warm air and circle, raptorlike; float higher and circle again, then disappear from vision into great heights from which they would glide and glide. Not that they can't flap far and fast: these are strong butterflies. But it would take way too much energy to go so far under their own steam.

Instead, the migrants descended frequently to drink nectar, not just to refuel for the next leg, but also storing up, constantly converting sugars to fats, building lipid reserves to get them through the long winter. And this is where I found them: sneaking up on a bank of color—asters, sunflowers, milkweeds, rabbit-brush—I always tingled in hopes of seeing great orange vanes unfolding over the flowers. Refreshed, they took off again. Before night fell, the wanderers sank through the cooling air in search of shelter. I watched them seek out the lee side, the morning-sun side, of a Russian olive, a locust, a willow; and I bedded down among them.

Sometimes in the early morning, the air too cool for butterfly flight, I scanned the leaves still heavy with night and shadows, looking for my leaders. That long, pale, apricot wedge of the sleeping butterfly's underside—sometimes I could make it out, more often it blended into the leaves as it was meant to do. And then a magic degree would arrive and the wings would spread, first a cinnamon smudge, becoming ripe persimmon, finally straight-out citrus as warmth struck, and . . . it was gone! As lepidopterist-writer Jo Brewer described them in her wonderful book *Wings in the Meadow*, like "wings of flame, rising to the sun." If I was lucky, I saw where, and I too was away.

Following rivers, a built-in sun compass, and likely the earth's magnetic field, the emigrants press on, making anywhere from a few to a hundred miles a day depending on winds and weather. My own route was more tortured; no one can follow the wind in a straight line. No one can do what these ones do. Icarus tried but flew too high, and look what it got him—a serious dunking, and a blue butterfly in his name. As his father Daedalus made it to Sicily on his waxen wings, so do most of the milkweed butterflies reach their forest resorts, where they hunker all winter long. Only with spring (about Valentine's Day in California, the equinox in Mexico) will they finally mature and mate, with the fervor and abruptitude of an orgy. And then they are gone, the mountain fastnesses and coastal groves shedding their tawny mantles as quickly as they grew them in fall. Now monarchs drift and skip back into the milkweeds' range, laying eggs as they go, and dying along the way. Their offspring carry on, and theirs. Thus the continent fills again, until by high summer the entire range has been retaken.

But I've gotten ahead of myself—where did these go, the monarchs I followed for more than nine thousand miles before I got home again for Halloween? As it turned out, most of the western monarchs I tracked bore away southeasterly rather than toward the southwest as the old maps said they should. They took me down the Columbia, up the Snake, and out into the Great Basin, where a big male materialized over the Bonneville Salt Flats: a living flame streaking across a world of ashen white. Down the Colorado, across Arizona, through the Chiricahuas, out over the saguaro-lands. Ultimately, on a rainy October day, I watched monarchs shooting the border, well west of the Continental Divide. One year later to the day, a monarch I tagged on the Columbia River turned up in Santa Cruz. So some western monarchs enter Mexico, while others populate the foggy coast, and the eastern and western populations are not after all monolithic quantities unto themselves that never shall meet. Heading back north along the coast, I felt I was beginning to catch a clue as to how this continental dance is choreographed.

One more puzzle piece soon fell into place. The California monarch population crashed to nothingness in 1994, then bounced back the next year. Lincoln Brower connected this remarkable recovery with a striking westward shift of returning warblers in the spring of 1995, and proposed that remigrating monarchs may have bent westward also, repopulating California. He theorized that West Coast monarchs may be subject to periodic extinction with drought and climate shifts, and depend upon refreshment from Mexico. This synched nicely with my findings, showing that the Californian and Mexican populations are intertwined, and their conservation must go hand in hand.

When the monarchs reach their respective destinations, they face radically different challenges, both biological and political, though their basic needs are the same. In order to make it through the winter, preserving their genes from one season to another, the wanderers require a narrow set of circumstances—theirs is truly a knife-edge ecology. Too cold, and they freeze in numbers greater than the population can withstand; too warm, and they fly too much, burning up fat they'll need to fuel the winter and the return flight, however far they get. Brower and Calvert found that this balance may be upset by any factor that opens the protective forest canopy to the harsher influences of wind, rain, snow, and cold by night, to intense sunshine, desiccation, and overheating by day.

In Mexico, even the selective, tidy forestry as practiced in former years may cause these effects; the much more intensive industrial logging seen in Michoacán today has even more baleful consequences. But there lies the conundrum of the wanderer: one person's butterfly tree is another person's job, meal, lodging, or gain.

I thought, back at the time of that first visit, that I had seen few more poignant sights than monarchs glazed with ice, frozen on the ground beneath the trees, having failed to reach the safety of the cluster the previous sundown. And I thought I'd seen the worst that intensive commercial logging can do, in the Pacific Northwest rain forest. But the vision of a clear-cut where once stood a temple of trees cloaked in the richest raiment imaginable, seemingly woven of golden threads but actually spun from base weeds far, far away—this transcends poignancy. It says, what kind of a world is this, where the greatest gifts of evolution fall away, not in their own time through natural selection, but as innocent witnesses to the unholy marriage of poverty and profit?

While Michoacán has too few resources for too many people, a common situation for the exploited poor everywhere, California presents the odd spectacle of too many people with too many resources. Pacific Grove, Santa Cruz, and Santa Barbara, hot spots for the West Coast monarchs, are three of the most affluent communities in the world. The challenge in Michoacán is maintaining a decent livelihood for the *ejidatarios* while sustaining the essential needs of the monarchs. In California, it is a matter of mediating between the aesthetics of those who want mansions and those who prefer parks, between native plants advocates who insist on removing eucalypts and others who know that monarchs depend upon eucalyptus roosts since their native coastal groves were cut.

You could say that for one group, this is a life-and-death issue; for the other, a luxury. For the monarchs, caught in the middle, survival is the only issue. Yet, viewed as a common denominator, they could help plot common cause—if not reconciling grossly mismatched economies, at least providing a focus for those who care about both people and the rest of nature in both cultures. It wouldn't be the first time mere butterflies have shown the way to higher ground.

During the 1980s, Brower and I cochaired the Xerces Society's Monarch Project. Again and again, we wandered the maze of Mexican bureaucracy in search of a plan to protect the monarchs while ensuring the livelihood of the local people. After the frustration, intensity, and wretched air of the capital, we retreated to the cool high forests and the balm of the monarchs, never failing to be renewed in spirit and commitment by the cause of all the commotion: the butterflies themselves. I couldn't wait to hike into the Arroyo Barranca Honda, a colony then known as "Julia." As we dropped through the scent of yerba buena floating over the blue lupines and scarlet salvias, and the sun came over the far sierra, we stopped before a sky-high scrim of gilt sequins—a cool forest fire of living, moving cinders arrived on the wind like sparks from a far blaze—and then we stepped inside. For the next several hours, we were never out of sight and sound of millions of fluttering, gliding, whispering wings.

Some worried that if many people came, the forests would suffer from the threat of real fire, the soils from trampling, the monarchs from disturbance. But inevitably, people would come. After all, tourists have flocked to the much smaller California sites for more than one hundred years, creating a substantial tourist trade on the Monterey Peninsula and in Pismo Beach. So it was natural that ecotourism would be promoted as a source of alternative income for the locals deprived of subsistence by forest set-asides. I have led a number of tours to the sanctuary, and the effect has seemed generally positive.

I shall never forget standing on the high *llano des los Conejos* amid a warren of astonished naturalists as dark stuffed "bags" of butterflies burst into fireworks that fluttered down all around us, alighting on hats and hands and faces with their streaming eyes. Time and again I have witnessed the magical power of *las monarcas* to transcend daily cares, refresh a blunted sense of wonder, or arouse a deeper love for life.

Coming down the trail at El Rosario with a group of thrilled *norteamericanos*, sharing cold Cerveza Victoria and quesadillas hot off a vendor's grill, life seemed good. But I have begun to wonder. The *muchachas* who sell Chiclets and postcards to the visitors seem to have lost the shy and giggling demeanor of their sisters who did the same in earlier years. Their pitch has become more urgent, their faces hardened like the children who sell Chiclets and notions on the median strips of Guadalajara expressways. Over at the Sierra Chincua site, expert *caballeros* delight in riding up and down the mountain hawking horseback rides to foot-weary pilgrims. But the thick dust their ponies kick up can't be good for these boys, and it certainly isn't good for the suffocating monarchs or the pulverized vegetation. At El Rosario, local men jockey cattle trucks full of sightseers up steep, rocky roads from the towns of Ocampo and Angangueo. Guides are eager to hurry visitors around the trails, and when they find dead tagged monarchs, they no longer present them to the scientists as gifts: they know that each tag is now worth fifty pesos—a lot of money where there are few other means of making a living. Ecotourism is indeed helping to some extent. Vendors' stalls serve the many visitors while providing an outlet for monarch-related arts and handicrafts, and guides earn a decent day's wage. But sometimes I wonder whether an impoverished farm economy has simply given way to a poor tourist economy.

On one of my most recent visits to El Rosario, I sat back in a branchwork bench beside a well-watered lawn put in by an entrepreneurial resident of the village. The monarchs must come down daily for water, a scarce quantity; by providing this wet green expanse, the villager had created an oasis both for thirsty monarchs and winded visitors who, for one peso, can step off the steep high trail, sit down, and watch thousands of monarchs sipping and swirling.

Basking in this mental massage of monarchs, I was taken back to another time and place of bliss among the butterflies. It was some fifteen years ago. Butterfly scientists and conservationists had gathered at the Esalen Institute on the central Californian shore, hopeful of coming up with a plan to protect West Coast monarchs. After an intensive work session, we'd retired to the hot soaking pools perched between the wild coast and wilder mountains of Big Sur. Sea otters crunched abalones a few yards away, and monarchs from Esalen's own colony floated overhead like paper umbrellas in a mai tai sky. Recalling that other idyll I realized that the sheer delight monarchs bring us is much the same everywhere; but we return the favor with a gauntlet of challenges that changes face, if not severity, as soon as the travelers pass the invisible borders we scrawl across their flight plans.

Now when I return to Sierra Chincua or Santa Cruz and watch the monarchs bundled in the foliage like hanks of golden fleece; to the country ditch in Colorado where as a boy I saw what Nabokov described in *Pnin*: "their incompletely retracted black legs hanging rather low beneath their polka-dotted bodies"; or to a special spot in the Columbia Gorge where I almost never fail to find monarchs in season, gliding among two species of milkweeds sheltered by pioneer locusts and Russian olives, I ask myself—what *are* monarchs, really, to inspire all this fuss?

For a start, monarchs are certainly our best known, best beloved butterflies, recalled by generations as a bright memory in the classrooms and the fields of home. Lately, some treat them as mere geegaws. Butterfly profiteers rear monarchs for indiscriminate release at weddings and other events, smearing our picture of their natural movements, so critical for conservation. When our de facto national butterfly becomes nothing more than a living bauble, its power is sucked away like the color of dead wings left to bleach in the sun. But for others, this insect is still the very heart of the land: the bringer of spring from the south, the essence of a summer meadow, as much a part of the autumn sky as drifting milkweed floss, the promise of flight to spite the winter. And it is always the Monarch of the Americas: the best catalyst since migratory waterfowl for real cooperation between Canada, the United States, and Mexico in service to conservation.

Beyond all these roles, the monarch serves as a powerful metaphor. To different eyes, it represents the meeting place of desire and need, of property and poverty, of power and helplessness. And the fact that we could actually lose it from our fauna gives this one butterfly an emblematic significance that no species could ever want: the monarch stands for every fine and delicate thing that philistine force and greed would gladly eradicate from this bruised and beautiful world.

Finally, the wanderers are the most wondrous emanation of life I know. To transnavigate a continent, borne aloft on a bit of flimsy tissue, directed through all the valleys and ranges, over all waters and winds, by a poppyseed of instinct and sense. To find the small, special places that lend them safety, twenty million strong at rest in a snowy mountain forest. Then in spring to climb, two by two in their nuptial flight, on their "wings of flame, rising to the sun." And to carry on, and on, all over again. Even in their frozen death the monarchs healed me, and I know I will fight for them as long as I live.

The Journey Home

(Foreword to *John Muir's Last Journey*, Island Press, 2001)

Many people believe that after John Muir lost the battle over Hetch Hetchy to Gifford Pinchot, he curled up under a rock and died. But this was not the case. He moped, then took heart, and set off on an epic journey long postponed: to see the distinctive trees of South America and South Africa. He kept extensive notes and drawings toward a future book, but the book never happened. At least, not until the writer and scholar Michael Branch got hold of the rough manuscript and brought it into being as an elegant and thrilling book. I was given the humbling honor of introducing John Muir's last book—all the more so, as he had been my college idol.

When I went off to college in the mid-1960s, my greatest desire was to be like John Muir. The Rock of western conservation was well known among the young environmentalists at the University of Washington. We recognized Muir as a true radical, at a time when many of us were playing at radicalism. Also as a genuine naturalist, which was what I most aspired to become. I probed dusty secondhand bookshops on University Way for his writings, grew my beard long out of honorific emulation, and affected a Muirish exultation in my journals. My jottings, embarrassing to read today, produced neither good writing nor good mimicry; but at least they were honest in praise of both model and topic.

A fond conceit, this, and doomed from the outset; yet in many ways, John Muir guided all I did. We had Muir's Yosemite in mind, for example, when our Conservation Education and Action Council fought for the North Cascades National Park. Focusing my revolutionary fervor on ecology as well as war, I joined Seattle Audubon Society and the local chapter of the Sierra Club, and these brought me still closer to the person of John Muir. The Audubon board meetings took place around an immense dining room table in the Capitol Hill home of Emily Haig, grand dame of Seattle conservationists; Sierra Club retreats also revolved around Emily, as we congregated in her country cabin on Hood Canal. When we broke for coffee and cookies at Emily's sideboard, or to gather dinner from her own oyster beds, I gazed on her eggshell face with its honeysuckle smile and conjured on this one astounding fact: Emily Haig had belonged to the Sierra Club in San Francisco while John Muir was still president! She had known the man.

When Emily Haig shared her memories of John Muir, I shivered with a sense of reflected glory such as only a twenty-year-old idol-worshipper could manage. I recall her telling of Muir's bright eyes, his youthful stride and spring, and his indefatigable energy when brought to bear upon conservation battles. Not that he had much ready appetite for fighting or politicking. He would far rather be afield, measuring the advance or retreat of glaciers, triangulating trees, plumbing the spiritual luminosity of the Range of Light. Even then he was a celebrity for his books, but he didn't seek such exposure. For him to actually write about experience rather than live it was tantamount to torture. As a young woman in the club, Emily told me, she especially enjoyed the outings, and they were the president's favorite part too. Even so, Muir recognized the powerful force the Sierra Club might exercise in the conservation colloquy of the times. He had no idea how important it would become under a certain successor.

David Brower came north to meet with Seattle wilderness advocates soon after he had left the executive directorship of the Sierra Club and founded Friends of the Earth and the John Muir Institute. A creature of the crags as well as congressional hearing rooms, Brower had not only climbed the same peaks as Muir, but also followed his example as longstanding leader of the club. Like his predecessor, Brower had experienced a great victory and a burning loss. If beating the scheme to dam the Green River was his Yosemite, then losing the struggle for Glen Canyon—inundated beneath Lake Powell—was Brower's Hetch Hetchy. But while the loss of "the second Yosemite" would be Muir's last campaign, Brower went on to lead the successful resistance to dams in the Grand Canyon. After we met with Brower in Seattle, I imagined the historic encounter in the nearby Olympic Hotel between Muir and Gifford Pinchot—founder of the Forest Service, leader of the "greatest good for the greatest number" school of conservation, and Muir's Hetch Hetchy nemesis. Out of their fateful and bitter joust would come the major dialectic of American environmentalism. But even people who know this much have little idea of Muir's overall import.

My own sense of John Muir broadened greatly in the years that followed. Walking in the California grove of coast redwoods that bears his name (where Brower once took Rachel Carson), or flying over Alaskan glaciers that he had scaled without a single piece of modern equipment from REI, I gained a feel for the kind of world for which he fought and the terms on which he came to the land. But it took a summer as ranger-naturalist in Sequoia National Park, hiking over some of the same sugar-stone granite passes and cirques where John O'Mountains had walked, to drive home the depth of his commitment and its effect. On Morro Rock, a miniature Half Dome, I watched a white-throated swift carry a feather sky-high and drop it for another to catch, over and over, and wondered if Muir had seen the same in Yosemite. On ranger walks in Giant Forest, I paused for silence in the very glade where Muir loved to listen for what his friend John Burroughs called the "religious beatitude" of the hermit thrushes. We too heard that sweet fluting. Another walk rounded Crescent Meadow, John Muir's favorite. Rambling that emerald curl, beneath the spires of Sierra redwoods, I palped the reverence for the wild that drove John Muir to become something he might never have intended: a campaigning scientist, rather than the contemplative naturalist he might have preferred.

In doing so, Muir set the pattern for those who followed—Aldo Leopold, Rachel Carson, E. O. Wilson, and all their lot—those who have possessed both the knowledge of the natural world and the refined love for its elements that, together, turned their consciences toward selfless activism on behalf of ecological reform. For it wasn't as much his friendship with presidents, his rhapsodic language, or his reputation as the Sage of the Sierra that saved Yosemite and inspired the conservation of biodiversity ever after. It was more the fact that John Muir truly was a rigorous scientific observer and a pioneering, original student of the landscape: its geology and glacial history, its plant communities, its ecological wholeness.

Muir combined a truly Thoreauvian attention to his surroundings with the robust physicality of Teddy Roosevelt and the inclusiveness of Gilbert White, the father of natural history; and he blended them all with a literary exuberance that caught the imagination of readers and politicians alike. John Muir also had a broad worldview, concern and curiosity for the whole globe spinning in his mind. Hence, his ultimate desire to see where he had not yet been. All these elements emerge in this celebratory account of his improbable, final adventure.

Popular belief has it that Muir's last years were eclipsed by his failure to save Hetch Hetchy Valley from inundation by thirsty San Francisco: an inglorious finish to a glorious life, a final darkness at the end of the Range of Light. Yet, that wasn't all there was to it, as *John Muir's Last Journey* shows. What a surprising, thrilling discovery! A whole chapter in the man's life, almost unknown, a great gift rendered with scholarly precision and literary elegance by Michael Branch. And how like Muir, to take off for far climes, alone, at seventy-three. The great gift of this remarkable book is the wonderful knowledge that John Muir's final years were rewarded, enlivened, and brilliantly illumined—you might almost say redeemed—by one final, phenomenal field trip.

I never succeeded in becoming much like Muir. For one thing, lacking his litheness and comfort with gravity, I do not climb rocks. For another, no one could really be much like this Scottish American original. But in reading his South American and African travels, so long deferred, so abundantly enjoyed, I realize anew how proper a model Muir was, and still is, for anyone who loves nature. For he did love, more than most have any idea how to do. He loved his family, friends, and all life. He loved the colors on the sea and sky, and the gift of sight he almost lost. He especially loved big round things: the clouds, the trees, the granite domes—the world itself.

A journal entry from the *Araucaria imbricata* forest of Chile says it all: "My three companions slept under tarpaulin tents, strangely fearing the blessed mountain air and dew." No one was more comfortable in the wild world than John Muir: his whole life was a journey home. We should all give thanks for the grace of going along on the last leg.

Reincorporation
(*Hipfish*, 2001)

Along with other frequent contributors to Orion, *I was asked to write my reflections after 9-11. I didn't particularly want to do this. Thea and I had flown to San Salvador on September 13, 2001, to help lead a butterfly watching trip in El Salvador and Guatemala. We found even the normally thronged localities, such as the great ruins at Tikal, almost devoid of travelers. But I didn't want to write about that, as our experience was a good one, if melancholy. Eventually I thought of something to say that was suitably somber, and that I doubted anyone else was likely to express. But* Orion *turned it down; I guess it was too visceral for them. In the end* Hipfish, *of Astoria, Oregon, gave my thoughts a place among those of other artists.*

Since the September enormities, three thoughts that I've not seen elsewhere expressed have come to mind.

Thought the first: perhaps no great loss of life has ever pulverized and dispersed the bodies of the victims so thoroughly, with the exception of Hiroshima, Nagasaki, and maybe Dresden and its like. To me, quite apart from the basic, incomprehensible circumstances, this is what distinguishes this disaster in my mind—not merely the numbers of the dead, which have been matched or exceeded by Bhopal, many wars, and any number of earthquakes and floods. While some may find this reaction morbid if not macabre, I take actual comfort in the thought that—while our lost loved ones are often prevented from reintegration with the elements of the earth for almost geologic time, carefully interred in fiberglass coffins and concrete vaults in their chemically embalmed state—the sad, sad departers in those big buildings will be incorporated in fluid and living things very soon. Some will join the Gulf Stream, some the marshes of Staten Island. Someone's elements will be taken up by horseshoe crabs in Delaware Bay this very season. Someone else's carbon will replicate in the leaves of beach tansy on Fire Island, their calcium be bound in the eggs of herons in the New Jersey Meadowlands, their nitrogen carried in a harrier over the grasslands of Jamaica Bay, in no time at all. Someone's molecules are on their way to Mexico right now, metamorphosed from dust on a Manhattan milkweed into what monarch butter-fly-writer Jo Brewer called "the wings of flame, rising to the sun." For me at least, there is some redemption to be found here.

Thought the second: Who would have guessed that those big buildings would actually fall down from the injuries inflicted? Yet the high supporting members melted, and the collapsing weight above brought down the whole. I see a met-aphor in this that could help us in the days to come. Neither can most people imagine that the insults inflicted upon ecosystems could realty undermine the whole show, let alone bring about collapse. Yet we have already weakened many of the higher members of the structure: wolves, whales, grizzlies, tigers. And just as the earlier WTC bombing would have accomplished the same end with much greater loss of life, had it succeeded in severing the foundations, we are busily at work chipping away at the foundations of our high-rise ecosystem: the plants and small-scale life. How better to dignify this irreconcilable calamity, than to take it as an allegory for our overarching, underbracing house of life?

Thought the Third: The subsequent concern has been largely for chemical and biological terrorism. It will come as no news to many, though they might not have thought of it in these terms, that we have been conducting potent chemical warfare against our own people for decades. That, in fact, is putting it mildly. "Better living through chemistry" has brought us many wonders, true enough. Yet the undeniable cancer swarms, the omnipresence of pollution, and the peo-ple's inculcated cavalier attitude toward strong poisons lining their superstore shelves leave us in no doubt: we are our own victims of chemical terrorism. Genetically modified crops could, in time, create another insidious enemy from within, with full governmental complicity and encouragement. This thought receives a sharper edge from the recent revelation by concerned scientists of the close relationship between *Bacillus anthracis* and the widely used and modified *B. thuringiensis*, or "BT," and their apparent ability to exchange genes when they come into contact. As one respected Swiss scientist put it, "If you start thinking about gene technology and bioweapons, one's day is ruined." As our authorities prepare their response to chemical and biological terrorism, we would do well to direct their attention to the domestic threat that Rachel Carson named long before September 11, 2001.

These are my meditations in the aftermath of great loss.

The Rise and Fall of Natural History

(*Orion*, 2001)

Having awarded their august John Hay Medal to E. O. Wilson, the Orion Society was much influenced by Wilson's autobiography, Naturalist, *and all it stood for. An issue of* Orion *was dedicated to the theme "natural history," with major contributions by Barry Lopez and Scott Russell Sanders. This essay was my contribution to the pot. It was later included in a book edited by Lopez,* The Future of Nature *(Milkweed, 2007). While suffering academic woes in the 1960s, I had no idea that the ordeal would become grist for strong convictions and durable prose.*

In the early summer of 1916, my grandmother boarded an eastbound train in Seattle to take her first job. Grace Phelps earned her teachers' credentials in the embryonic University of Washington, then just a handful of buildings plunked down among old-growth forest. Once certified to teach in the young state, Grace easily obtained a position at Lake Chelan, a remote town at the foot of a glacial lake set deep in Washington's Cascades.

The journey involved a Great Northern locomotive through the mountains, a river steamer on the undammed Columbia River, and a stagecoach for the steep and rocky passage around a gorge below the lake's outlet. When she finally arrived in Chelan, the school board was there to meet her, all three of them. As Grammy told it, she stepped down from the stagecoach, directly onto the hem of her long traveling skirt. Her stern employers looking on, the young woman went down, scraping her knees. But she was obliged to smile as she was helped up by her principal, who told her there was no need to show such obeisance upon arrival at her post. Miss Phelps would meet that grim visage at least once more during her year in Chelan: when she was chastised for leading botany walks on Sundays.

The problem, of course, was the Sundays, not the subject. In those tight-laced times, the Sabbath was not to be broken for purposes of instruction, unless it was for Sunday School. But as for botany walks—well, they were commonplace, practically anywhere in the country. For those were the times when the subject of nature study was ubiquitous in American schools. Naturalists such as John Burroughs and Asa Gray were among the most respected people in society, and natural history was considered a high and worthy calling. The notion that an educated person would have a basic acquaintance with local flora and fauna was widely held, and broadly practiced.

My grandmother, though interested in nature all her life, would not have been described in those times as a "naturalist." While always extraordinary in my memory, she was just an ordinary teacher in this respect: along with the other standard subjects, she taught the close and direct study of nature. This was completely in tune with the times. Gram's period on the UW campus was barely after the heyday of the Young Naturalists' Society—a band of pioneer Seattle men and women dedicated to the study of natural history in all its forms. Their patron was Arthur Denny, cofounder of the university; Orson Bennett "Bug" Johnson, the sole professor of science, led their field studies and forays.

Leap forward now to the fall of 1965, when I arrived at the University of Washington in search of a fundamental education as a naturalist. Now there were many more buildings, and the old growth had retreated far away. I made my way to Johnson Hall, long the home of botany and zoology on campus, in search of what might remain of "Bug" Johnson's legacy. As a lad of arid eastern Colorado, I might as well have landed on a new, unexplored planet, a would-be naturalist's paradise. Nearby ravines and marshes, the Olympics and Cascades on either horizon, all promised endless immersion in natural history.

But I needed an academic framework for the studies I had in mind. My first intoxicated look at the university catalog revealed a plethora of natural history classes: birds, mammals, insects, local flora, lichens and mosses, mushrooms, marine invertebrates, paleontology, astronomy, on and on. The only problem was, you couldn't actually take those courses; at least, not many. And you certainly couldn't major in them. They were intended for "dessert": after you'd filled your plate with "hard" sciences such as math, physics, chemistry organic and inorganic, physiology, cell and molecular biology, and the like, you might be able to squeeze in one or two field-based classes as electives. The first year I nearly flunked out of the university as I skipped chemistry labs to bird Union Bay in a canoe. Two or three times I changed majors before I finally found a way through the byzantine university apparatus and a sympathetic dean who helped me dowse a degree out of the place. All along, I got to know the professors who signed my way into the courses I longed for. They became lifesaving mentors, coconspirators in erecting my illicit major, and lifelong friends.

For starters, there was Melville Hatch, "Bug" Johnson's legatee as keeper of the museum's insect collections, master of the region's vast beetle fauna, and scholar of Darwiniana. I took the last courses of his half-century teaching career. The professor's great jowls wagged beneath a puzzled grin as he lectured on the very changes that would ensure he was the last of his kind. Another zoologist, Frank Richardson, taught splendid bird and mammal classes. His pipe and white Hemingway goatee were traits shared with a close friend and colleague in botany, Arthur Kruckeberg, founder of the Washington Native Plant Society and sponsor of our ecology action club. Down the hall from Art in Johnson Hall dwelled Daniel Stuntz, kind and gentle professor of mycology who specialized in psychedelic *Psilocybe* but would never take them. His laboratory was packed instead with edible mushrooms and German pastries for the benefit of hungry students. These and other professors in geography, geology, forestry, and elsewhere gave me exactly what I needed.

And they were on their way out. Most were older, or being encouraged to retire early. The only young naturalist on the faculty, shortly after receiving the outstanding teaching award for his magnificent classes in field natural history, was denied tenure; the department wanted superstar lab candidates who published frequently in all the right journals. A few profs interested in complete organisms survived by being strong on theory. But the majority of new appointments had little connection with the field, and as they came in, the old courses disappeared one by one from the catalog. Soon it would be impossible to assemble a curriculum such as I had gleaned.

The University of Washington experience was not unusual. Throughout the country, the attrition of academic naturalists has been progressive over the past half century. It would be easy just to call it a shift in pedagogic styles and a predictable development toward an always elusive modernity. But this is too facile, especially when the full consequences of the purge of the naturalists are considered. Two main concerns seem evident to me.

First, a populace less familiar with its nonhuman neighbors is one whose own impacts are unlikely to be noticed and moderated by choice. Ecological ignorance breeds indifference, throttling up the cycle I call the extinction of experience: as common elements of diversity disappear from our own nearby environs, we grow increasingly alienated, less caring, more apathetic. Such collective anomie allows further extinctions and deeper impoverishment of experience, round and round. What we know, we may choose to care for. What we fail to recognize, we certainly won't.

Second, many of the naturalists were systematists and taxonomists—the very men and women who recognize, describe, and catalog the organisms of the earth. At a time when taking account of biodiversity has never been more urgent, we have lost much of our capacity for training and employing such people. Along with the naturalists went most of the courses and jobs in systematics, leaving the great institutional collections that sustain and contain our store of knowledge in grave jeopardy. Taxonomy grew unfashionable as laboratory research brought more prestige, glamour, and grant money—especially grant money—to the universities. Biologists David Wilcove and Thomas Eisner consider the institutional rejection of natural history to be one of the biggest scientific mistakes of our time. But this isn't the whole story. To see what happened to natural history, we must revisit the time when botany walks were de rigeur and butterfly nets wouldn't rate a second look on a campus where half the students today have cell phone implants and the other half wouldn't know a Douglas-fir from a dogwood.

Natural history came to the new world with the colonists, who brought an educated and needful interest in the products of the earth. Of course it was already here, since native populations everywhere have been superb naturalists, or else perished. But that native knowledge was soon dispersed and eradicated, leaving a once well-known biota to be rediscovered by the likes of the Bartrams, Clark, Townsend, Nuttall, and their vigorous ilk, trained in the Linnaean tradition. George Washington and Thomas Jefferson were both excellent naturalists. A lively, experimental curiosity in plants and animals was nothing unusual; it was simply one component of the engaged citizen's life.

The nineteenth-century naturalist reached its apogee in the person of Jean Louis Rodolphe Agassiz, a Swiss geologist and zoologist who developed the comprehensive Museum of Comparative Zoology at Harvard University. Agassiz liked to say, "If you study nature in books, when you go out-of-doors you cannot find her." According to a later naturalist of acclaim, David Starr Jordan, Agassiz brought about "a complete revolution in natural history study in America . . . not a category of facts taken from others, but the ability, through contact, to gather the needed facts. As a result of his activities, every notable teacher of natural history in the United States for the second half of the nineteenth century was at some time a pupil of Agassiz or of one of his students." In 1873, in Buzzard's Bay, Massachusetts, he initiated the very first summer field station for natural history study and teaching, the model for hundreds of institutes since.

The close study of nature had its economic and exploitative side: the various state natural history surveys that sprang up in the 1800s were not concerned solely with an intellectual interest in the kindly fruits of the earth. The agricultural depression in New York State in 1891–1893 drove many people off the land and into New York City. A program in nature study was begun at the Cornell College of Agriculture as a first step in interesting children of the country in better farming. For fifteen years the director was Professor Liberty Hyde Bailey, a student of Agassiz's and a respected zoologist. In 1903, Anna Botsford Comstock took this over, writing leaflets for teachers and students, organizing Junior Naturalists' clubs and correspondence courses. She would bring the nature study movement to its fullest degree of development over the next thirty years.

The program received a heartening response from thousands of students all over New York. Comstock's goals clearly went far beyond the initial hopes, amounting to no less than an ecological context to general education for all students. She believed "the reason why nature-study has not yet accomplished its mission, as thought core for much of the required work in our public schools, is that the teachers are as a whole untrained in the subject." To remedy this lack, in 1911 Comstock published a large book called the *Handbook of Nature-Study,* replete with hundreds of lessons as well as relevant poems, photographs, and vignettes.

Nature study on the New York plan, now that its manifesto was everywhere available, took off all over the country. Anna Comstock's *Handbook* became one of the most universal texts in the American classroom, and it was not the only one of its kind. I have collected dozens of titles, published mostly between 1890 and 1940. They take different approaches, some more didactic than others, others baldly emulating Comstock's form and style but seldom as well written. What they share is a devotion to the idea of firsthand experience with the animals and plants under study. Clifton Hodge, in *Nature-Study and Life,* called this kind of direct contact "the sheet anchor of elementary education, all the more necessary as modern life tends to drift away from nature into artificialities of every sort." And that was in 1902! What would he think a hundred years later, when children are more likely to recognize a Palm Pilot than a palm tree?

The implicit goal of all these books and the movement that inspired them, along with the Audubon Nature Clubs that followed, the novels of Gene Stratton Porter, the philosophy and writings of Theodore Roosevelt, the essays of Joseph Wood Krutch and Edwin Way Teale, and an entire culture of nature study, is just this: *essential nature literacy.* In a shocking line that seems hyperbolic today but may have been quite true in 1911, Comstock claimed that her weighty work "does not contain more than any intelligent country child of twelve should know of his environment; things that he should know naturally and without effort, although it might take him half his life-time to learn so much if he should not begin before the age of twenty."

And that's where things stood between the World Wars. Not that every citizen came out of public school a naturalist, nor every teacher a gifted guide. But there was a time in this country—the time when my grandmother led botany walks in Chelan—when a general familiarity with the fauna and flora around us was considered by consensus to be a worthwhile educational goal, and the naturalists were still highly respected in the universities.

So what happened? The answer isn't simple, but I believe it has to do with three main developments: the rise of highly quantitative, experimental, and specialized scholarship—the so-called hard sciences; the depopulation of the countryside and rise of the cities and suburbs; and World War II and the subsequent Cold War. The signs that nature study was on the defensive are already apparent in the publisher's foreword to the 1939 (24th) edition of Comstock's *Handbook*, which would still be printed into the late forties: "Some readers of the *Handbook* have suggested that the new edition be oriented away from the nature-study approach, and be made instead to serve as an introduction to the natural sciences. . . . But the nature-study approach has been preserved. The kernel of that method of treatment is the study of the organism in its environment, its relation to the world about it, and the features that enable it to function in its surrounding . . . The promising science of ecology is merely formalized nature-study . . . The truth is that nature-study is a science, and is more than a science; it is not merely a study of life, but an experience of life."

Science, however, did not agree. As mathematics penetrated deeper into every province of science, the descriptive and empirical nature of natural history began to look subjective to its critics. The fact that Mrs. Comstock and her followers admitted poetry and, horror of horrors, emotion, into their range of responses to the natural world planted them firmly beyond the pale of objectivity. The catchword that arose was "rigor" (and more recently, "robust"). How could an observation be robust, possess rigor, if it was merely "anecdotal" (the final condemnation) instead of experimental and statistically significant? In the end, what doomed the naturalists was exactly what Comstock celebrated in her work: in her long experience as a nature-study teacher, she wrote, she had "never been able to give a lesson twice alike on a certain topic or secure exactly the same results twice in succession." Since repeatability is a fundamental canon of the modern scientific process, this admission is anathema. "Natural history" became not only unfashionable, but derogatory; "naturalist" came to be a pejorative, or at best a quaint condescension.

It is worth examining the charges against the naturalists. Indeed, many of them permitted personal impressions into their work. Others attempted to minimize this, like Joseph Grinnell at the University of California in Berkeley, who required field notes to be kept in a prescribed manner to reduce bias. This brought a degree of observational rigor to field studies, but there was also plenty of slop and cheap sentimentality in the less thoughtful precincts of the genre. Since nature study was oriented toward the young, anthropomorphism was often employed. Sometimes, as in Thornton Burgess's *Bedtime Stories,* this was done with great skill alongside observation to convey the actual behavior of the animals. But all too often, nature stories descended into moralizing or emotional pandering, with animals as handy foils, wholly out of character from their namesake species. A vigorous debate arose over purported "nature faking" when John Burroughs and Theodore Roosevelt accused Ernest Thompson Seton, Rev. William J. Long, and others of setting up wildlife dramas in their books that never actually occurred in the wild, just for commercial effect. While Burroughs himself, Enos Mills, John Muir, and similar writers were keen and careful observers, their high-flown language nonetheless turned off the more hardheaded natural scientists in the academies who conflated honest sentiment with sentimentality.

The fact that many university naturalists rebelled at the increasingly quantitative nature of academic science and did not possess the tools for performing multivariate analyses and other tests of statistical significance inevitably furthered the gap. This allowed their modernist colleagues to portray them as soft and hopelessly outmoded, if not outright unreliable. The scientists had a point. A better kind of science had become available, at least as far as demonstrating the reality of perceived results. When the old guard failed to embrace these techniques (often for lack of the necessary math and, later, computer skills) they appeared to be fuddy-duddies or dilettantes, treating the natural world in a popular or superficial way. Many of the newer generation rejected the notion that results of value could be gained through observation of organisms in their habitats in the absence of experiment, manipulation, or statistics. They came to regard the old school as stuffy and intransigently old fashioned, to be rooted out if unable to adapt to the new terms.

However, the blame cut both ways, and the revolution threw out the best with the worst. The fact that the lab scientists frequently knew next to nothing about the organisms they studied as molecular or cellular "systems" or mathematical models made them defensive and unnecessarily hostile toward the naturalists, whose knowledge they sorely could have used. Just as the scientists saw the naturalists as oversimplifying amateurs, the field people saw the new professionals as reductionists ignorant of the actual ways of field and forest. As one teacher with a foot in both camps put it, how sad to have lost a healthy collegiality between the young turks on the cutting edge and the old farts with all the facts.

Things might have gone differently. The highly respected biologist Marston Bates, in his 1950 book *The Nature of Natural History*, argued that natural history and the erudite-sounding term "ecology" both "apply to just about the same package of goods." He rejected neither, and felt that the most important task confronting natural history was to find "appropriate experimental methods." But as experimental biology complexified the subject too far for anyone to be a successful generalist in the Jeffersonian manner, specialization ruled. Medicine and genetics helped to drive research away from the whole organism and into the cell and the molecule, thus out of the field and into the lab. Natural history was placed on a high, dusty shelf as a romantic artifact.

When the Second World War arrived, resources shifted to support a kind of science that delivered specific results: bombs capable of precise mayhem seemed a higher priority than classifying beetles. Children learned to identify aircraft profiles instead of songbirds. The aftermath left science in thrall to the national purpose of winning the Cold War. And then came *Sputnik*, the first Russian satellite and the coup de grace for the nature study movement. After 1956, advanced math programs arose around the country. Biology classes shifted toward the microscope and away from the field. Meanwhile, urban flight left a much-depleted population of rural residents in close daily contact with the countryside, even as the Victorian popularity of collecting the artifacts of nature was fading. The objective of a nature-literate citizenry was quietly forgotten.

So is natural history really dead? Certainly not. Only one member of the University of California system still retains the title Emeritus Professor of Natural History, but there have always been fine scientists who were also professed naturalists—people such as Rachel Carson, Loren Eiseley, Paul Ehrlich, Jane Goodall, Bernd Heinrich, Gary Paul Nabhan, and E. O. Wilson, who entitled his memoir *Naturalist*. Many fine ecologists of lesser renown have invigorated universities today, men and women who know that basic, real-world observation can be undertaken with rigor; they just can't teach much natural history as such, or call themselves naturalists too openly. Some departments where natural history may be performed at a safe remove from the old field's associations, and with more numbers involved, have adopted the ungainly label "organismal biology." Other schools buck the trend. The Evergreen State College in Washington offered the best of natural history and field instruction for its first thirty years, though this may be fading as the first wave of faculty retires.

The University of Vermont has a field natural history master's program, and Texas Tech University has just created such a major for undergraduates. But overall, few classes in field natural history are available. Though statistical cladistics and DNA studies are breathing new life into classification, pure systematics is as outre as ever. Unpaid adjuncts and amateurs perform much of the curatorial and classificatory labor in the museums, where a serious crisis looms in the apprehension of biological diversity. The main lepidopterist on "Bug" Johnson's old turf today is a truck driver, and the primary authorities on West Coast earthworms are a mother and son who receive no support for their important work. Who will tell us what we are losing, when we can no longer name the pieces—most of which have not even been described?

As for the children, some think environmental education has taken up the slack for the long-extinct nature study movement, but I don't believe that's the case. I have taken part in a great many EE programs, attended lots of conferences, observed numerous facilities. This is some of the most important work being done today, and the level of dedication is off the scale. I have only praise for the professionals involved. Yet there are fundamental differences between the old way and the new, and the new is by no means always better. For starters, nature study always and fundamentally stressed direct contact between student and organism. The point was to emulate the discoveries that country children would make on their own, enhanced by information to put the finds in context. Anna's lessons were meant to get children out, or to get the actual live materials into the classroom. Nowadays, secondhand connection is the rule, via games, lab specimens, and computers. Enter the Internet, its vastness of information making vicarious field-tripping instantly available. This can be a good thing, in proportion. But most teachers agree that no website can substitute for a spiderweb, while scintillating pixels on a screen will never replace the scintillant scales on a butterfly's wing. The virtual is even more remote from real life than cells and molecules. Still, all too often, teachers see no choice. That one-on-one, kid-and-creature chemistry largely went out with the slate board.

Second, nature study at its best happened regularly, often daily, and at every level. Environmental education, if funded at all, frequently takes place only during certain grades for brief spans of time. Typically, sixth graders will have an outdoor educational experience for one week—and that's that, except for bits and pieces fitted into other studies here and there. Standardized testing further marginalizes EE, since it doesn't figure into the all-important test scores. Few schools expose students to frequent and regular nature studies these days. And if they do, the outings and materials are likely to be sponsored by a timber company or resource agency and consist largely of propaganda.

Third, and of great importance, is the difference in approach to plants and animals today. Nature study premised itself on the assumption that boys and girls would become acquainted with their local flora and fauna by name, features, and habit. What birds flew and nested near the school, and how did they feed? What plants sprang up, outside the garden? Who sang in the spring chorus at dusk? But today, I see students coming out of school with no appreciable knowledge of their nonhuman neighbors: every evergreen is a pine, all brown birds are sparrows; and if a spring chorus is to be heard at all, a frog is a frog is a frog. Instead of the names and traits of different species, EE tends to concentrate on the "big picture" of ecological roles, functions, habitats, relationships, and patterns. Laudable goals, except it is like watching a play with no cast list! And is therefore liable to seem meaningless.

I generalize, of course. Splendid, knowledgeable teachers and exceptional facilities and programs do exist. However, many field trips more resemble recess in the woods than wood lore. Kids at one EE camp I visit each spring are so hyped to get out that they run and yell much of the time, while wildlife makes itself scarce and teachers resort to quasi-military and summer-camp routines to keep them (literally) in line. The few kids I find eager to learn a little natural history are swamped by the escapee tumult of the rest. Ropes courses and Ritalin are not what Anna Botsford Comstock had in mind. But then, as she found, uninformed teachers cannot teach nature with passion or results; few teachers today know any natural history at all, because they had none in high school or college.

The unavoidable facts that available habitats have retreated from the vicinities of most schools; that field trips have been truncated for reasons of liability, distance, and budget: and that students are so many, all make it much more difficult to ensure direct contact today. Consider too the hugely reduced access of children to wild places in their free time, whether because of safety concerns, Nintendo, or sprawl, and the conclusion seems inescapable that we are further than ever from a vision of a people on intimate terms with its cohabitants. While naturalist activities such as bird and butterfly watching grow in popularity as leisure pursuits, summer field institutes proliferate, and the National Audubon Society is investing in new nature centers all over the country, these still involve trivial numbers compared to mall shopping, football, or NASCAR racing.

We are not likely to return to nature study as it once was. Human society has become vastly more complex, even as the natural world has been simplified. During our nation's two previous fins de siecle, naturalists sat as president, and were admired for it. This is patently not the case now, when the relevance and rightness of good natural history teaching has never been greater but its estate never more distanced from the main affairs of the land and its leaders.

Our environmental professionals are superbly trained in engineering, management, and theory, yet seldom have any intimate knowledge of the working parts of the systems they measure, monitor, and care for. Likewise, the quality of ecological research being done in the universities and field stations has never been higher, but its context has never been narrower for most practitioners. Even the nature interpreters in our parks and preserves tend to know far less about the denizens of their precincts than the practice of communicating about them. Anna Comstock said "it is absolutely necessary to have a wide knowledge of other plants and animals" in order to understand our relations to any one kind. As one kind of animal ourselves, in deep need of righting our relations with the rest, a fundamental acquaintance with flora and fauna should be common knowledge. But when the people we delegate to study, manage, and interpret the natural world are unversed in its parts and ways, how is the ordinary citizen supposed to achieve ecological literacy?

What I most fear is how direct experience flees before these winds of change, along with a nuanced, responsive awareness of the very earth we inhabit. In his 1908 book *Nature-Study*, Frederick L. Holtz wrote that the child's interest in nature "is the outcome of curiosity, wonder—and is the complement of the social interest in bringing him into right relationship with the world." As the distance grows between a tiny priesthood who know small parts of nature very well and a massive population who know next to nothing about the whole and not even the names of their neighbors, a right relationship with the world seems more and more elusive. Today, when children have all too many stimuli and all too few opportunities to experience bald wonder, many seem to lack any real interest in nature. Yet I believe, along with Carson and Wilson, that wonder is innate in the very young, waiting only to be ignited before the cheap tricks of modern life damp the fuse. Nothing can light the flame of fascination in a child like another living thing.

It may be the naturalists who save us in the end, by bringing us all back down to earth.

Fat with Frits

(*Oregon Humanities*, 2002)

When Oregon Humanities *asked me to write to the theme of "wealth," this saying of an old butterfly collector friend leapt to mind. The piece later appeared in an issue of* Whole Terrain *devoted to "gratitude and greed." Except for the episode with Ken Tidwell and the stinging nettles, which I can still feel fifty-five years later, it was fun recalling field trips rich in fritillaries, and flitting with them into the territory between true wealth versus too much.*

It was forty years ago in Utah's Stansbury Mountains when I first heard the phrase.

I was a high school wrestler and lepidopterist, and I'd made friends with an Air Force Academy cadet with the same enthusiasms and the remarkable future officer's name of John Justice. John had invited me along on a butterfly-collecting trip that summer. He left Colorado Springs, picked me up east of Denver, and we headed up to the foot of Mount Elbert, over Wolf Creek Pass, and down to the lowlands at Pagosa Springs, camping and collecting along the way. We explored cool, dewy morning meadows for orange ips and checkerspots; hot, fly-ridden sage flats for Stretch's satyrs; blackrock rims for Baird's swallowtails.

Each time the bag was good, furnishing enough specimens for a study series with some left over for swapping with fellow leppers elsewhere, John summed up the action with a pithy statement standing for sufficiency plus: "Great!" he'd say, "we're fat with *bairdii*!" or, "Good goin'—now I'm fat with *stretchi*." One night I awoke to a big flight of huge, rare, mauve-brown and olive Glover's silkmoths around the embers of our campfire. In my somnolant state, I'd failed to apprehend their rarity, and awaken John. When he heard what he'd missed, then confirmed it from bat-dropped wings, he was inconsolable. "We could have been SO FAT with *gloveri*," he wailed, and never let me forget it.

John, much stronger and tougher than I, made me wrestle him in a lep-friend's peach orchard, giving me the first asthma attack of my life from the orchard grass pollen. A few days later, in Utah's Wasatch Range, another butterfly pal named Ken Tidwell took us collecting among the aspen groves. He introduced me to stinging nettle by slapping my wrist with it so I wouldn't forget. But it was all worth it when we got into the Stansburys and filled our envelopes with the rarely collected *Speyeria egleis linda*—a lovely, green-and-mercury ventered fritillary— and half a dozen other species of silverspots. Though our take was prodigious, it consisted mostly of males (almost redundant in the population) and made not a dent in the masses on the wing. Even so, perhaps already wimping into more of a watcher than a catcher, I was sated. I had way more new and exciting material than I'd have time to spread and label for weeks and plenty to exchange with my academic pen pals in Romania, Rhodesia, and Wisconsin. I was ready to be home when we rolled back in to Denver at the end of our road trip. John's parting words, as he turned south for the academy, were these: "Good trip, Bob. Man, are we ever fat with frits!"

I thought of that recently as I flew over the Stansbury Mountains on my way home for an early spring break from a teaching job in Utah. There was the smoking turret of Kennecott Copper, where leathery-handed Ken had worked; and there, the range itself, and its canyons where lovely *linda* still flies in summer. Shuttling down from snowy Logan that morning, flying out of Salt Lake City in the midst of the Winter Olympics, I made out nothing of the city's once-in-a-lifetime fest and chaos but even more National Guardsmen and -women in the airport than usual, lots of folks decked out in Olympic logo togs, and still more studded with dozens of colorful metal pins. Olympic pins had been the big thing in the Utah papers, along with judging scandals and traffic jams. Green Jell-O pins were the most sought after. Collectors, without nets, came from afar to buy, sell, and especially to trade pins. In the airport lobby I saw people garlanded, swaddled, and armored with chain-mail suits of pins depicting every event and everything else from Brigham Young to Utah fry sauce, each with the requisite field marks of the five Olympic rings and the 2002 logo like a multipronged electrical plug. The best-decorated collectors had a kind of a smile, a slight, self-satisfied lift and twitch to the corner of the mouth that I thought I recognized. Once aloft, looking down at the Stansburys, it came to me: They were fat with pins.

Nowadays, in our culture, few would equate or express "having it" with "fat." Affluence, or its perception, comes in many colors. We may feel rich in trade goods, hoarded foodstuffs, apparel and array, or toys and accoutrements. Of course, nothing speaks "well off" louder to most folks than plain old money. But not fat. If anything, the moneyed distance themselves from blubber much more than the have-nots. Obesity is an American specialty, but even more so for the poor. So while showing off folds of fat might remain a statement of affluence for some island peoples, it has come to mean the opposite here. Yet the metaphor remains—if not in the traditional sense of storing away sustenance for the lean season, then by way of corpulent display of opulence.

To me, there is no more blatant sign of the reigning plutocracy than the spare tire of pretentious macrohouses that girds most cities today. While traditional mansions tended to be sturdy brick Tudors or Queen Annes set on modest lots along urban parkways, these contemporary castles of conspicuous consumption occupy acres on the suburban fringe, sprawling beyond sprawl. As an Austin friend put it while showing me one twelve-thousand-square-foot excrescence, "These people have an edifice complex."

I plainly admit my bias here. As an independent writer for twenty years, an existence designed to maintain a standard of living approximately that of a graduate student, I have always been one to seek a sense of well-being outside the fiduciary realm. Since I no longer collect butterflies except a little for research (and then mostly catch-and-release), I no longer get fat on frits in the same way. But a day minted in yellow and blue and butterfly-bush purple, when I can anticipate loads of bright wings on the buddleia, is a day I feel positively loaded. The knowledge that a patch of native bleeding hearts is spreading in our little woods under the influence of our care, furnishing host plants for parnassian butterfly larvae, as well as a broad swatch of spring pink and a spicy-sweet redolence on the April air, makes me almost guilty with the gluttony of expanding interest on investment.

When we have firewood stacked beyond our foreseeable needs, food on the shelves and in the garden well past first frost, and a colorfield of twenty-four Steller's jays beneath the cedar's umbrella; while health holds and old cars still run well; with a canoe in the shed and miles of unexplored rivers in easy reach; with good books aplenty lined up to read both in my own crammed stacks and in the library that the Philistines have not yet managed to shut down, not to mention in devoted independent bookstores holding out in nearby towns, I consider myself affluent beyond all need or measure. If I can pay my bills too—gravy!

I reckon this could sound smug, or be mistaken for an argument that people should be satisfied with what they have. The fact that I've always been of modest means and taken material satisfaction in nonmonetary goods says nothing whatever about the greater need of the many who actually have too little. What it may speak to—not as example but by way of contrast—is the growing clot of those who have too much.

For I do believe beyond all doubt that the acquisition, concentration, and exemplification of wealth—more than religious schism, more than tribalism and nationalism, even more than egoism—will be our undoing. The fast-breeder appearance of enormous private vehicles on the lots and highways, the eruption of those plasterboard palaces in place of the fruited plain, the proliferation of pure, product-driven plenitude—these are signs of decadence far beyond the usually touted marks of a fading culture. This is true simply because no species can persist beyond the means of its ecosystem, and no finite system could support forever the rate and degree of our collective consumption. Nor, as we have seen, will the rest of the world tolerate our stilling presumption.

But it is not just appetite, or the injustice of misallocation, that bugs me. It is the shade and timbre of our surreal sense of priorities. How can it be, I ask myself again and again, in this time of unprecedented personal wealth among more Americans than ever, when taxes are being cut and arsenals fattened, that we lack the cash for some of the most basic functions of a sane and civilized society? As I write, budget proposals commonly call for the dissolution or shrinkage of libraries, many teachers earn less than a living wage, Congress is debating the abolishment of long-distance passenger trains, and on and on.

From the biblical eye of the needle to Midas to Enron, our folk literature is full of cautionary tales about the toxicity of wealth. But our myths still reward heroes who kill the dragon to seize its golden hoard. What if the dragon, instead of something evil, is the generative and protective force of nature? What if the gold isn't there to be seized, but stewarded, succored, and shared?

I don't suppose it likely that many will adopt my model of affluence—replete in the knowledge that the world once gave Thomas Tallis and still has Bob Dylan, surfeited with the possibility of good art and good food and drink and good company, wealthy with a roof and an old woodstove and a family I love. In a phrase, fat with frits. But I can at least hope that our species' concept of wealth may one day come to mean happy adaptation instead of endless acquisition. Hope like that, after all, is the ultimate luxury.

Postcards from the Pleistocene

Saving Hendrickson Canyon

(Holding Common Ground, EWU Press, 2005)

It took a coalition of Willapa locals over twenty years to protect the last old-growth forest patch in Wahkiakum County. The invitation for this essay gave me the opportunity to tell the long tale. A nice postscript is the fact that the former bassist for Nirvana, Krist Novoselic, has bought the quarter-section adjacent to Hendrickson Canyon, effectively doubling its size. He and his wife Darbury keep an eye on goings-on at Hendrickson, as voluntary stewards for the Washington Natural Heritage Program.

In 1973, as Deep River resident Jack Scharbach could see, logging had ruled in the Willapa for many decades. The watersheds in the Willapa Hills—the low, rainy coastal range in southwest Washington—had been cut over, leaving a tatterde-malion landscape of recent clear-cuts, young plantations, and extensive second growth. But the forest behind Jack's place was different. He wandered freely in those deep woods, getting to know the ridges and ravines intimately. The elk got fed up with his following them, and one day a large bull charged him. He knew it was a special place he'd landed.

Jack had happened on the only stand of original forest in all of Wahkiakum County. The old-growth in Hendrickson Canyon stood out like a pompadour in a company of chrome-domes, so bald were the surrounding sections of private timberlands. The canyon, in contrast, belonged to the people of Washington. The Department of Natural Resources (DNR) administers the state forests on behalf of a number of trusts. Hendrickson came under a "university trust," one desig-nated to produce income for the five state universities. Luckily its stumpage had never been put up for bid.

Washington Natural Heritage Program biologists Reid Schuller and Rex Crawford confirmed Jack's find and recommended Hendrickson for protection. When I learned about this, I rushed to see the canyon. But the maze of logging roads that pierced those shaven acres proved so convoluted and the maps so contradictory that finding the forest turned out to be a real challenge. Several failed forays made it easy for me to imagine how Sasquatch can live undetected in the tangle of successional forest around Mount St. Helens. My search also showed how tiny the leavings really are, that they can be secreted among the immensity of the second growth, despite the size of their great old trees. Once I had located the place, many field trips followed.

Now, when I think of Hendrickson Canyon, I think of which flowers were blooming, what birds were singing, and who saw and heard them with me. During one late-autumn outing, bright chanterelles and even oranger polypore fungi daubed the secret places with unexpected color. Penny-whistling winter wrens shattered the same silence the varied thrush only shivered when it gave its hoarse call, like a whistling through spit. Slanting great cedars hung draperies of moss mixed with their own lacy foliage, a green screen to the pinched winter light that rarely reached the ground through the canopy of conifers. Winter was on its way out when I took my friend and mentor Charles Remington, of Yale's Peabody Museum of Natural History, to see the trees. We sought the wood roach, a creature merging evolutionary traits of both roaches and termites; we found many-legged myriapods—centipedes and millipedes—attenuated marvels of nervous organization. There were isopods, related to common "pill bugs" or wood lice, their young collected around their legs in a display of parental care uncommon among invertebrates. And there were snail-eating ground beetles, their mandibles elongated to reach into coiled snail shells, and several species of their prey, notably the Vancouver green snail. Charles collected a rich bag of insects. I promised to keep searching for the wood roach.

Spring seems the liveliest time in the forest, and our expeditions center on that season. My wife, Thea, and I took to the canyon to catalog trees one March. Hendrickson is the truly mixed forest of the very old Willapa inland—some spruce, some cedar, a lot of hemlock, and remnants of Douglas-fir. The largest tree we found that day, in fact, was a massive Douglas-fir. We lounged by the big tree's base and pondered the wealth of the uncut woods, a treasure not measured in board feet but in the number of notes in a winter wren's song and the legacy of leaflets in the carpet of oxalis shamrocks spread before our boots. When we learned this tree stood a little outside of the trust parcel, and it later fell to a logging contractor who also bulldozed the nearby stream, we were shattered.

The next spring outing to Hendrickson found a band of old-growth pilgrims assembling at Swede Park, our home in Gray's River, on an April morning. Elizabeth Rodrick of the Washington Department of Game's Nongame

Wildlife Program had come to see the forest as a possible habitat for northern spotted owls. The party included Carol Carver, Wahkiakum County extension agent; David and Elaine Myers, local photographer and master gardener; old-tree tracker Bob Richards, and others. The hoped-for owls failed to respond, the habitat too small for them to breed. But we found amphibians—red-legged and chorus frogs and several salamanders. A small, spring-fed stream led to a spruce and cedar cleft where a pond stood, its water roiled by massing newts. Caddisfly larvae dragged their shelters across the newts' gelatinous egg masses. We reached a broad ridge carpeted with grass-green oxalis and single-flowered wintergreen, with its heavenly scent, overhung by cedar snags from a fire. Remains of three deer could have been cougar kills, as they were not far from where I had once seen the big chocolate-colored cat. Reluctantly we rounded the ridge and stepped back out to a clear-cut and cars.

The year at Hendrickson came around with a late-autumn excursion in search of spiders. Our arachnologist friend, Rod Crawford, extended Professor Remington's invertebrate list with his own careful survey of spiders and other microfauna. In a brief circuit of one lobe of forest, tangential to the main old-growth stand, Rod found twenty-two species of spiders and six kinds of harvestmen, including one new state record and one old-growth indicator species. All this, on a rainy day, after most of the natural activity had shut down for the season.

Besides enjoying and studying the canyon, we accelerated efforts to protect it. In 1983 we got a resolution, from the Columbia-Pacific Resource Conservation and Development District, that urged DNR to reserve the canyon as an old-growth natural area. In 1984, the Wahkiakum County Democratic Convention passed a similar resolution. In 1985, the Wahkiakum County Board of Commissioners did likewise when Joe Florek (a logger), Bob Torppa, and Kayrene Gilbertsen all voted for the measure. The commissioners went on record as "supporting the preservation of the Hendrickson Canyon Old-Growth Forest to protect the same from being destroyed or severely impacted by the encroachment of man for uses other than educational and conservation purposes." Even so, Crown Zellerbach opposed the Hendrickson designation sub rosa, apparently just on principle, or maybe because a preserve plunked down beside their managed land would be inconvenient.

The fact that old-growth indicator spiders occur in the canyon might not impress anyone in the local tavern, but the heritage idea made sense. Dennis Nagasawa, neighbor, fire chief, and local DNR man who kept a protective eye on the stand, told me that cones had been gathered from big trees in Hendrickson for seed recovery. Developed through natural selection over ages, the genes in those seeds are postcards from the Pleistocene, phone calls to the future of forestry. You can't buy them from Burpee's. So we gathered solid local support to save our last, best Willapa forest.

Bert Cole—longtime commissioner of public lands, in the cockpit at DNR, one hand on the controls and the other on a chainsaw—yielded to Brian Boyle, whose fresh set of policies emphasized the unique qualities of state forestlands. Among these, Boyle adopted a plan for a number of so-called Old-Growth Seral Stage Deferrals. If granted, Hendrickson's deferral was to last until 1993; after that we hoped to dedicate this special place as a state natural-area preserve. In the end, though, only twenty-five acres of Hendrickson made it into this program.

We kept up the pressure. Professor Gordon Alcorn of the University of Puget Sound, eleven-year chair of the Scientific Area Advisory Committee, came to see the canyon with us and sent the commissioner his enthusiastic vote for protection as a Natural Area Preserve. The 1987 legislative session passed the Natural Resource Conservation Area Act, providing another means for removing ecologically significant trust lands from the timber harvest schedule. The next year the Wahkiakum County Commissioners, at our request, again wrote to Commissioner Boyle, asking that Hendrickson be considered as a Natural Resource Conservation Area. John Edwards replied for DNR that it was indeed a candidate.

A new commissioner, Jennifer Belcher, was elected on a conservation platform. She maintained the temporary administrative withdrawal for Hendrickson. But she was feeling pressure to make more state timber available for sale; formal preserve dedication would have to be garnered if we were to rest easy. At a one-on-one lobbying session with Commissioner Belcher at a fund-raising function of The Nature Conservancy, I gestured broadly and swept a glass of red wine all over her blue jacket, just before her speech. The commissioner, fortunately, had a sense of humor, and promised to send me her dry-cleaning bill. Not long after, when we shared a podium at a conference, she wisely kept her distance.

Late in 1994, Commissioner Belcher wrote to tell me that her office was "currently putting together a legislative packet to obtain the necessary funding for trust land transfer" for Hendrickson. But just as the site gained the top position in line, the legislature approved no funds for the transfer program, and we went back to writing and lobbying for another five years.

Meanwhile, a kerfuffle arose over the natural-area preserves. Some local people in Grays Harbor County, upset over potential restriction of their hunting, objected loudly to a proposed preserve on Elk River. Their howls alerted some politicians who introduced legislation to abolish or trim back the program. It failed, but the episode managed to put the state heritage protection effort on the defensive. Once more I asked the Wahkiakum County Board of Commissioners to pass a new resolution in favor of a Hendrickson Canyon reserve. Led by Esther Gregg and including Ron Ozment and Richard Marsyla, the county commission again came through with key support. So did the Gray's River Grange, of which I am a longtime member. Finally our district senator, Majority Leader Sid Snyder, a Democrat from Long Beach, gave his vital endorsement. Early in 1999, the legislature not only passed the appropriation, but placed Hendrickson Canyon in the top "must acquire" category—largely because of the key local support we had garnered.

On a vile day, just before Thanksgiving in 1999, we attended one last hearing before a DNR fiscal officer in the Pacific County courthouse. Opponents bantered about how we might all be spending the holiday together if the storm got any worse. The mood hardened as testimony began. A Pacific County commissioner with feet in both logging and real estate, a diehard opponent of state preserves, railed against removal of any land from either the tax base or the timber supply. How absurdly tiny our request was, I pointed out, compared to the hundreds of thousands of acres in the industrial forest estate, and how petty the argument against it. Fisheries manager Ed Maxwell spoke of the key importance of protecting the few remaining undamaged headwaters, when millions were being spent to restore damaged salmon streams all over the region. If it is cut, he said, it will be gone forever. Trees will come back, but not the forest, not in our time. When a Columbia tugboat crewman, Dan Toelkes, got up and shared from the heart his hopes that this one bit of woods might be spared as a token of what this place once was, the examiner had no doubt about the quality of local sentiment. The winterdark room, just then, felt like victory. But one hurdle remained, and it was a high one.

The outcome still had to be approved by the Natural Resources Board in Olympia. The board meeting came more than a year later, in early December. With it, a new and unexpected problem arose. Because the canyon is home to nesting marbled murrelets, a threatened species that came into prominence after the northern spotted owl, state appraisers rated its price tag very low. This meant the university trust would receive little value for the land and timber. There was a real danger of the board's turning down the transfer on that basis.

At Commissioner Belcher's request, in-house economists had devised a bold scheme to apply substantial economic value for noncommercial habitat—a real advance in DNR thinking that promised to take the agency discourse beyond bare stumpage prices—but this new initiative threatened old-fashioned thinkers. The outcome would prove critical, not only for Hendrickson but for several other trust land parcels that were on the agenda as well, including old-growth additions to the Nemah Natural Resource Conservation Area and Willapa Divide Natural Area Preserve, located respectively west and east of our site. I'd been warned there might be disagreement, and I had almost stayed away from this meeting; I didn't think I could stand another let-down.

One member, the dean of the University of Washington College of Forest Resources, who turned out to have a remarkably brief tenure in that position, was wavering and seemed to be leaning against the initiative on the faulty theory that the land might be worth more later. The same Pacific County commissioner was furious that he had not been allowed to speak at this late date. Jennifer Belcher was chairing the Forest Board for the last time; after eight years in a job guaranteed to piss almost everyone off, she was not amused by the waffling and whining. Showing that she held no grudge over the red wine, she muscled the vote through in one of her last acts as Commissioner of Public Lands. On December 5, 2000, after a campaign of more than twenty years, Hendrickson Canyon finally was saved as a Natural Resource Conservation Area.

A celebration followed at the Fishbowl Brewpub in Olympia. Most of our Willapa old-growth campaigners came along. So did Laura Smith and Jennie Lange of The Nature Conservancy, an organization that had been key in getting the trust lands package through the legislature and the agency. Jack Scharbach joined us too. When Jack had first told me about Hendrickson Canyon, he had little hope of its protection; after all, every stand of trees in the Willapa Hills seemed bound to come before the saw one day. Now the deal was done. We lifted pints to the forest, to our friends, and to persistence, warm in the knowledge that at least in this small corner, the forest of our homeland would stand.

How to Love a River

(*Hipfish*, 2005)

Living along the Lower Columbia River in recent decades has meant living with the constant threat of carbon, in all of its merchantable forms, coming here for processing or storage before shipment abroad. Oil trains, coal depots, and pipeline after pipeline bear down on the Columbia's banks and other shorelines of the Pacific Northwest. This piece addresses just the first of several liquefied natural gas (LNG) terminals that were proposed for the Lower Columbia. As the battles over LNG were joined and began to gain momentum, the snappy arts magazine Hipfish *polled writers resident to the estuary on what the river, its plight, and its protection meant to them.*

When I was a kid, another kid named Sam Hart lived down the block. Sam Hart was famous for a special talent he possessed. I knew several boys who could burp on demand, some even to a melody. But Sam Hart was the only one I knew who could fart on demand. Hart the Fart, as he was inevitably known, made a party trick of passing gas at a lit match, launching an impressive blue jet. I don't know how much this skill helped Sam get girls; not much, I'd guess. But Patty Vido once attended a make-out party at his house to which I was not invited; I could hear the music from my bedroom, and it drove me crazy, as I had a mammoth crush on Patty Vido. Someone, everyone, was in there kissing Patty Vido, and all I had was the scent of the snow through my window screen and the beat of the hi-fi on the night air. But I took comfort in the fact that at least I wasn't famous for my flatulence.

For Sam's part, maybe some kind of popularity was better than none. In any case, I couldn't help but think of Hart the Fart when I learned of the Calpine liquefied natural gas scam proposed for the Skipanon Peninsula. How to say something fresh about the Great River of the West? When you stack up the literature of the Columbia, it seems it must all have been uttered already. There are the logs kept by Haswell, Boit, and Hoskins on Captain Robert Gray's *Columbia Redeviva*, followed by Vancouver's logs and Richard Nokes's *Columbia's River*. There are the economical effusions of Lewis, Clark, and their interpreters from

DeVoto through Ambrose, Botkin, and Ziak. Washington Irving's *Fur Traders of the Columbia River*, Woody Guthrie's "Roll On, Columbia," and Chuck Williams's *Bridge of the Gods, Mountains of Fire*. Thomas Nelson Strong's *Cathlamet on the Columbia*, Julia Butler Hansen's *Singing Paddles*, and Keith McCoy's *Melodic Whistles in the Columbia Gorge*. Archie Satterfield's *Moods of the Columbia*, Archie Binns's *You Rolling River*, and Murray Morgan's *The Dam*. More recently a great spate of Columbia books has flowed forth, including Richard White's *The Organic Machine*, Bill Dietrich's *Northwest Passage*, Blain Harden's *A River Lost*, and Susan Zwinger's *The Hanford Reach*. And don't forget Sam McKinney's *Reach of Tide, Ring of History*, Robin Cody's *Voyage of a Summer Sun*, Craig Lesley's *Riversong*, and even Pyle's "Ring of Rivers" in *Wintergreen*.

And yet, there is more to say. Maybe no one has recorded the exact way the current shifted in the lee of Tenasillahe Island yesterday when a raft of common mergansers took wing. Perhaps the scent of cottonwood balsam when the wind from the Gorge shifts away from Camas has never yet been captured. I don't suppose any writer has plumbed the depth of black in the sunken shadow of Beacon Rock, or taken down the dialogue where the Willamette and the Columbia finally meet, again and again and again.

Nor has the river's capacity for insults been fully recorded. We suffer no lack of documentation of dams, no gaps in the catalog of cataclysm, no dearth of dope on dioxins. I have sacrificed a perfectly good butterfly net to catching an oil-soaked murre from a spill spit out the river's mouth; I have tugged invasive loosestrife from wapato beds, and written letters about dredging and dumping the spoils of this particular water war. You'd think the Columbia had already taken our best shot at screwing it up, from Hermiston's nerve gas to Hanford's nuclear waste. Apparently not. Now comes the Calpine LNG juggernaut, mainlining toward Warrenton and Hammond like a blue flame for the ages. And this is why Sam Hart, famous in Hoffman Heights, Colorado, in 1960, comes to mind when I contemplate this new enormity shuffling on our doorstep.

If it makes its way in, get ready for a Sam Hart Special, and I don't mean a party trick. With an accidental incineration radius of a thousand yards and a burn zone of a mile or more, this is a new neighbor that can kill—a lethal genie that can't be stoppered, once out of its acrid canister. The epic shortcomings and monumental risks of the LNG misadventure are well known and described by other writers more knowledgeable than I. But this wickedness cuts beyond the immediate mischief of eviscerating a pleasant peninsula, endangering its populace, and placing a critical estuary and its uses in immense jeopardy. The knavery extends into territory so near the wild heart of the entire region that many cannot even conceive how persons of right mind could contemplate such an outrage with a straight face and a whole heart.

Our big river—second biggest on the continent—has suffered clots, stents, bypasses, and all manner of noxious plaque; has weathered dilution, pollution, and solution with every kind of foul infusion; has labored under logging silt and rip-rap, isotope and nucleotide, squaw fish and sewage sludge, while watching its salmon slip like so many silverfish down the bathtub drain. But this big aorta of Cascadia has never before invited full-scale thrombosis with open arms.

Or maybe I'm all wet, and in this sublimely mercantile age, LNG is just the ticket. After all, the Upright Apes of North America, Second Coming, have enflamed the Cuyahoga, oiled the Ohio, quicksilvered the Quebec, hog-tied the Tennessee, PCB'd the Hudson, slimed the Potomac, DMZ'd the Rio Grande, out-right stolen the Colorado, leaded the St. Lawrence, sacrificed the Sacramento, laked the Snake, petered out the San Pedro, concreted the LA, reversed the Labrador, radiated the Savannah, massacred the Missouri, and just plain mo' fo'd the Mississippi. Why shouldn't we all get behind this one grand chance, the very best yet, for first-rate, top-flight, full-scale Calamity on the Columbia? Why should the Cuyahoga be the only watercourse that gets to burn?

Of course, it wasn't, not really. There was also Whatcom Creek, in Bellingham. When Olympic Pipeline Company's pipe ruptured, a bombing wall of gasoline spewed down the streambed, preceded by a pressure-cloud of explosive vapors. Two ten-year-old boys playing with a bottle rocket ignited the fumes and lost their lives horribly. In an ultimate betrayal, a teen named Liam was fishing his beloved creek, only to be incinerated, as the ecosystem was baked beyond func-tion. Have the Port of Astoria Commissioners forgotten this event? Did they even notice? Perhaps they should be required to study the tragedy of Whatcom Creek in all its grim detail, for this is what happens when a gassy new neighbor goes bad: the very air can kill you, when it becomes flammable. And with LNG on the Skipanon, the losses would be many more than those three unutterably unlucky lads.

Americans are not alone in their river-blindness, nor even very special; con-sider the Danube's blues, the wretched Rhine, the ruined Nile, the disgorged Yangtze. But we have been particularly energetic at the task, seldom missing an opportunity to show heroic contempt for rivers. That's been the easy part: the hydraulic-placered canyons of Colorado and California, the diverted flumes that gave rise to Denver and Las Vegas, the entire Southeast stripped of the richest fauna of pearly mussels in the world. Hurting rivers takes no great imagination. Chemical plants and concrete have made easy work of that part of what often resembles a hate-hate relationship. Want to endear a river to its people? Slap a freeway along its shore—hey presto! No, the real challenge is the one taken up by the few who would love our rivers.

Not so few, really; in fact, maybe most, if they only knew it. Anyone who has ever dunked a worm or cast a fly, raised a topsail or stoked a stinkpot, sailed a board or dipped a paddle; anybody who has set a net from bowpicker or sternpicker, walked the deck of a tug or barge as sunrise breaks free from heavy fog, soaked a toe at the shore or wished to be an otter while flailing away at a mediocre breaststroke—any such a one must know in at least a rudimentary, brain-stem sort of way what it is to love a river. Maybe everybody loves rivers. But will we ever learn how to show it?

To love a river well, like a person or a place or anything else, means to attend. To pay extraordinary attention. All the time. To dive deep into the flow of water, time, and land that together lay this river down where it is and not somewhere else, flowing some other direction. It takes fingering the bits of shell and crayfish carapace and mayfly exuvium that wash ashore; following the ripples downstream as they race, then spend themselves on the beach; watching the rafts of western grebes and tundra swans, the canvasbacks that collect for a few days a year in Young's Bay, the scoters and the scaups and the sea lion nuggets known as buffleheads. And there is more to it than that. You have to imagine the pilots climbing the sides of ships in storm; drop the sneer for the folks on the paddle-wheelers long enough to realize that this may be their first time on a big river; and consider what it once meant to sleek the current in a canoe beside sea otters, beneath condors. If you can do all this, and then take it into your heart in a thousand other ways, you can say that you are beginning to love the river in a way that its own giant heart might recognize. And if, doing all this, you can still imagine casting a vote for Calpine, then you need professional help—maybe a heart transplant, for starters; then a brain. For the soul, I'm afraid there's no help, or hope.

Because it can only be this that led our elected officials to sign such a devil's deal: a deep and abiding inability to love the very entity they are sworn to manage, to nurture, to protect, for all of us who huddle here in the Columbia's lap. And so it falls to the rest of us, who have chosen to live (not die) along these damaged (but not yet dead) waters, to embrace what's left of the Great River of the West as our home. Just because a watercourse has been sorely compromised does not mean it is no longer worth revering. Indians still wash their dead in the tepid but living Ganges. Athabascans yet fish the Yukon between the banks of melting permafrost. Visiting Philadelphia, near the mouth of its besmirched river, I was struck to see the gray water lit up by thousands of flowers and fruits. As black children skipped stones on my shore, residents of South Philly on the other side dressed the river in a summer festival transcending all sludge and chemicals.

For all of its burdens, the Columbia yet retains its essential character—especially our share, the tidal reach. Despite the jetties and the dredges, never mind the spoils and the wakes, the big river carries on in a state worth embracing—and saving. When I say it is up to those of us who dwell here, we voluntary riparians, to love the river enough in the absence of any such impulse from the commissioners, I mean we must exercise that embrace. And in doing so, one collective utterance must issue from our love-struck throats: NO, we must say. No, we won't have this. It shan't happen, not here not on this river that we love. We must send them packing, wishing them all bad luck elsewhere. And when we've done that, we must go out, onto the water, along the shore, or into the hills above; look this river over, breathe in the fresh estuarine air, and say, "Yes. That's how."

The Beauty of Butterfly Nets

(*Wings*, 2006)

Noting the yawning absence of butterfly watching in our outdoor scene, I was the first in this country to write books about it, in 1974 and 1984. What I had in mind, and advocated, was an appreciative, nonconsumptive approach to enjoying butterflies, overdue as a parallel to birding, and just as rewarding. I thought that people who discovered butterflies would become natural allies for butterfly conservation. I saw this development as complementary to catching butterflies, which remains necessary for conservation biology and serves to introduce many children to a love of nature. Others took the ball and ran with it. But as always seems to happen, they redefined the goal in absolutist terms: cameras and binoculars only—no nets. Hence this essay.

It is in many ways apt that this piece should be penned on a Friday the thirteenth, the day between Charles Darwin's two hundredth birthday and St. Valentine's Day. The thirteenth, because an unlucky day to me is one when I don't get outdoors in direct contact with nature. Valentine's, because this essay is really a love letter to one of my favorite tools and field companions. And Darwin Day, on account of the simple and certain fact that our all-time greatest naturalist might have merely toiled in quiet obscurity as a country vicar, had it not been for his butterfly net.

When Darwin cut theology classes at Cambridge, he did so to collect beetles and chase swallowtails at Wicken Fen. That's what led him astray, ultimately to his voyage on the *Beagle*, to the Galapagos, and to his residence at Down House where *On the Origin of Species* was written. Things are not too different in our time: E. O. Wilson didn't need a net to study ants, but he made clear in his memoir, *Naturalist*, that his carefree days afield with his insect net were the hours that made him who he is. The godfather of the Karner blue butterfly (*Lycaeides samuelis*) and a great literary recorder of the "individuating detail," Vladimir Nabokov, put it this way: "The ordinary stroller might feel on sauntering out a twinge of pleasure . . . but the cold of the metal netstick in my right hand magnifies the pleasure to almost intolerable bliss."

Some readers perhaps find it odd to read an encomium to the classic collecting implement in a journal devoted to insect conservation. But this is no contradiction, as was recognized in the earliest days of the Xerces Society, when its collecting policy was carefully crafted. When collecting presents an actual conservation risk with overzealous pursuit of rare or highly restricted species, we of course oppose it. But this is an uncommon event. For the most part, aerial insect populations in particular are reproductively adept, elusive, and highly resistant to overcollecting. Besides, as anyone who has actually tried to catch butterflies knows, a human being wielding a net is one of the most inefficient predators you could design. On the other hand, in order to conserve something, you have to know exactly where it occurs. The great contribution of the net-wielders is in building and updating the database of invertebrate distribution. This is why, as counterintuitive as it may seem to some, butterfly nets have been among our most important instruments for insect conservation.

But that is just one reason we should appreciate these simple and centuries-old implements. True, our field guides, state butterfly atlases, and rare-species surveys have commonly depended upon specimens in hand. More and more these days these functions are being conducted with binoculars and digital cameras instead, and that's all to the good when it serves the purpose just as well. But it doesn't always. The fact is, many butterflies—especially certain blues, skippers, and rare varieties only subtly differentiated from more-common types—require close examination for positive identification. For these it doesn't help to have an approximate ID; positive recognition is essential.

For example, during my recently completed Butterfly Big Year, I was looking (among other things) at the responses of ranges to changing climate, and I certainly saw some dramatic examples. But, at one spot in arid north Texas, I thought I had found a species abundant more than a hundred miles north of any previous records. Surrounded by my field guides, I still couldn't determine the species for sure from my notes, or from photographs. Even the national authority on the group had to dissect a specimen to be certain which of two species it represented—and in the end, he was able to determine that it was the one that belonged there after all.

So the reliability of occurrence data is essential—and often it is still the net that sifts good data from bad. Nets are seldom weapons of mass destruction and need not even be lethal. I do a great deal of my field survey and teaching with harmless catch-and-release. I find that people make a deeper connection when they can examine a creature up close, from every angle, and then carefully release it to a flower, or a child's nose. This practice, employing net, tweezers, and a light and practiced touch, gives a far more satisfactory encounter for a group than a fleeting glimpse from yards away.

And that brings us to my favorite reason for loving butterfly nets: they are the cheapest, simplest, and most effective environmental education tools ever invented. Give a child a pair of binoculars or a camera, and he will be occupied for a moment or two, before setting it aside. But give her a net, and watch her go! Besides, the argument that all interaction with butterflies should be conducted solely through optics is an elitist one; most kids can't afford close-focusing binoculars or a good camera, but they can often pull together twelve or fourteen bucks for a basic net from BioQuip—or make one themselves, as my friends and I always did. To this day I chiefly use a net fashioned from a Colorado cottonwood branch—an artifact from my youth—that I named Marsha. I made Marsha almost forty years ago, and she has had a hard life (described in detail in *Walking the High Ridge: Life as Field Trip*). Yet she is still with me, a beloved friend who has helped me introduce butterflies to thousands of children and their parents.

Kids love nets because chasing insects is *fun*. It also brings the chaser face-to-face with exciting, novel, always-surprising *life*. Talk to any number of biologists, doctors, wildlife managers, and other life-science professionals, and the preponderance of them will tell you that catching bugs was a vital early stimulus for their engagement with nature. And consider the current crisis of children's disconnection from the living world, articulated in Richard Louv's book *Last Child in the Woods: Saving Our Children from Nature Deficit Disorder*. Most kids used to wander freely and catch fireflies in a jar—or crawdads, or polliwogs— and, through those encounters, learned to connect with the land on which we all depend. These days, their attachment to electronica almost from birth, their parents' fears for their safety, and the loss of accessible habitats close to home means that this fundamental experience of roaming freely is now rare. Where will our future conservationists and biologists come from, when kids no longer chase grasshoppers in real life? Well, there is no more effective defense against nature deficit disorder than the butterfly net! That's why the Lepidopterists' Society has initiated the Outernet Project, to get free nets into the hands of curious kids, and to get them outdoors with knowledgeable mentors.

Now, some people oppose the use of nets outright. With the exciting rise of butterfly watching and photography in the outdoor-recreation repertoire, an either/or mentality has too often crept into people's attitudes. Since my *Watching Washington Butterflies* (1974) and *Handbook for Butterfly Watchers* (1984) were among the first books to push these activities, I accept some responsibility for this trend. However, I have always promoted watching and photography *alongside*—not *instead of*—responsible netting. I continue to preach mutual tolerance in this regard and an ecumenical approach among watchers and catchers, as parallel parts of the community of butterfly lovers.

For my own part, I have carried both my binoculars and my netstick (when appropriate) for several decades, and I feel naked without either one. They can be wonderfully complementary means for exploring the living world. During the Butterfly Big Year, I used Marsha a great deal—as net, yes, but also as companion, and walking staff. But I also employed Akito, a beautifully engineered, extendible and collapsible Japanese net, given me by a fine lepidopterist of the same name; a basic BioQuip wooden-handled net, easy to jump out of the car with; and a little foldable job known as Mini-Marsha that fits into a pocket for times when I need both hands. I used them all—or none. When investigating endangered species, such as the Uncompahgre fritillary above thirteen thousand feet in Colorado's San Juan Mountains with Xerces director Scott Black; in parks and preserves, where nets were not welcome; or when in company with watchers uncomfortable with nets, I relied solely on my binoculars. The point is, all of our appliances for apprehending nature, taken together, are like a good toolbox: more than the sum of their parts. When a butterfly in the bush just won't do, a net in the hand, deftly and gently wielded, may be just the right tool for the job.

Watching and photographing butterflies as a recreational pastime now draws increasing numbers of enthusiasts. But to me, doing away with butterfly nets, as some advocates of butterfly watching would like to do, would be a great mistake. Many butterfly watchers, like most biologists, began with a butterfly net, and learned much of what they know on the end of it. Many will go on to enjoy butterflies through ground glass instead of gossamer mesh; more power to them. My wish for all children is that they may know the delight of a sunny day afield in company with the bright wings of summer. If that should involve a net, more power to them, too.

Always a Naturalist

(*Courage for the Earth*, Houghton Mifflin, 2007)

In 2008, Houghton Mifflin published a centenary appreciation volume for Rachel Carson, compiled by Peter Matthiessen. Courage for the Earth *gave me the opportunity to write about two of my main inspirations, Rachel Carson and my mother, and how they came together in my life if not in their own. I was gobsmacked to learn of Carson's prescience about the evolution of a western chimney swift, an idea I'd come to through my own observation, only to learn that she had anticipated it based on slim evidence sixty years before. That's the kind of naturalist she was. In recent years, I've been delighted to sleep in the Rachel Carson dormitory at the National Conservation Training Center in Shepherdstown, West Virginia, and to handle Rachel's magnifying glass in the US Fish and Wildlife Service archives held there.*

During my first years of college, attempting to major in natural history in a hard-biology department, I trolled the secondhand bookshops up and down University Avenue in Seattle for any nature books I could afford. These were usually thumbed-through paperbacks with turned-down pages and broken spines, but they still worked: they could still be read. I picked up everything from Sterling North's *Rascal* to Marston Bates's *The Forest and the Sea*, *King Solomon's Ring* by Konrad Lorenz, and *Curious Naturalists* by his mentor, Niko Tinbergen. After a quick read I boxed up many of these books and sent them to my mother, who shared my interests, in Denver. When I visited her the following summer, I would bring them back to Seattle, along with other titles she'd gathered from used bookstores on Colfax Avenue, to bolster my growing horde of natural history books: antidote to mathematical biology, counterbalance to my chemistry textbooks.

The last time I visited Mom, in the summer of 1967, she was reluctant to let go of all the books I intended to take back. "Won't you leave me any?" she pled, and I realized that my greed was overwhelming my sensitivity for her own needs. Besides my shame at that moment, what I remember most clearly are the books that caused my mother to let me know how she really felt: her Rachel Carsons.

She so loved *The Edge of the Sea*, *The Sea Around Us*, and *Under the Sea-Wind* that my presumption in removing them triggered her tearful outburst.

On reflection, I am not surprised that these were the books that mattered most. Rachel Carson once wrote that "it isn't at all surprising that I should have written a book about the sea, because as long as I can remember it has fascinated me. Even as a child long before I had ever seen it . . . I used to imagine what it would look like, and what the surf sounded like." So it was for my mother. She grew up in Seattle, came to love the seaside best, but moved to Colorado young and always felt marooned there. I caught this condition from her and fled to the coast for college. We schemed that I would eventually help her return to Washington. Meanwhile, along with Anne Morrow Lindbergh's *Gift from the Sea* and Hazel Heckman's *Island in the Sound*, Carson's oceanic trilogy kept her alive. That moment—when she wouldn't let those paperbacks go—may have been the first time I witnessed how much a book, or an author, could really mean to a reader. I left those books with her, of course. But Mom did send me home with another book of Carson's, her final, posthumous title, which had recently been published. *A Sense of Wonder* seemed to speak to everything I was trying to do, and to all my callow but earnest hopes as a young conservationist.

That autumn, in a botany class, I met Thea Peterson, who would become my wife many years later. In our first conversation we discovered that we shared a strong interest in conservation. Thea told me, and still maintains, that *Silent Spring* was the most important book she ever read. "She showed me how I wanted to live my life," Thea said. I ran out and found a copy of *Silent Spring* on the Ave, and quickly saw what she meant. As we and our peers worked on conservation issues as student activists, watched the banning of DDT and other pesticide reforms take place before our eyes, and eventually witnessed the comeback of bald eagles, ospreys, peregrine falcons, and brown pelicans, we thought of Carson. She was an absent patron saint, like Muir, Leopold, and Krutch, and a very present inspiration along with giants still living at the time such as Brower, Abbey, Udall, Douglas, Peterson, Teale, and Mardy Murie.

Much later I learned how Rachel Carson had accidentally become the great public interpreter of the seas. I had the pleasure of hearing the story directly from Paul Brooks, the longtime Houghton Mifflin editor, when my own editor at that house, Harry Foster, took me to meet Brooks not long before he died. Parts of the tale are also recounted in Brooks's intimate portrait of Carson, *This House of Life*; his literary memoir, *Two Park Street*; and Linda Lear's biography *Rachel Carson: Witness for Nature*. During a weekend house party at Edmond Wilson's Provincetown, Cape Cod, summer home, the great critic, his daughter, Rosalind, and various others were strolling an outer beach. Horseshoe crabs were in, tumbled about in great numbers and crawling over one another. Some of the guests, concerned and thinking them stranded, began tossing the animals back into the water, until one companion explained that they were trying to spawn on shore and the well-meaning guests were interfering with their progress. Someone present lamented the lack of a good book to educate caring but uninformed people about such common life at the seashore. Rosalind Wilson, then an editor at Houghton Mifflin, reported this episode to Paul Brooks the following Monday morning. At that time, Brooks was in discussion with Rachel Carson about a book of historic bird illustrations by Louis Agassiz Fuertes, for which she hoped to write the text, if Houghton would publish it. An admirer of Carson's first, little-known book, *Under the Sea-Wind*, Brooks asked Carson if she might be interested in writing instead such a book about oceanside life. Thus was born *The Edge of the Sea* and, eventually, *Silent Spring*. I love this story, especially the way it illustrates the power and primacy of natural history through Carson's life: how an intimate acquaintance with the natural world is vital not only to living with it, but for informing and motivating environmental conservation. We take this connection for granted now, and it should seem self-evident to any biologist. But prior to Carson, *The Edge of the Sea*, and *Silent Spring*, few really acted on this fact.

I have imagined that the naturalist who knew what the horseshoe crabs were about might have been Vladimir Nabokov, then still a close friend and frequent guest of Wilson's. Though Nabokov did occasionally visit the Wilsons in Provincetown, there is no evidence that Carson and Nabokov had any such oblique connection. Yet in a certain way, I believe Rachel Carson embodied a particularly Nabokovian view of the world. In a *New York Times Book Review* appraisal of a volume on Audubon's paintings of butterflies and moths, Nabokov asked a rhetorical question: "Does there not exist a high ridge, where the mountainside of 'scientific' knowledge meets the opposite slope of 'artistic' imagination?" I say rhetorical, because such an ambidextrous habitat is exactly the territory Nabokov occupied. As both an accomplished (and still admired) lepidopterist and one of the greatest fiction writers ever in two languages, Nabokov knew full well that an individual could thrive in both atmospheres. He professed to be less concerned about giving his readers too much science than with failing to fully inform his science with his art. He spoke happily of "the precision of poetry and the art of science."

Nabokov was not the only scientist of substance who also visited his full intelligence and subtlety upon his literary output—we think of Goethe, Loren Eiseley, and Lewis Thomas—but I know of no one who strode that rarefied ridge as sure-footedly as Rachel Carson. This was no accident; in fact, it was part of her own credo. In her acceptance speech at the National Book Awards ceremony in 1952, she challenged "the notion that 'science' is something that belongs in a separate compartment of its own, apart from everyday life." She said that "the aim of science is to discover and illuminate truth. And that, I take it, is the aim of literature, whether biography or history or fiction. It seems to me, then, that there can be no separate literature of science." This accords with my own view that the term nature writing is a redundancy.

Unlike Nabokov, Carson walked the ridge between art and science as a writer of essays, where the distinction between reflection and refraction is even muddier than in fiction and requires even greater rigor to maintain. Yet her values, lyricism, metaphor, and poetry never degrade or detract from her wealth of deeply informed fact. "My own guiding principle," she said in that 1952 address, "was to portray the subject of my sea profile with fidelity and understanding. All else was secondary. I did not stop to consider whether I was doing it scientifically or poetically; I was writing as the subject demanded. The winds, the sea, and the moving tides are what they are. If there is wonder and beauty and majesty in them, science will discover these qualities. If they are not there, science cannot create them. If there is poetry in my book about the sea, it is not because I deliberately put it there, but because no one could write truthfully about the sea and leave out the poetry."

Reviewers agreed. The *New York Herald Tribune* said of *The Sea Around Us* that "it is a work of science; it is stamped with authority. It is a work of art: it is saturated with the excitement of mystery. It is literature." And as *Time* described *The Edge of the Sea*, "again author Carson has shown her remarkable talent for catching the life breath of science on the still glass of poetry." Yet quite apart from the lyrical peace she found in her beloved Maine tide pools, and in writing about them, Rachel Carson also carried her art and her science into a bitterly hostile political arena—something Nabokov assiduously avoided, and for which she was both vilified and lionized, and even called a follower of some "cult of the balance of nature." As Paul Brooks put it, "She was not at heart a crusader. But at last she decided that if it were to be done, she would have to do it herself." So she did, and in consequence, the very health of the earth was changed.

When my college friends and I threw our enthusiasm toward conservation as well as against the Vietnam War, we had every expectation that our efforts and optimism would be rewarded. If not so naïve as to expect ecotopia, we really did believe that the kindly earth could be saved through activism and education. And we had reinforcement in that direction. The North Cascades National Park for which we battled really was created and its high valleys and peaks protected. We kept dams out of the Grand Canyon. While others were marching to take over the president's office and demanding peace and justice, we marched to the former marshland that the university had leased to the city as the Montlake Dump, occupied it, and demanded topsoil and trees; as a result, it has become one of the great urban wildlife habitats. The Wilderness Act, the Clean Air and Clean Water acts, and many other glorious victories ensued. Jimmy Carter doubled the size of the national park system through the Alaska Lands Act, and of course, thanks to Carson, DDT was banned. We had no reason to believe that conservation would not ultimately win the day.

But perhaps we should have read our Paul Ehrlich and Rachel Carson more closely. She suffered from no false hopes. In a 1953 letter to the *Washington Post*, reprinted in *Reader's Digest*, she criticized the Eisenhower administration's sacking of Albert M. Day, a dedicated director of the US Fish and Wildlife Service, and other conservation professionals, in favor of patronage hacks. "These actions within the Interior Department fall into place beside the proposed giveaway of our offshore oil reserves and the threatened invasion of national parks, forests, and other public lands," she wrote. Had she lived to see it, she would have been dismayed but not surprised when along came Reagan, Watt, Hodel, and the Sagebrush Rebellion; the *Exxon Valdez*, Bhopal, Love Canal, and Three Mile Island; Bush I, Iraq I, and the Timber Salvage Act; Monsanto (one of Carson's fiercest attackers), ADM, and GM crops like BT corn and Roundup-Ready soybeans; Bush II, Iraq II, and the general attack on the EPA and all other environmental fronts. In light of our current environmental dark age, where the "war on the land" masquerades as the "war on terror," the way Carson ended that letter could not be more eerily prescient: "It is one of the ironies of our time that, while concentrating on the defense of our country against enemies from without, we should be so heedless of those who would destroy it from within."

Another tragic irony of environmental history was that Rachel Carson herself perished young from a kind of cancer that has proliferated to plague proportions in the organophosphate era that she helped hold back. Along with Peak Oil, global climate change, and a population of three hundred million Americans have come thousands of new chemicals on the market, and cancer swarms in numbers undreamed of in Carson's day. Maybe the indicators—robins dead on the lawn, ospreys cracking their own eggshells—aren't as obvious this time around. But the number of toxins released into our air, soil, and waters is greater than ever, and the amoral chemical combines show no compunction over this condition. We can't be sure that any given cancer belongs to the legacy of our toxic load, but it is beyond reason to imagine that many do not. When my wife, Thea, confronted ovarian cancer several years ago, she might have owed it to any number of factors. And beyond question, her recovery stands in debt to intensive modern chemistry involving derivatives of natural substances such as taxol and platinum. For this I am intensely grateful. But that we are forced into a Faustian contract involving sophisticated chemical fixes for the sour fruits of an ever-more-chemicalized world strikes me as an unacceptable trade-off. The hopes of current and future sufferers of a polluted planet owe largely to this one woman who effected great change. But the sad fact is that forty-five years after the publication of *Silent Spring*, we need Rachel Carson more than ever.

In Shepherdstown, West Virginia, stands the National Conservation Training Center of the US Fish and Wildlife Service, Rachel Carson's one-time employer. This magnificent facility, all stone and wood and set in a campus of woods and meadows, has three dormitories. These are named for great figures in wildlife conservation: Ding Darling, Aldo Leopold, and Rachel Carson. Hers is a name that will never be forgotten, wherever anyone so much as thinks of conservation. And her gentle, percipient presence is a judgment upon all who would wreak enormities upon the land, air, soil, water, and sea. Especially the sea. How her own views evolved on the ocean's future should instruct us all.

In a 1942 letter to her publicist describing the general plan of her first sea book, *Under the Sea-Wind*, Carson wrote, "The ocean is too big and vast and its forces are too mighty to be much affected by human activity." But by 1960, in view of the dumping of nuclear wastes at sea, she had changed her mind. In her preface that year for the revised edition of *The Sea Around Us*, she said that "although man's record as a steward of natural resources of the earth has been a discouraging one, there has long been a certain comfort in the belief that the sea, at least, was inviolate, beyond man's ability to change and to despoil. But this belief, unfortunately, has proved to be naive." And she concluded: "It is a curious situation that the sea, from which life first arose, should now be threatened by the activities of one form of that life." In this she was sadly right. Absent speedy and radical change, the oceanographer Jeremy Jackson expects an impoverished, slimy soup, inhabited chiefly by a monoculture of adaptive jellies called salps, to replace the hugely diverse wonderlands described in Carson's books.

Just as she arrived at an understanding of how we are harming the high seas themselves, Rachel Carson intuited the reality of global climate change. As she wrote to Dorothy Freeman, "It was pleasant to believe, for example, that much of Nature was forever beyond the tampering reach of man—he might level the forests and dam the streams, but the clouds and the rain and the wind were God's—the

God of your ice-crystal cathedral in that beautiful passage of a recent letter of yours. It was comforting to suppose that the stream of life would flow on through time in whatever course that God had appointed for it—without interference by one of the drops of the stream—man. And to suppose that, however the physical environment might mold Life, that Life could never assume the power to change things drastically—or even destroy—the physical world."

But she was coming to know better. Climate change was one of several subjects she might have pursued in depth, had her time not run out. She even anticipated, slightly slant, the title of Al Gore's film on the subject, *An Inconvenient Truth*. In a speech to the National Women's Press Club in 1962, having cited the monetary control that chemical companies exercise over pesticide research results, she asked this: "Is industry becoming a screen through which facts must be filtered, so that the hard, uncomfortable truths are kept back and only the harmless morsels allowed to filter through?" And Carson's shift in understanding went well beyond anticipating the critically injured seas and skies of today. She began to see the capacity of her species to actually endanger itself. "But the sea," she wrote, "though changed in a sinister way, will continue to exist; the threat is rather to life itself."

It was life, after all, that ultimately enthralled Rachel Carson, in all its ways of being. Brooks's biography, *The House of Life*, is well named. Above all, Carson was always a naturalist. This shows in her long, warm friendships with Edwin and Nellie Teale, Roger Tory Peterson, and others who built their lives largely around a passion for animals, plants, and habitats beyond the strictly human realm. Both Carson and her mother, Marion, benefited from the peak of the American nature-study movement, and it shows throughout her life and work. The maritime books speak for themselves in this regard on every page. But so does almost everything else she wrote. Even the personal letters Carson addressed to her dear friend Dorothy Freeman and other correspondents contain frequent passages describing the texture, color, smell, and inhabitants of her best-beloved places, such as the shore forest in Maine she called the "Lost Woods." From bird walks and tide pool crawls wrested from a busy schedule to the topics of her occasional articles and lectures, close attention to the living world informed Carson's whole being.

Those who identify the writer chiefly with intertidal creatures and DDT are often surprised to discover the breadth of her interests in natural history. I hope I've never defined her in such a narrow way; yet I was recently caught up short by a surprising example of her amplitude as a naturalist. Thea and I had spent an early evening in Portland, Oregon, watching the swirling descent of Vaux's swifts into a tall school chimney where they roost for a fortnight or so during their migration.

Like the residents of Austin, Texas, who assemble at dusk to watch the Mexican free-tailed bats fly out from their roost beneath the Congress Street Bridge, locals had gathered with picnic baskets and telescopes, and a festival atmosphere over-ruled the rain. A Cooper's hawk alighted on the rim of the chimney, scaring off the swirl, and now and then it hopped in and grabbed one of the already alighted swifts. Then it flew off with the sacrifice, while the others resumed their impres-sion of smoke curling into the smokestack backwards. Flying out myself the next morning, I spent the next couple of evenings bewitched by the related chimney swifts screaming through twilight towns in Kansas and Oklahoma, and dropping at last into their night-roost stacks.

Chimney swifts, like the European bird known in England as the swift, once must have roosted and nested in hollow trees, prior to the loss of such features from the countryside and the fortunate adaptation of the birds to their anthropo-genic alternatives. Vaux's swifts, which still nest largely in hollow trees but often roost in big smokestacks during migration, are beginning to nest in chimneys as well. The first example I heard of took place in my own valley. It occurred to me that we are witnessing the evolution of a western chimney swift in our own time. Coming home, intending to write an essay on these marvelous birds and pretty sure my insight was not wholly original, I searched for any prior obser-vations along these lines. And where did I find the most compelling one? By accident while working on this piece. Right there in Linda Lear's compilation *Lost Woods: The Discovered Writing of Rachel Carson*, I found Carson's 1944 essay "Aces of Nature's Aviators," on the adaptations and migration of chimney swifts. "Ancestors of the modern chimney swift lived in great hollow trees," she wrote. And "the western cousin of the chimney swift—Vaux's swift—only of recent years has begun to make the transition from trees to chimneys." And "an occasional swift may be snatched by a hawk as the birds are circling above a chimney, prepa-ratory to entering for the night." So there it was—aced by Rachel Carson! Except one can never be scooped as a naturalist, only anticipated and given shoulders to stand on for the next, further vantage. Demure as she was, Rachel Carson's shoul-ders have proved as broad and sturdy as any in all of American natural history.

One striking example has arisen recently, with the publication of a book I consider as important as any since *Silent Spring*. I am speaking of Richard Louv's *Last Child in the Woods: Saving Our Children from Nature-Deficit Disorder*. Like Paul Brooks and Rachel Carson with *Silent Spring*, Louv's edi-tor suggested his author's book title—or in this case, the subtitle, which is catching on in a similarly incendiary style. Louv's vital premise is that our culture, and the future of conservation, are being profoundly compromised by the radical loss of everyday contact between children and the outdoors. Though this baleful condition has never been put so well or so forcefully, Louv's ideas have their antecedents, which he graciously acknowledges. One of the earliest and most resonant of these was Rachel Carson. She first iterated her ideas along these lines in an essay for Woman's Home Companion titled "Help Your Child to Wonder." The piece was later expanded and published as a book, with photographs, under the title *A Sense of Wonder*, the book my mother had given me. The phrase *sense of wonder* may be as famous as the term *silent spring*, but relatively few know that they came from the same source. At its heart is Carson's wish that every child in the world have "a sense of wonder so indestructible that it would last throughout life, as an unfailing antidote against the boredom and disenchantments of later years, the sterile preoccupation with things that are artificial, the alienation from the sources of our strength." Richard Louv's book shows chillingly how those very states of preoccupation and alienation have nearly come to pass and suggests ways in which we might get back toward Carson's dream.

I have felt close to this woman for much of my life, and looking over our lives, it's not hard to see why. Like her, I was born far from the sea, yet felt captivated by it. Even the jacket illustration of my 1959 paperback copy of *The Edge of the Sea*, adorned with the bright pink mouth of a king conch, a green crab, a sea star, and a scattering of shells on a golden beach, filled me with longing. When I actually got to the coast of Maine for the summer of 1963, not far from the very shores that she and Dorothy most loved, and three years later to the wilderness beaches of the Olympic Peninsula, Carson's tide pool tales told me who I was seeing, what they were doing, and how to look more deeply beneath the surface of the water, beneath the surface of things as they seemed. Though our experiences were offset by years, I eventually learned that we had shared certain friends, mentors, and inspirations, critical boosts, publishers, and convictions. I'd love to have known her. I'd love to have walked a tidal reach with her. Though, like my mother and many others, I almost feel I have.

Maybe I never felt this propinquity more keenly than when I was working on *Chasing Monarchs*, a narrative of following the migration of monarch butterflies. I was reading *Always, Rachel* at the time and came across one of her last letters to Dorothy Freeman, when Carson knew she probably hadn't long to live. Carson had just lost a dear cat and was about to leave her beloved Southport, Maine, likely for the final time. Freeman took her to a favorite place at the end of the island, where they encountered masses of monarchs nectaring on goldenrod. Afterward,

Carson wrote to Freeman, "Most of all, I shall remember the Monarchs, their unhurried westward drift of one small winged form after another, each drawn by some invisible force." I thought this one of the loveliest descriptions of monarchs I'd ever read, right up there with her contemporacy Jo Brewer's wonderful phrase in *Wings on the Meadow*: "these wings of flame, rising to the sun." Carson continued, "We talked a little about their migration, their life history. Did they return? We thought not; for most, at least, this was the closing journey of their lives." Yet this had been "a happy spectacle," she wrote. "And rightly—for when any living thing has come to the end of its life cycle we accept that end as natural. For the Monarch, that cycle is measured in a known span of months. For ourselves, the measure is something else, the span of which we cannot know. But the thought is the same: when the intangible cycle has run its course it is a natural and not unhappy thing that a life comes to its end." She concluded, "That is what these brightly fluttering bits of life taught me this morning. I found a deep happiness in it—so, I hope, may you."

The rest of my mother's books came to me all too soon. Natural cycles or no, her life, like Carson's, ended way too early. Rachel Carson lived from 1907 to 1964; Helen Lee Miller from 1916 to 1967. They were both gifted naturalists and writers. Though their lives largely overlapped, their experiences could hardly have been more different except for their suffering before they died and their joy when they came under the spell of a shoreline and the central place of natural history in their lives. They never met, yet Rachel Carson kept my mother good company in the last years of her life. An intensely private person always denied much privacy, Rachel Carson was vitally important in millions of lives. She remains so in mine.

Volcanic Blues; or, How the Butterfly Tamed the Volcano

(Into the Blast Zone, Oregon State University Press, 2008)

In the summer of 2005, a passel of writers and scientists (including Ursula LeGuin, Ann Zwinger, Fred Swanson, and Jerry Franklin) camped and confabbed on the shoulder of Mount St. Helens, in celebration of the twenty-fifth anniversary of her eruption. Our ruminations were collected, and this was my contribution. I continue to study the way the butterflies come back.

An old tale from somewhere around the Pacific Rim of Fire relates how a village was threatened by a fierce volcano. The People importuned the volcano spirit, but she only puffed more steam and ash at them. Eagle and Raven also appealed to the volcano to spare the village and the forest, but the volcano rebuffed them too. They flapped raggedly back down the mountain, singed and covered with ash, and shrugged. Finally, a mere butterfly fluttered up the long steep slopes to the volcano's crater and delivered her own petition in her tiny voice. This time the volcano heard, and giving Butterfly time to get out of the way first, promptly erupted. She spared the village, but leveled about half of the forest. Butterfly was happy, for she knew that without a good eruption now and then to clear the deep, dark forest, the meadows and sunny slopes that her kind needed would cease to exist. Eagle and Raven and People had asked only for safety; Butterfly had asked for renewal. Or if there is no such tale, there ought to be.

In eastern Washington and throughout the arid West there occurs a group of small blue butterflies known as the dotted blues (genus *Euphilotes*). Well under an inch in wingspan, the males of these rapid-flying mites are pale to deep blue above, the females mole-brown or gray, both chalky white below and peppered with the black dots of their name. Bright lunules, pale orange-juice to fire-engine red, line the rim of the hindwings on both sides. All *Euphilotes* depend solely upon species of buckwheat (*Eriogonum*) for their larval host plants. We've long believed we had two species of these butterflies in Washington, assigned to *E. battoides* (the square-spotted blue) and *E. enoptes* (the western dotted blue). But in recent years, with close study of host plant relationships and DNA, the picture is growing more complicated. It seems that particular species of blues have evolved in intimate (and obligate) association with not just buckwheats in general, but specific types of buckwheat, and we have more kinds of blues than we thought.

The Washington species long assigned to *E. enoptes* has turned out to be *E. columbiae*, the Columbia blue, formerly regarded as a subspecies. Lepidopterists Dave Nunnalee and David James, one a retired scientist, the other a state entomologist, have been rearing all of the butterflies resident in Washington. They have found that the pillbug-sized caterpillars of Columbia blues exploit northern buckwheat (*Eriogonum compositum*) early in the flight season, then use the later-flowering tall buckwheat (*E. elatum*) as summer progresses. The larvae tend to match the colors of the flowers they graze, appearing pinker or creamier depending on their chosen buckwheat. The true *Euphilotes enoptes* seemed to be restricted to California and Oregon, feeding on bare-stemmed buckwheat (*Eriogonum nudum*), which looks like a small version of *E. elatum*. Andrew Warren, of the McGuire Center for Lepidoptera and Biodiversity in Gainesville, Florida, is another of the lepidopterists who has been figuring all this out. When a graduate student at Oregon State University, Andy urged butterfly folk north of the Columbia to try to locate *Eriogonum nudum* in Washington; if we could do so, he thought, we might well find the actual *Euphilotes enoptes* also, as a new species for the state.

Loving this sort of a challenge, my botanist wife, Thea, and I tracked down the known records for bare-stemmed buckwheat. There were only two in the University of Washington herbarium, and a couple of others in separate databases, including one from a Washington Native Plant Society foray to the Dark Divide, east of Mount St. Helens, that we'd actually been along on. Come spring, we found the Yakima County site for the plant that had been recorded by our old UW mentor, Art Kruckeberg. There was the buckwheat, in tight, pink bud and cold, wet rain: no butterflies, to be sure. But a fortnight later the bloom was out, crowding the roadcuts above the deep canyon with creamy little flowers on their smooth green stalks. Crossing the road we whooped with joy, as minute flickers of azure gave away the newest-known member of the Washington butterfly fauna.

We would see many dotted blues that day, all *E. enoptes*, most of them nectaring or laying eggs on their rare host plant. But were there any more, elsewhere? The other *E. nudum* record from the UW herbarium was an old one from an unspecified location in the Goat Rocks Wilderness Area, west of where we'd found the plant and its butterfly. We hiked into likely habitat in fog so thick it might have been shed by the eponymous goats. The only buckwheat to be seen was the cushion species known as *E. pyrolifolium* for its leaves, shaped like those of pears.

We searched farther, as did Dave Nunnalee and others. Only a few patches of the plant turned up, near White Pass. It began to seem as if the plant might be as rare as the lack of records suggested, and the butterfly just as limited.

It was the middle of July, and a pack of scientists and writers gathered for several days of camping, hiking, jawboning, eating, drinking, and storytelling on the slopes of Mount St. Helens. A little late arriving, I was taking the curves of Forest Road 99 with some celerity. A few miles short of the meeting place, I rounded the thirty-third curve or so and took in the spectacle of an entire slope of what looked for all the world like bare-stemmed buckwheat. "What?" I said. Then, braking hard, followed up with "Holy shit!" It must be pearly everlasting, I told myself. That redoubtable native plant upholsters vast areas of the blast zone, and it is not entirely dissimilar, at speed, from my nudie cutie. But when I pulled over and got a good look, there was no doubt: this was *Eriogonum nudum*—lots of it!—blooming weeks later at this higher elevation than in our Yakima County location, though most clusters had blossomed by now, with still a few pink buds to go. Between the point where the plant kicked in and the turnoff to the camping site, I saw acres of it, if the verges and cuts had been flattened out: vanilla drifts against the milky white ash. I wondered how the plant could be so abundant here, in one of the most-studied ecosystems in Washington, and yet so rare in the herbaria and lists?

Around our campfire that night, I put the question to Charlie Crisafulli, Forest Service ecologist for Mount St. Helens National Volcanic Monument. Charlie told me that he knew the plant well, but hadn't appreciated its rarity in Washington outside the monument. His theory was that it had come in on road-building material during post-eruptive construction. That seemed plausible on first consideration, since bare-stemmed buckwheat loves well-drained, disturbed slopes such as roadcuts. From there it might have spread out into ashfields. However, given the plant's spotty (to put it generously) distribution in the state, the chances of a gravel source containing its seeds or roots seemed highly unlikely to me. Besides, as I would see later, the buckwheat was so well established along so many miles, and so far beyond the road margins, that such a degree of spread in the years since the roads were rebuilt seemed equally improbable. But the question also seemed moot: How could you know?

Given our schedule and the deteriorating weather, my chances to look for buckwheat blues didn't look good. The third day began with wild weather and a cold, saturated wind like the drooling howl of some deep-sea beast. The company split up into groups depending on which of several possible hikes they favored.

Two of us, Ursula Le Guin and I, opted instead for a general look around at a number of sites. Fred Swanson, consummate forest ecologist and visionary who strongly believes in the happy meeting of art and science, kindly accommodated our whim. He drove us to Windy Ridge, Meta Lake, and a number of viewpoints in between, sharing history in deep and recent time as few could. Ursula pointed out this declivity, that prominence that caught her eye, and that we could well imagine she had invented out of the mist. Fred showed why he loves the place so damn much. I spotted the odd wind-tossed bird. We had a ball. Then we headed way up north along the Green River to the far edge of the monument, hearing the history of forests felled by architectonic forces and chainsaws, the latter fortunately arrested before their all-too-obvious lines pushed any farther upvalley.

I'd noticed plenty of the buckwheat on the way up the Green River road. And then, on the way back down, lo! The sun came out! Fred said there was time for me to have a look, so I hopped out of the car and made my awkward way up the loose pumice slope between bleached "driftwood" and pearly everlasting, taking care not to step on the buckwheats blooming among them, but swishing them with my net bag to put up any insects stirred by the latent sun. A quick flitter that might have been a small, gray female blue was more likely a fly. But then there was a definite blue flash, big and bright. I'd disturbed it from a buckwheat head. The butterfly rose over me, then dropped downslope to another cluster, where it settled and commenced to nectar. I moved that way, trying to keep my footing. But the unstable substrate crumbled, threatening to disturb the butterfly. I could see that my best chance would be a controlled fall, or a targeted plummet. I leapt, swinging my net as I passed the blue, then flipped it over and turned my attention to landing upright on the road below. I made it, and I had the butterfly. Ursula later told me that she watched my abrupt descent of the steep ash-pitch with a combination of amusement and considerable alarm. Gratifying "wows" escaped Ursula and Fred as they viewed the brilliant, foil-blue wings of my quarry. Then they left me to walk the buckwheat verges and ravines down to the main road, flicking my net. But the day cooled again, and I saw no more blue, either above or on the wing.

The insect I'd caught was not a dotted blue; it wasn't even a true blue. Though *Lycaena heteronea* males flash the deepest, most shimmering cerulean of any of our blue butterflies, this species actually belongs to a related group of lycaenids (gossamer wings) known as coppers. This we know from its wing veins, genitalia, and other structural traits. Twice the size of a dotted blue and silvery white below, the blue copper closely resembles the fiery bronze copper (*L. rubidus*) except in color: mere hue, whether pigmented or prismatic as in these iridescent gems, can evolve rapidly, while structure is much more stable over time. But like the genus *Euphilotes,* and unlike most other coppers (which tend to develop on docks, *Rumex* species), the blue copper feeds solely on species of buckwheat as a caterpillar. In this case, it must have been using *E. nudum.* The only other species of buckwheat known to occur in the monument, *E. pyrolifolium,* grows on high, blast-protected outcrops of the mountain, subalpine habitats such as in the Goat Rocks, and blue coppers, chiefly resident east of the Cascades in dry habitats, are not known to employ that species. This was the first record of the blue copper in Skamania County, and the first occurrence well west of the Cascade Crest, a range extension of some forty miles. While some butterflies are mobile, quickly colonizing new territory, they tend to be generalists with widespread, weedy food plants. In contrast, *L. heteronea* is a sedentary host plant specialist, seldom found far from the nearest buckwheat.

The surprising discovery of blue coppers at Mount St. Helens allows us to make an educated guess about the source of the mystery buckwheat on the monument. Even if *E. nudum* had indeed come in with road gravel, the chances of copper eggs or larvae coming with it, or a gravid female copper finding it there, seem vanishingly small. Parsimony suggests that both the plant and the butterfly were there in the first place, and survived the eruption of 1980. More than survived: in the case of the bare-stemmed buckwheat, at least, absolutely thrived. Supposing it was present but restricted before (as the lack of records suggests), the post-eruptive conditions—thousands of acres of new, dry, hot pumice slopes much like the gravelly screes and roadcuts this plant loves—allowed a rapid adaptive spread known as "ecological release." The blue copper has presumably advanced with it.

Further sunny summer sampling bore this out. The following summer I found a female blue copper at the Clearwater interpretive overlook, and yet another buckwheat-feeding species, the acmon blue (*Plebejus acmon*) along the Green River. *Euphilotes enoptes,* the western dotted blue, has not yet turned up on the Monument, but we'll continue to look for it. Its occurrence there along with the other two buckwheat butterflies would cinch the case for *E. nudum* predating the eruption at Mount St. Helens. Perhaps, in the right season and weather, this "new" Washington butterfly will swarm over waving fields of buckwheat on Loowit.

I am a biogeographer, and the distribution of plants and animals—why they occur here, why not there—is of infinite interest to me. But there are larger implications here than dots on a map. By chance, I conducted the last butterfly sampling on the mountain prior to her 1980 eruption. While I found a nice array of butterflies near the former Timberline campground—snowberry checkerspots and northern blues in abundance, a few others—the diversity (as one would expect in a young alpine habitat) wasn't high. And then almost all that habitat, I thought, was scarified by the blast. Subsequent surveys have found that all the species I'd tallied in 1979 have recovered, but have noted few others. So I had long believed that Mount St. Helens had little to offer in the way of butterfly surprises.

Then in the fall of 1997, Thea and I found American painted ladies prolific on Johnson Ridge. Though its larvae feed on the widespread pearly everlasting, *Vanessa virginiensis* is a distinctly uncommon butterfly in the state. Conditions here on the pumice desert must have proved perfect for both species, the ladies abounding on a blanket of everlasting. Since then, Charlie Crisafulli has found Edith's checkerspot larvae defoliating Cardwell's penstemons on barren-looking Windy Ridge. And then the blue copper. Clearly, more life survived the eruption than I'd expected, a fact I've heard over and over from the scientists. And just as clearly, Loowit holds out more potential for butterfly discovery than I had guessed.

We know other examples of Cascadian butterflies not only favored by periodic vulcanism, but actually evolving in concert with the volcanic landscape. The "sand plains" left behind by the ash-plume of massive Mount Mazama's great blow, east of its surviving caldera, known as Crater Lake, have long been recognized as harboring a distinctive fritillary butterfly. This was finally named *Speyeria egleis moecki* for its discoverer, Arthur Moeck, by Paul Hammond and Ernst Dornfeld in 1983. And then in 1995, veteran lepidopterist Harold Rice discovered a truly minuscule blue on a truly tiny buckwheat on the same Mazama ashfields. Hammond and Dave McCorkle named it *Philotiella leona* for Harold's wife and collecting partner, and I designated it Leona's little blue in *The Butterflies of Cascadia*. *P. leona* is almost invisible as it darts over the sandy flats, both the summer air and the pyroclastics nearly as hot as when Mazama erupted.

What else might be lurking in these vast and challenging fields of fire? What butterflies—not eradicated, but rather renewed, have proliferated, even evolved through this natural act of so-called destruction? And what would the giant copper mine proposed for Goat Mountain, up the Green River just outside the monument, mean for the butterflies and their buckwheats? If I were the mining boss, I would watch out for that tiny butterfly. This is a longer, more complicated version of that old tale about the volcano and the butterfly; but the moral is the same.

World without Violets

(*Orion*, 2009)

When the news broke about the Oxford Junior Dictionary *abandoning many of its words pertaining to natural history and the living world, I was only one of many who responded with shock and outrage. The imagined conceit that, in doing so, the editors of the OJD might actually excise these features from existence gave me the idea for this riposte. Indignation is always a good sharp spur, or saddle burr, to the essayist.*

The best-known lexicographers of English, Samuel Johnson and Noah Webster, differed in obvious respects: the good doctor, toast of London's beau monde and king of the coffeehouse intelligentsia, versus the Connecticut Yankee bent on making a distinctively American language. But they shared a fundamental belief: that their respective dictionaries should honestly represent the worlds in which they lived. Locked up with no other books to read but theirs, you could get well clued in to the England or the United States of their times.

Working on that model, let me paint today's English-speaking world by the lights of the current *Oxford Junior Dictionary* (OJD), published by Oxford University Press (OUP). It is a world without violets. Spring comes unannounced by catkins and proceeds without benefit of crocuses, cowslips, or tulips. Summer brings no lavender, melons, or nectarines, and autumn is absent of acorns, almonds, and hazelnuts. Winter must be endured without the holly and the ivy, the wren or the mistletoe. Brooks have no buttercups or brambles on their banks, but then there are no brooks, either. Woods exist, sans fern or fungus, willow or weasel, porcupine, beech, or sycamore. Scotland has no heather; Ohio, no dandelions. Heron and raven have followed the passenger pigeon into oblivion along with magpie, pelican, and stork. If this world has song, it is not that of thrush, lark, or canary. Neither leopard nor newt are known here, and you will search in vain for cygnet or cheetah. On the bright side, starlings and gorse are nowhere to be seen; but neither are bluebells. Scan the waters forever and you will never see an otter, a beaver, or a kingfisher.

On the other hand, in OJD-world you'll have no trouble locating blogs or chat-rooms. Celebrities are there, spending euros. You can check your voicemail on your broadband MP3 player and send attachments with bullet points, all while bungee jumping if you so desire, without fear of blackberries below—not that kind, anyway. There is a food chain here; a very short one.

The blueprint for this lonely world lies in a set of words deleted from the latest OJD and a parallel set of terms newly included. These came to light when a concerned British mother compared editions of the popular teaching tool and, appalled, called the papers. OUP responded that the volume must be kept small for small hands, so when new words are added to keep up with the times, old words must come out. Sharp howls of protest arose from people who hold to the quaint belief that an essential societal good comes from young people getting to know—or at least know about—their natural surroundings.

Of course, lexicography is not the same thing as geography. Beavers are still out there, even if the OJD seems to have done a better job of extirpating them than John Jacob Astor and the Hudson's Bay Company combined. What gobsmacks me is the depressing rationale for the changes. Vineeta Gupta, director of children's dictionaries at OUP, told the *Daily Telegraph* that the added words respect what children are learning, based on trials conducted in schools. Ms. Gupta asserts that changes in the world are responsible for changes in the book. So is this where these children are growing up—in a world ungraced by otters?

Or might it be the other way around: Could changes in the book be responsible for changes in the world? Could the press prove mightier than the leghold trap when it comes to beavers? That probably flatters the OJD, which does not, after all, occupy every child's bookshelf (speaking of quaint concepts). Nor is it the curious child's only source. As my friend David Branch replied when I told him of this affair: "A seven-year-old who doesn't know a Willow from a Walnut, an Apricot from an Almond, or a Turnip from a Tulip could be in deep gorse and never know it. BUT he could text his way out! All may not be lost if these words appear in the Wikipedia software installed on the kid's PDA . . . and just think of the trees that would save!"

Even so—Yo, Oxford? Dunce cap for you! Look it up in the OED.

Evening Falls on the Maladaptive Ape

(*Moral Ground*, Trinity University Press, 2010)

When she was compiling the monumental collection of commentary on climate change called Moral Ground, Kathleen Dean Moore asked me to contribute. I resisted for a long time, in the belief I had nothing original to add. Kathleen persisted. I asked her if I might write exactly what I felt, and that it wouldn't be very nice. She said sure, and welcome—"Everyone is being way too polite." Not one of my cheeriest essays, with perhaps my darkest ending ever, this is at least honest, and anything but polite.

If I were a giant clam, instead of an ape, and if I lived on the Great Barrier Reef, and if clams were in charge, my moral choice would be clear: to do something about it. "It" is the fact that the Great Barrier Reef, as we know it, is likely to be history within brief decades, due to warming and acidification of southern ocean waters. Even as other ocean currents slow and the great North Atlantic gyre slugs up into a polluted sump, ice caps melt, and Bangladesh and Bikini slip slowly beneath the water's lap, that country of corals—the Great Barrier Reef—is expected to collapse as a living, functioning system.

So, as that clam, what is this thing I should do? Actually, in order to examine a moral choice, you need two things: a moral outlook and ethical agency. *Tridacna gigas*, you guess, gets by without a moral framework, and, being sessile, it surely lacks agency. So while it would be nice to do something about it, I really can't: I guess I'm off the hook. When crown-of-thorns sea stars occupied our reef, just as when hungry Pacific lionfish (escaped from broken aquariums during a hurricane) recently infiltrated the Atlantic, we clams and such really were left with only one choice: adapt or die.

Now, shedding my giant crenellated turquoise-mantled shell and donning my ape-suit once more, things become more complex. We so-called higher primates do possess a moral sensibility, or what passes for it, or so we tell ourselves. At the very least we know what such a trait should look like. Even chimps seem to express a knowledge of what's "right" and "wrong." What's more, they act on it.

Yet their agency is limited to interpersonal relationships: they can't pass laws, exercise regulations, levy taxes or credits, extend or deny permits. In the end, for them too, it's adapt or die. And more and more, it's looking more like die, unless Jane Goodall & Co. can help it.

But *Homo sapiens*—named by Linnaeus in an extraordinary act of optimism, especially for a Swede, as "all the same and smart"—has not only his morals and an elaborate ethics derived from them, but also an astonishing degree of active agency. Since the big bamboo scaffolding of human enterprise, like the Barrier Reef, ice cap, and rain forest, is in early to mid-collapse, it is worth asking whether said sapient ape has more than a clam's chance to do something about it, more than a chimp's chance of making it.

Agency cuts both ways. It is our big brains and opposable thumbs, after all, that brought everything—clam, coral, ice, and ape—to this pretty pass. So can our technical and manual powers translate into actual ethical agency that's up to the task—speeding the currents on their way, jump-starting the gyres while cleansing their load, cooling the ice, caring for the corals? It might very likely be too late for all that, and just too hard a task for us; but if it's not, will we? The evidence elsewhere (war and torture on every hand, for example) is not encouraging. In addition to morals and agency, we have several other traits that might belong largely if not exclusively to humans, among them rue, regret, dread, and hindsight. Combined with moral sense, intelligence, and agility, they surely should drive an ethical response to our crumbling scaffold. But can they?

The key question might be, how have we come by our morals and ethics? I can imagine only three sources. First: they were bestowed by a higher power. Many, maybe most, folks believe that we have a moral imperative to "be good"—a mandate from on high, delivered up from some power outside ourselves, mainlining morals straight to our hearts. Others, happy with happenstance as the whole show, require no rule maker or referee for their cosmos. To my mind, any intelligence that bestowed a moral system on just our species among millions, plus the tools to wreck it all, would not be worth the term; and any god remotely satisfied with the results to date would be a risible god. But such a provenance is surely the handiest, when it comes to self-justification: when "God is on our side," anything goes.

Second hypothesis: we bestowed our ethical construct upon ourselves. This seems clearly to be the case, at least in part: our laws are laws of men (mostly *sensu stricto*), though often erected in the name of whatever indulgent or vengeful deity their authors contrive, the better to meet their needs and desires. And just as clearly, this hasn't worked out, except to create, empower, and maintain privilege, beggar the poor, and plunder the common weal. For those ends, such self-published ethics have worked very well.

The third possibility is that our morals and ethics have evolved, biologically and socially. This too seems obvious to a certain extent, since dogs, cats, elephants, cetaceans, great apes, and maybe others all demonstrate elements (I won't say rudiments) of a moral outlook: decency and affection toward others, loyalty, and suchlike. This is hopeful, as it suggests that human behavior could conceivably evolve into something worthy of itself. Aldo Leopold posits such growth in "The Land Ethic," comparing a time when chattels might be killed on whim with ethical impunity, to a modern era of greater restraint or compunction. Today Leopold might question whether we have come much past the chattel-wasting days, what with Mexican drug cartels in Juarez, systematic rape in Uganda, bomb-belts and drone missiles at wedding parties in Afpak Iraq, and bulldozer brigades in Palestine, as "Thou shalt not kill" becomes "except when thou needest to."

In calling for a land ethic, Aldo took his vision a step further. He dared hope for a time when we would see, agree, and act on the idea that "a thing is right when it tends to preserve the integrity, stability, and beauty of the biotic community. It is wrong when it tends otherwise." He thought the way to get there would he to "quit thinking about decent land-use as solely an economic problem," to "examine each question in terms of what is ethically and esthetically right, as well as what is economically expedient." Many might regard such a shift as even less likely than mass observance of the Golden Rule, and so might it be; others would see it as a narrow side-issue of the larger dilemma, even peripheral. Yet it seems to me that such an ethic as Aldo describes would be the only sort of moral resolve that could conceivably give comfort and relief to the current crisis. An ethic based on concern for future human generations alone doesn't strike me as having much heft, since it hasn't stemmed our excesses against one another so far. But an ethic founded on the well-being of the supportive fabric might have a chance.

I think our moral and ethical equipment is largely self-contrived, built upon an evolved capacity, more jury-rigged than refined, and better developed in some than in others. So while the individual will, desire, skill, and devotion for doing so may all be in place, our collective power to repair the reefs and waters, currents and gyres, clouds and caps may be no more effective than the corporate efforts of clams: not only because the task is so large and intractable, but also because the overall ethic is so feeble, and its agency so malleable. And because alongside our clear capacity for honesty, generosity, mercy, and cooperation lurks our apparent imperative for power, greed, and domination. The friction between them is what poet Carolyn Wright calls "our struggle for the preservation of compassion and decency in a perennially fallen world."

And what was this fall? As I see it, it was a two-part tumble. In more than a merely metaphorical way, it was first the very one implied in Genesis: sex. Not doing it, but doing it for eons in the absence of Planned Parenthood. For the very unrestrained mass of the combined peoples of the whole wide world is that from which we probably cannot return to our prelapsarian grace: the six billion were three when we last turned around, and will be twelve when we next take a look. Then there was industry, the removal of the people from the land to the factory, and, in particular, our embrace of fossil fuel. Rudyard Kipling already had it right in "The Gods of the Copybook Headings": "In the Carboniferous Epoch we were promised abundance for all / By robbing selective Peter to pay for collective Paul." Or as Fritz Schumacher put it in *Small Is Beautiful*: "As the world's resources of non-renewable fuels—coal, oil, and natural gas—are exceedingly unevenly distributed over the globe and undoubtedly limited in quantity, it is clear that their exploitation at an ever-increasing rate is an act of violence against nature which must almost inevitably lead to violence among men." As it has.

Schumacher didn't know about the coming violence to the climate, but he did write that "in the excitement of the unfolding of his scientific and technical powers, modern man has built a system of production that ravishes nature." One who intuited remarkably early that the ravishment would extend to the very elements was Vladimir Nabokov. In a 1974 interview, he said, "Pollution itself is a lesser enemy of butterfly life than, say, climatic change." In my own travels all across the United States in 2008 in search of butterflies, I saw a number of examples that corroborated his prescient fears. The Uncompahgre fritillary, for one, barely teeters on the roof of the San Juan Mountains.

I am even more angry than sad at how much will be lost before complexity arises again. Extinction events are nothing new, but this one didn't have to happen. The grand evocation of diversity that we know, or call it the "Creation," could have lasted a lot longer, and we could have stuck around to enjoy it. But my anger isn't yet widely shared. It will be, and if it takes longer than I live to get there, I won't mind missing that point. A world without *Tridacna*, or the reefs to hold them? A world without pika geeking from the high rocks? Count me out. I'd rather be a clam.

For us too, it is a matter of adapt or die—there is no way out of that circumstance for any organism. Yet our flimsy ethical condition, regardless of political persuasion or economic system, still thinks perpetual growth and ultimate good are compatible. They are not. As Fritz Schumacher put it, "Greed and envy demand continuous and limitless economic growth of a material kind, without proper regard for conservation, and this type of growth cannot possibly fit into a finite environment." Nor is it merely a matter of greed and envy. As we saw in the recent economic implosion, the entire social system suicidally depends on perpetual growth. Kipling wrote, of the old values and verities, that "we found them lacking in Uplift, Vision, and Breadth of Mind / So we left them to teach the Gorillas, while we followed the march of Mankind"—directly into the lap of "the Gods of the Marketplace," where we engage in carbon trading to pay back Peter. Maybe the gorillas, or some other ape, could make a better job of it next time around.

In spite of the worst we can do, the tatters of nature we leave behind will carry on. All insults will be redressed by a jealous earth and atmosphere, and in time, coyote may give rise to a dozen new canids. Collembola might found whole new orders of invertebrates, with lifeways beyond our imagining. And if some sort of upright ape is among the array, it might not bear much resemblance to those who pulled the plug, pushed the plunger, pulled the trigger on the chamber that, oops! really was loaded.

Our moral sense is really the collective genetic and social experience of what's good for us and what isn't. Just like any other species, we are subject to natural selection of the most advantageous traits for the species in the long run. And that can change: love without issue, anathema once, has become heroic and adaptive. Evolution never before encountered self-interest such as ours, empowered by such powerful tools for planetary alteration: the ability of the individual animal or group to frustrate the good of the whole. To my mind, the greatest reason for bringing an ethical response to bear on annealing the damaged climate is to give evolution a fair shake in the next iteration.

Our moral imperative to turn down the heat is merely our mandate from nature to adapt—to survive. But fat chance we've got, now. For this species, and the many others we are dragging down with us, it is late in the game. Cap-and-trade is unlikely to do the job, especially if economic and population growth remain the order of the day. With luck, the smart and humble adherents of the small and the local may survive to have another go after the larger collapse, may even thrive under the uncomfortable and inconvenient conditions to come. But I doubt very much that the culture we know will long persist, absent truly radical changes in the way it works. We are the maladaptive ape, at twilight. Evolution will mock our tardy rage.

A Nat'ral Histerrical Feller in an Unwondering Age

(*Way of Natural History*, Trinity University Press, 2011)

Following a series of regional conversations on the revivification of natu-
ral history, Tom Fleischner, professor at Prescott College and founder of the
Natural History Institute, compiled a volume of essays on the discipline's
future. I didn't want to rehash "The Rise and Fall of Natural History." Feeling
I'd had my say in the matter, at first I declined to be included, as with the
previous piece. But, déjà vu, Tom asked me to reconsider, and to write from
the standpoint of a "deep naturalist." Believing I am anything but, I said I
would write if I could take the opposite approach, and speak of our collec-
tive ignorance and its consequences. Some felt that I was too harsh, perhaps
even discouraging, about how little most people know their neighbors. But it
seemed to me that the sin would rather be in failing to disclose the depths of
our shared ecological illiteracy, bitter though the pill may be. And the ending,
I believe, is very positive.

> One touch of Nature makes the whole world kin.
> —William Shakespeare, *Troilus and Cressida*

For anyone seriously interested in North American butterflies in the first half of
the twentieth century, the primary reference by a long shot was W. J. Holland's
The Butterfly Book. Published in 1898 and revised in 1931, its final 1950's impression included my own copy. The charm and interest of Holland's big tome, hardly
a field guide, were much enhanced for young readers by a series of "Digressions
and Quotations." These ranged from the author's own recollections of important
moments with butterflies, to verse by Hugo (translated by Eugene Field), Ella
Wheeler Wilcox, and "Mrs. Hemans." Vladimir Nabokov, a stern critic of "old
Dr. Holland," dismissed these marginalia as "stale anecdotes . . . and third-rate
poetry." Lowbrow though they may be, these bits made the ponderous work more
fun, and like many a young lepidopterist of the era, I practically memorized them
through successive rainy-day readings.

One such piece, "Uncle Jotham's Boarder" by Annie Trumbull Slosson, tells in stylized dialect the story of a summer boarder at a rural farmhouse, and his perception by his host. Uncle Jotham reported his guest's activities in anthropological detail:

> Well, true as I live, that old feller just spent
> His hull days in loafin' about
> And pickin' up hoppers and roaches and flies
> Not to use for his bait to ketch trout
> But to kill and stick pins in and squint at and all.
> He was crazy's a coot, th' ain't no doubt.

When the boarder tries to explain why he feeds "ellums and birches and willers" to boxes of caterpillars in his bedroom, Uncle Jotham concludes, "S'near's I can tell, 'stead of enterin' a trade, / He was tryin' to just enter mology." He continues:

> And Hannah, my wife, says she's heard o' sech things;
> She guesses his brain warn't so meller.
> There's a thing they call Nat'ral Histerry, she says.
> And whatever the folks here may tell her
> Till it's settled she's wrong she'll just hold that 'air man
> Was a Nat'ral Histerrical feller.

No matter how many times I read it, I always got a giggle out of the silly pun. It also served to remind me that I, too, was a "nat'ral histerrical feller," and that not everyone else was. But the verse also reinforced a message I got loud and clear every time I went out in public with my own "old bait net": one of surprise, amusement, and, often, even derision.

Most folks didn't know what to make of my passion. I lived in a 1960s suburban setting, but as Mrs. Slosson's fin de siecle rural verse suggests, country people shared that bemusement toward a naturalist in their midst with the suburbanites. For the most part, I withstood the cracks and hoots; but I've seen many other kids hang up their nets under the pressure of conformity, especially in adolescence. It helped me to know that I wasn't the only nature freak ever to be cast an incredulous eye. But it was another bit of Holland's borrowed verse that pointed me toward my lifelong objective—not just to know some "nat'ral histerry," but to inquire deeply of nature. His follow-up volume, *The Moth Book*, begins with this dialogue by Oliver Wendell Holmes in *The Poet at the Breakfast Table*:

"I suppose you are an entomologist?"

"Not quite as ambitious as that, sir. I should like to put my eyes on the individual entitled to that name. No man can be truly called an entomologist, sir; the subject is too vast for any human intelligence to grasp."

If it was a vast challenge that Holland and Holmes hurled my way, they also served up a useful corrective to my childish conceit: After all, if it was impossible to become a real entomologist, how could one hope to embrace natural history as a whole? But as I soon learned, this particular uphill road was full of delights. I might never get there, but I would have fun trying. Ultimately, the attempt would define my life.

There was a time when most members of every social band were pretty good working naturalists, or they didn't survive. But "civilization" meant compartmentalizing jobs and functions, so that the intimate knowledge of flora and fauna possessed by the people became the province of shamans, priests, and wise women. (The first such division of labor, following the hunter/gatherer fault, may have broken along gender lines: animal-savvy men versus plantswomen. Until relatively recent times, women in life sciences were much more likely to be found in botany departments than zoology.)

In their modern eras, most cultures have found natural history retreating into smaller and smaller crannies and obscure recesses. England seemed to be the one exception, where "countryside" pursuits remained more or less common until fairly recent times. But that was an aberration, and it has in any case faded. In general, contemporary culture has marginalized the naturalist with impressive thoroughness. After all, naturalists know what's going on out there, which gets in the way of progress.

There was also a time when professionals were trained and hired to attend to natural history for the rest of us: the systematists, curators, fieldworkers, professors, and so on. But that was Holland's time, and he was one of them, as director of the Carnegie Museum. From midcentury on, a purge of the naturalists occurred at many universities, in favor of molecular, cellular, and mathematical biology. The University of Washington conducted its final entomological field trip this past summer, after a century of insect instruction. Great museums went increasingly for big exhibits over basic study, neglecting their vital collections. Even as professional, academic natural history went into eclipse, the regular presence of outdoor subjects in the public schools (inspired by Anna Botsford Comstock's nature-study movement) withered to near nothingness, capped off by *Sputnik*. Environmental education has never managed to replace nature study, whereby a basic working knowledge of local fauna and flora was considered an essential part of education.

Now that we've come to a time when understanding all the working parts of the biosphere is more important than ever, the number of people charged with and compensated for doing so is smaller than ever. Most detailed biological survey and systematic study is now performed by amateurs who do it for love, as the term implies, in concert with a handful of holdout pros at the Smithsonian, the McGuire Center for Biological Diversity in Gainesville, and a few other overstretched institutions. One elder woman and her son possess most of the knowledge of West Coast worms. A volunteer devout is the primary authority on spiders of the Pacific Northwest. The greatest North American butterfly taxonomist is a swing-shift truck driver. They are not unusual. As Carol Kaesuk Yoon puts it in *Naming Nature: The Clash between Instinct and Science*, "We are willfully . . . losing the ability to order and name and therefore losing a connection to and a place in the living world."

Oddly enough, despite such trends, natural history has bounced back in the United States in some ways. Television and Internet features and series, bird-watching and feeding, butterflying, native plants and gardening groups are all popular and growing. The drive toward green has made nature fashionable again. But most of this attention is shallow. People too often ignore what they separate from themselves as "nature," and of those members who do notice or even celebrate it, few explore the real, living, more-than-human world in any depth. It's better than nothing, is about all you can say.

If Americans on the whole are profoundly ignorant about natural history, and they are, then most of the "naturalists" among them aren't much better. Most birders don't know their local flora. The majority of butterfly watchers of my acquaintance have little knowledge of other orders of insects, let alone other groups of invertebrates. Gardeners often have little sense of plant families, knowing nothing of the relatives and progenitors of their favorite flowers or veggies. Few modern hunters and fishers know many non-game species by name or habit. And children, the original naturalists, recognize many more corporate logos today than animals or plants, as recent studies have shown. Some enthusiasts cross over, such as birdwatchers who discover butterflies as a new challenge, jokingly known as "birders gone bad." The equivalent for butterfly watchers is to take up dragonfly-watching. But the majority of nature lovers tend to stick to familiar territory.

Last year, I traveled over much of the United States conducting the first Butterfly Big Year. One of my hopes was to conduct a broad overview of butterfly well-being. Aside from general development, the single factor most often cited for local or regional extirpation of rare butterflies was fire, wild or intentional. The lack of baseline data for pre-burn, fire-intolerant butterflies allows fires to go ahead with no awareness of their consequences—the pyrobotanists literally know not what they do. The Ottoe skipper has been wiped out of Iowa and much of the Midwest, largely by controlled burns—too hot, too big, too often—on state and private reserves. And that's just butterflies! What about the many more moths? The flies, wasps, and other pollinators? Let alone the cities of soil invertebrates. In fact, there is usually no one available to identify invertebrates, even if managers did attempt due diligence in baseline sampling.

Our culture neither values nor rewards, let alone trains and hires, well-versed naturalists. Is it any wonder that we are a nation (and a world) of natural history ignoramuses? Our ecological illiteracy achieves a scale no less than spectacular. Most nature writers, poets of the more-than-human, environmental studies professionals, landscape engineers and planners, and others whom we might expect to know better actually have very little natural history at their disposal. Among the worst are some of the so-called, self-described deep ecologists, ecopsychologists, and spiritual ecophilosophers.

In my experience, though nice enough folks with admirable ethics and intentions, many such people don't know squat about actual ecosystems. Next time you meet a "deep ecologist," ask him to explain the trophic levels in his backyard, complete with plot and cast. On your next walk with a person with ecoanything on her business card, ask for an introduction to the local flora and fauna. Some may be able to accommodate—but most? I am not putting down these people, practices, or professions, but their self-awarded titles often strike me as ironic, if not hubristic.

The plain fact is, there are very few deep naturalists, as I would define the term: someone with a working knowledge of a broad slice of the biota, and how the parts fit together with one another and their physical setting. After fifty-plus years of hanging about with thousands of biologists and nature lovers, I can think of just a handful who even come close: Dennis Paulson in Seattle, John Alcock in

Phoenix, Roger Hammer down in Homestead, Bill Leonard up in Olympia come to mind_humble aspirants all, who would probably not accept the title I am giving them. I'm sure there are many others I don't know. But serious practitioners of the principles Ann Zwinger exemplifies in her splendid book *The Nearsighted Naturalist* are, by any measure, few.

Lately, programs have arisen to certify naturalists, along the lines of Master Gardeners. It's a nice idea, designed to increase people's confidence in teaching others. But no one knows enough to even ask the test questions. I have always said that anyone out of doors with open eyes (and/or ears) and mind is a naturalist, and I believe it. That lets most folks out, right there. But a deep naturalist (let alone a Master Naturalist—ha!) would have a passable knowledge of many groups of organisms, their lifeways, and the processes that bind them together, as well as geology, climatology, and much more. Do you know many such? Any?

I do know many experts on given groups of organisms. Perhaps it is asking too much of anyone to know a lot of groups, habitats, and phenomena, like asking Joshua Bell to also be Dr. John and Merle Haggard. But what's to keep one from trying to know something of everything out there? Perhaps what we need is a better class of dilettantes.

At this point, I should make it very clear that I consider myself a dilettante when it comes to most aspects of natural history, if not an outright ignoramus. People think I know a lot about nature, but I snort at that. Perhaps I do, compared to most, but that only reinforces my depressing point. I know "a lot" about butterflies, but far less than fifty or one hundred people I could immediately name, and a great many more I don't know. And though I know my local birds, plants, mammals, mollusks, herps, some moths, fish, and a few others, I know very little about our magnificent fly fauna, our lichens, or the water bears that surely clamber through our anonymous, sopping mosses in winter. No one else does, either. How dispiriting! That flying termite at my feet, that moth, that midge . . . who are they? I thirst to know them all—not just their names, but something of their lives.

It would be unreasonable to expect many people to seek a really deep knowledge of natural history. The sheer quantity of ecological information is daunting, to be sure. Besides, the banal details of quotidian life won't allow it, with most of us who are "caught between the longing for love and the struggle for the legal tender," as Jackson Browne so perfectly put it. The stupidifying effects of contemporary culture take care of the rest of the possibility for many, by miring their spare time in trivia. But in a culture that hopes to stick around for a while, is it too much to ask its members to get to know a few of their nonhuman neighbors? A bird a week, a plant a month, a beetle a year—it's not that hard.

For my part, I aspire someday toward the middle rungs of deep natural history. But this is no competition. In my Butterfly Big Year, I attended to every other group I noticed as well to some extent. With the help of field guides, book and human, I noted around a thousand distinct animal species (though I didn't have a name for every one) along with countless plants. This was satisfying, and put again a question I've often asked: How do people survive sans natural history? The nature I know has saved my life, over and over. It also lets me know how much I don't know, and causes me to crave a deeper immersion than I've known so far. We can never know it all, but there's nothing to keep us from becoming better acquainted with our surroundings, a little bit every day.

I used to imagine an island—I knew one or two that would nicely suffice—on which I would camp and try to get to know every single occupant over the years. But islands are hard to come by, difficult of access and supply, and lack certain elements, thanks to island biogeography. Now I live on a kind of an island—a little three-acre pie-slice of land between two roads and a creek. It is an old Swedish homestead, known as Swede Park, in the southwestern Washington rain forest. I told its story in *Sky Time in Gray's River: Living for Keeps in a Forgotten Place.* People think I know its natural history in depth, but I laugh. I would love to. And maybe I will yet make the attempt.

I am sixty-two—with luck, I've got maybe thirty or forty years left. What to do with it? More and more, natural history is what makes sense to me. I have fought many conservation battles, and will continue to do so, as quixotic as it often seems. But I have grown anaphylactically allergic to committees and almost all meetings. I have lost most interest in distant cities. I gave up TV in 1969, and the Internet, largely, forty years later. I spend much of my time perforce before a screen in order to write, and I just don't feel the need to entertain myself in the same posture.

Without a doubt, the Internet offers vastly greater information about natural history, and closer communication among naturalists. The superb www.butterfliesofamerica.org is just one example. However, I've watched many colleagues dissipate much of their available time and energy in ephemeral e-mail fusillades and repetitive, unrefereed disputation. I will surely use the Internet for specific information search and concise communication, but I refuse to devote to it much time that could be spent out of doors.

As for my work, teaching is a fine and two-way thing. But done too much without refreshment, it can also keep one stationary and static, locked into present knowledge and its repetition: fine for some, but it pales for me. Literary distinction, too, is illusory—if someone reads what I write now and then, is affected by it, and responds, I am deeply gratified. That's the best part of the practice, and the most I can reasonably hope for. Of course I will keep on writing. But it is no profession to depend on in material terms, nor is it an adequate end in itself, at least for me. I love my family, my friends, my dwelling place, and my library, and I hope and intend to devote a goodly portion of my time and attention to all of them, as long as I remain able. What else does that leave?

What I would really like to do is to devote most of my days—as fits nicely with the many outdoor chores an old place like this requires—to the deep study of this tiny slice of the world. The fly fauna here is phenomenal: I've always wanted to become a dipterist. And the other insects—I don't even know our bumblebees, for cripe's sake! Or most of our moths, or mosses, nor even all the mollusks. This is simply sinful, after thirty years here. As one who is called a naturalist, what I most want now, is to really become a naturalist.

A young writer friend, to whom I recently explained my ambition to become a deeper naturalist, asked me, "To what end?" That made me think. I suppose at a time when activism has never been more needed, the pursuit of pure natural history (like pure art) might strike some as self-indulgent, even merely masturbatory: harmless enough, but unhelpful to the revolution, useless to the resistance against our clear and present crisis. Or is it? Just as pure (or basic) science has come up with essential solutions at least as often as applied science, so has unpremeditated natural history revealed what we've needed to know again and again. Who knows when a given encounter, closely observed, might uncover some generality that applies to specific questions or problems all over? For example, the long search for the cryptic nest of the marbled murrelet finally led to mossy boughs in remnant old-growth forests near the northwestern coast. Along with its famous fellow old-growth obligate, the northern spotted owl, and its lesser-known cohort, the Hemphill's jumping slug, the murrelet now drives much of Pacific Northwest timber management policy through its natural history. At the very least, if communicated, each naturalist's findings add to the simmering pot of knowledge that might someday allow us to behave in an adaptive manner after all.

But must any such practical justification really be invoked? Isn't it enough that the pursuit of deep natural history is one of the surest paths toward an entirely earthly state of enlightenment? In a 1969 interview with Robert Tabozzi, Vladimir Nabokov said, "The emotion of recognizing in an alpine meadow a butterfly one knows to be different from another and whose special comportment one observes—this emotion is a feeling in which the scientific and the artistic sides join in an apex of sharp pleasure unknown to the man walking under trees he cannot even name."

Surely the inability of even educated people to name the trees they walk beneath presents a distinct and timely danger to our culture and its future, if any. Where, in a populace innocent of sincere acquaintance with its extra-human neighbors, is the ability to live well in our shared neighborhood to come from? And where will conservationists come from, when the young no longer meet the world in special places of dirt and leaf and water and crawler? I believe with burning urgency that our ecological illiteracy is not only lazy, self-impugning, and solipsistic to the max, but also ultimately suicidal.

Yet the ignorance of the population at large is not what this essay is really about. It is about how I, or anyone, might aspire toward lesser ignorance. After all, it is important to remember that depth is a relative thing. For one person to learn his neighborhood birds might be the objective; for another, the butterflies in her garden. No one need feel compelled to attempt the impossible. The point is to get to know a few new lives, then take it as deep as you want. Intimidated by the bounty of life that they can never hope to know in its entirety, most folks give up before they ever make a start. Others pick up a field guide, and begin.

Two Essays from Billy Meadows

(from *Letting the Flies Out*, New Riverside Press, 2011)

In 2010, I was the Werner Writing Resident at Billy Meadows, the old Blue Mountains Forest Service outpost that then served as the base for the summer writing workshop called Outpost, sponsored by Fishtrap. While I wrote mostly poetry that summer, these two prose pieces emerged. Happily, the first event described took place during the visit of my late wife, Thea.

I. A Mountain Lion

We saw a mountain lion today. It was the second time for each of us, in 126 years of watching, all told. We were driving the 46 road on the top of the Oregon side of the Wallowa-Whitman National Forest, edge of the Hells Canyon National Recreation Area, in the stretch between Cold Spring Ridge and Buckhorn Overlook. We'd stopped several times on our way from the Billy Meadows guard station to luxuriate in the deep orchid shag carpet of *Allium*, or to parse the blue butterflies at the mud beside a stock tank or over a mound of buckwheat bloom.

Thea's other one came in the rocks in late summer beside a reservoir between Laramie and Cheyenne, a fleeting but definitive and thrilling glimpse. My first puma crossed a narrow logging road before me in the Willapa Hills, alder to alder in two or three seconds and bounds.

I've always had a jones for *Felis concolor*. I've duly lamented houndhunters, treers, bounty hunters, and their like. I've reveled in lion tales such as Jim Halfpenny's account of one puma batting a weathervane atop a Boulder resident's rooftop, like a whirring cat toy. And I've rued stories of latter-day lion attacks on joggers and children, never known before, brought on by the incursion of suburbia into lion habitat, because such accounts go badly for the cats. I've read of people tracked by curious pumas, and one who sat still until the animal approached, sat, actually permitted petting, and purred deeply. I've petted one myself, but it was captive and spoiled for release, part of a teaching collection at the Cincinnati Zoo, so it didn't really count, but I loved feeling its broad head, dense pelt, and fat tail just the same.

That's what tipped me off—that amazing tail. When the animal entered the road, my thought was first, "Wow, there's somebody's golden retriever." But there was no such somebody: the only people we saw the livelong day were one Forest Service employee on patrol and one rancher steaming toward town. There were no retrievers abroad on the land.

By the time the beast reached the centerline (a fir twig in the dust, midway across), the penny dropped. I saw the big head, and the sooty mustache. I saw the long, lean torso, tawny, not reddish like that Olympic subspecies Willapa cat I saw before. And most of all, as the puma *loped*—not dashed, not flashed, but only *loped* across in front of us at forty or fifty feet—I saw that singular tail: almost as long as the animal itself, as thick as a lodgepole pine bough, as curved down and up again as a pipe-cleaner model of a mountain lion's tail. Tipped in black, like a girl's pigtails in a pioneer school in these parts, dipped in the inkwell by some loutish lad.

"Oh my god!" I yelped, a quaver in my voice. And there loped the great cat. *Loped*, not ran, not slinked, not skedaddled, but loped, with all deliberation, never looking our way. The arms and legs muscled forward in no great explosion such as the many deer and elk we'd spooked that day might fear, but at a measured pace. I tell you, that catamount *loped*. Its great paws came down in the dust, that impossibly long, thick tail stuck out and curled up at the end.

And then, several seconds after that dog bounded into the road in front of us, that cat was gone. Solid gone. I braked when I saw it, and backed to where it crossed.

"You won't see it anymore," said Thea, and of course, she was right. It might've been in Washington by then, or at least farther than I could ever follow.

Still to come were slopes of rose pink *Clarkia*, spattered among scarlet gilia and deep drifts of *Delphinium;* the unlikely beauty of red-spotted parnassians drifting among fields of purple-spotted mariposa lilies; *Aconitum* swales, cornflower towers, and back at Billy Meadows, a hose hanging from a stand-pipe for filling fire-wagons that was thick as that lion's tail. Later, stars, as many in the wilderness of sky as permitted by half a moon. And many another wonder in between.

But that puma, now; wasn't that just *it*?

II. But the Names Do Matter

For a group poem exercise at the Outpost workshop, the first line I offered was this: "That warbler in the high fir—I know it, I know it. So what the heck is it?"

The first five responses were: "My name is not vital; listen to my song." "I invite you to pause a moment—and not think—just listen." "Perhaps then I will call you by name. The name you have forgotten." "It's the song that matters and where the song comes from." "Whatever its name it finds food and shelter here. Could you do as well?"

All charming, thoughtful, and all have a point. But they also reminded me of an attitude I have frequently heard among friends, students, poets, and certain self-described deep ecologists: "Who cares what name people give it—it's the creature itself that counts."

Such statements often come from people who know few organisms by name, and are intimidated by the seeming hopelessness of ever learning them all. They remind me of people who, knowing they will never "catch up" on their reading, read nothing at all, at least not books. I have even encountered such behavior among aspiring poets and naturalists!

The responses to my first line imply an impatience with my desire to name the warbler, as if that were a distraction from the real work of just listening to its song. Taken further, such a reaction can seem almost contemptuous of the naming of animals and plants. When people go such lengths, they violate John Fowles's important and apt dictum from his novel *Daniel Martin*, delivered from the male protagonist to his lover who was impatient with his affection for the names of wild orchids and his wish for her to recognize a junco: "Why isn't it enough that I just love it here?" she asks. "That I don't want to know all the names and the frightfully scientific words." And he replies, "Because one shouldn't justify contempt from ignorance. In anything."

Hanging on the wall of the bedroom in Billy Meadows Guard Station are two broadsides: "Sabbath Poem IV" by Wendell Berry, about the golden-fronted warbler; and "Cormorants" by Gary Snyder. Both invoke the character of their place and time through the appearance and behavior of these particular birds. Neither poem would amount to much if they were simply called "Bird." For names *are* important; they matter after all. After invoking dozens of names in her poem "The Family Is All There Is," Pattiann Rogers concludes, "all brothers, sisters, all there is. Name something else." We dignify the members of our families with individual names. And the nonhumans living around us are all our neighbors, as well as our evolutionary relations. Don't we care more about our neighbors, when we know their names?

When we take the trouble to know an organism's appellation, we can tell its stories. The Northwest coast Indians did not speak of, carve, or pass on the stories of *anonymous* totems—raven, heron, beaver, bear—they all have names. (Exception: Athabascans refer to "the big brown thing" because the names of the grizzly bear and the Wild Man of the Woods are not to be uttered, a la "He who must not be named.") By knowing someone's distinctive handle, we can speak of his or her "individuating details," in Nabokov's great term. We can give "attention to the particular," which Snyder tells us "is never in vain," communicate about it, and our listeners or readers can know exactly to whom we are referring.

My first week at Billy Meadows has been graced by coyotes crying in stereo, as I once heard black howlers howl in stereo from a pyramid at Tikal in Guatemala; a hundred or more wapiti bedding down in the meadow below me after the bugled arrival of the bull and his herd; a mountain lion (aka puma, catamount, cougar, or *Felis concolor*) crossing the road before me, loping cool and slow; and gray jays=camp robbers=whiskey jacks coming to my picnic table in hopes of crumbs. Yesterday, a female or immature calliope hummingbird hovered over the red-topped bench I was using for a table on the porch at lunch. It probed all around the scarlet-painted wood. I held out a slice of watermelon, hoping the hummer would find it and drink; it tried to suck from the grooves in the table instead. And just now, next morning, at the picnic table out back again, I heard that same thrum as the minute humbird appeared again beside me, shoving its ice-pick bill into my red bandanna on the tabletop. I felt its tiny fan on my hand an inch away. Then it flew behind me and tapped me on the back, probing the red letters on my tee shirt. Don't stories like these deserve names to go by? And how can we survey, tally, account for, or manage land on behalf of the nameless?

"Stay together," writes Gary Snyder in "For the Children," "learn the flowers / go light." No one expects you to learn *all* the flowers or name all the birds, or to recognize all the butterflies. No one ever will. But you *can* pull out your Roger Tory Peterson and make the effort to become acquainted with one or two. You can get to know another neighbor each week, or month, or year. You can ask, "Who *are* you?" Because by knowing names, we grant each plant, each creature, the unique details of its own existence. No, never should we justify ignorance from contempt.

Not that I think my fellow Outposters were implying anything of the kind with their lines; I think they simply didn't want the song itself to be lost in the rush to put a label on it, and they're right, because we all know birders like *that*! But I also think they might have liked to know that the bird who delivered the sweetest song of all, the double-syrinxed, self-harmonizing, Pan-like piping we heard at the edge of the forest up behind the meadow, is named *hermit thrush*.

Parents without Children
Confessions of a Favorite Uncle
(*Orion*, 1995; updated for *Companions in Wonder*, MIT Press, 2012)

During one of the Orion Society's Forgotten Language Tours—far-roaming, barnstorming chautauquas of nature writers prowling the provinces to deliver the good word—the idea emerged of an issue of the magazine devoted to parenting. Both Marion Gilliam, the publisher, and I felt there should be a piece included devoted to those of us who have not reproduced yet have contributed to the lives of the young of the species. I volunteered and got the assignment. This is the version updated for a later book, in my grandfather years.

In my father's latter working years, single and still involved with my younger brother's well-being, he joined an organization called Parents Without Partners. He wasn't the first single parent in my family. All my grandparents, both his folks and my mother's, had been divorced in the 1920s, when broken families were rare. After my own parents divorced when I was ten, I lived with my father at first and then with my mother through junior high and high school. Unpartnered parenting was the norm in my family long before it became a common social pattern. I don't know whether that fractured background has anything to do with the fact that of my parents' four offspring, only one has had children of his own. For my part, I have come to think of myself as a parent without children.

Not that I made a conscious decision not to reproduce. On the contrary, I imagined bringing forth children who would benefit from what I had learned from my own scattered but diverse family. Of course, I envisioned children made much in my own mold, living rich childhoods bathed in nature, allowing me to relive my own early enchantments but with specific improvements—such as an intact family.

Nor have I lacked the circumstances for potential parenthood. Thrice blessed in marriage, I found in the first union that our ages, economics, college, and jobs militated against early childbearing. Far-flung travel, career hopes, and financial uncertainty put off pregnancy in my second marriage. Our irresolution saved me from perpetuating the family pattern for a third generation, and the great women involved went on to become mothers of great children. When Thea and I married, we too considered procreating, but she already had children and quite rightly wasn't sure she wanted to do it all over again just as her life was opening out. My reasons, by then largely sensual and sentimental, were insufficient for creating a new life with an ambivalent partner while in the midst of an over-stuffed, uninsured, half-spent life.

So I cannot say that my lack of biological children was the clear result of an ethical decision not to reproduce, such as the one announced by conservation writer Stephanie Mills in her famous 1969 college commencement speech at Mills College. Even so, influenced (like Stephanie) by Paul Ehrlich's *Population Bomb*, I decided that none of us had any business doing more than replacing ourselves. I admire Paul and Anne Ehrlich's symbolic withholding of baby presents after the second child, and as they do, I believe that our estate is at urgent risk from the balance-busting, super-sized proportions of the whole human population. So I felt fine, as a citizen of the ecosystem, having kept my genes to myself.

Still, a shade of regret must chill most of the childless from time to time. To see one's genes, mixmastered through meiosis with those of your loved one, expressed in the eyes and face and mind and toes of a baby; to experience the unmatched exultation that parents must feel when their own children jump into their arms for a hug or onto their laps for a story; to aid another life as only a parent can—these are large and real desires only poorly mitigated by the relief of not exposing one more child to the modern malaise or oneself to the fears and heartbreak that go along with the joys of parenthood. Yet no one remotely open to the immatures of the species can remain aloof from their gifts, their needs, their futures. So while largely reconciled to my role as one of this world's uncles, I find myself asking from time to time not only what I gain as a parent without children but what I can give to young I have not helped to conceive.

When I am afield with kids, on butterfly walks or hikes with their folks or just knocking about where families are likely to be encountered, I frequently receive a kind compliment from the adults. It used to go, "You'll be a great parent." As my beard became increasingly grizzled, the subjective gradually took over: "You'd make a great dad." Well, maybe and maybe not. If I were top-drawer dad material, making children might have been a higher priority than the things I have done instead. I think that what these parents are really reacting to is not only my genuine interest in their children and how they perceive the natural world but also the freshness that I, as a nonparent, can bring to the enterprise of taking in the world with children. In fact, my appetite for teaching and learning with kids is pretty finite; they wear me out. But in modest spurts, as ranger, teacher, friend, uncle, and finally stepfather and grandfather, I have been privileged to go afield with many other people's kids, giving their parents a little relief from the constant questions while giving the young 'uns the benefit of my unjaded enthusiasm. It should go without saying that, up to a point (when I can go home, kidless), the pleasure has been mine.

This has been especially true of my own blood kin. I have one niece, Heather, and one nephew, Michael. Their father, my older brother, Tom, once told me that he could not imagine my ever settling down to have children. "Then it's a good thing you have," I told him. And it is true. Tom and Mary furnished these great kids for all of us, is how my other brother and sister and I see it. Geography limits our visits, but whenever I can, I take full advantage of my collateral kids. When Heather and I walked up and down her neighborhood streets in Colorado Springs looking for the serpentoid caterpillars of two-tailed tiger swallowtails on green ash shade trees, and when she wrote to tell me about the black swallowtail larvae whose mothers had found the dill in her garden, I felt every bit of the buzz that parents must experience when passing on the details of the world beyond the back door, in any culture. When Mike accompanied me to a National Wildlife Federation Conservation Summit (a family natural history camp where I was teaching), broadening the bounds of his universe by a bit, I knew something of the sense of continuity that the elders know in passing on the secrets of the vision quest. I flatter myself that they will remember these days too; and as I watched them complete their formal educations, Heather in landscape architecture and Michael in the arts, I liked to think I made a contribution to these important people—small, but different from the daily donations their parents make to their lives. And when Heather married Pete and had children of her own, I became a great-uncle. When Grant and Jarrod showed me around their special fort, a cool crevice among pink granite boulders on the family cabin site north of Pikes Peak, I was able to tell them how their granddad and I made do with dens among dirt mounds and cottonwood thickets beside a ditch on the high plains.

I have never heard of a culture in which uncles and aunts are not accorded important roles in child development. These roles extend to highly stylized and vital kinship patterns in certain clan systems, as any perusal of Franz Boas or Margaret Mead shows. Such a function goes well beyond the genetics of actual siblings of the parents. The ability to perform an avuncular part in the lives of the next generation lies in all of us who, free of the demands of parenthood ourselves, have the leisure, the energy, the experience, and the desire to influence positively the lives of other people's children. This fact was driven home to me by the entries for an essay contest sponsored recently by my rural Grange. The subject was community and rural life, and we were looking for personal responses.

Some of the most striking essays came from boys whose fathers, uncles, and their bachelor friends had apprenticed them in the ways of logging, fishing, hunting, and country life, and from two girls who spoke fondly of the women in their church who had provided a circle of aunties to pass on the stories, skills, and lifeways of their Finnish immigrant community.

Reading these loving, earnest pieces, I felt as if I'd stepped back in time. But these were contemporary kids with computers and cars. Their ways of life might change as old livelihoods pass, and they might leave, but they will remember their grownup guides when their own chance comes. No one should be surprised that childless adults bring much that is good to the world by virtue of their freedom from parental responsibility and their concomitant energy, expendable income, and time. Many of our finest artists, writers, and social activists have borne great works from their intellects instead of children from their loins. The greater surprise is that many other creative persons have done both. Yet scarcely a generation has passed since young couples who chose not to bear children got nothing but grief, not only from parents eager for grandchildren but from society at large. This is still true in communities and creeds where childbearing is next to godliness or where family planning is suspect. But by now, when reproduction as a virtue in itself has become distinctly questionable in ecological terms and same-sex marriage is increasingly accepted as a love option in a world that desperately needs more love more than more people, the choice not to replace oneself can be seen as heroic rather than anomalous.

Opportunities for expression, personal development, and social participation clearly arise from the relative freedom that childlessness affords. Beyond these, I find myself asking what are the responsibilities of the nonparent? Aside from the obvious answers of providing relief, assistance, and moral support to the sainted parents, the best thing we can do (it seems to me) is to serve as vessels for the transmission of wisdom. While this role is terribly important in every area of civil and cultural life, it is nowhere more timely than in the passing on of natural lore. Books, TV, Twitter, Google Earth, environmental ed classes, and family vacations in national parks are all very fine. But there is no substitute for an elder who has been out there, knows a thing or two from direct experience, and is willing to share hard-earned knowledge with receptive and curious young minds.

Among the people who served this role in my life, I picture a spinster teacher or two, some gifted gardeners and bachelor lepidopterists, and my Great-Aunt Helen, who was a sturdy five foot six in pants and pumps, with high cheekbones hoisting her bright smile, and an intelligent forehead broad beneath the gray nimbus of her perm. Of course, my mentors included my parents and grandparents, den mothers, the fathers and mothers of friends, teachers, and other reproducers. But of the ones who really had time for me, not a few had no children of their own—like Aunt Helen.

I don't see such people as nonparents but as parents without children. Smart phones may be wonderfully interactive, but they are not interactive with the world. Not, in any case, as Aunt Helen was. Whenever she took me into the Front Range west of Denver to explore granite chasms, up to heavenly Boreas Pass that we considered our shared special place, to Western Slope ranches that had once been "ours," or just across from her Seventeenth Avenue apartment into Denver's City Park, I had her full attention. I had the benefit of her knowledge, experience, history, wit, and lore, freely offered up as perhaps only the dead-end elders can do. In this way, the dead end of mere genetics was short-circuited. I carry something of Aunt Helen and her all-encompassing love of the universe just as certainly as if it had been balled up in a double-dominant allele and passed to me in traditional gametic union, as it was from her sister, my grandmother Grace.

In *The Geography of Childhood*, the book he coauthored with Gary Nabhan, Steven Trimble wrote, "As parents, our job is to pay attention, to create possibilities—to be careful matchmakers between our children and the earth." I agree abundantly and would add that perhaps our job as parents without children is to augment those possibilities in ways that mothers and fathers might less easily be able to do by the very nature of their demanding role and sacrifice.

I have found, for example, that children sometimes show a special receptiveness toward grownups other than their parents. As novel personages free of the disciplinarian's burden, we may have open access to a child's enthusiasm that his or her parent might be denied. Three times one spring, young Tyler came along on my butterfly classes. Robert, his father, was his good buddy, and he participated as well. I wouldn't think to butt in to their outdoor idyll together. Yet the different dynamic Tyler forged with me—precisely because I wasn't his father—brought something to the forays that each of us could appreciate. When, too few years later, Tyler found himself in Fallujah as a Marine, catching some sanity along with the few butterflies in the compound with a hand-fashioned net, and later, home safe, pursuing further studies and a career in wildlife, I like to imagine that his butterfly-uncle had helped him out a little bit.

This power of the nonparent is an evanescent quality that wears thin with familiarity, but it can be a marvelous entree while it lasts—the stock in trade of nannies, aunties, and favorite uncles everywhere. Friends acting in loco parentis, if only momentarily, can help prevent "parent burnout." When Thea and I went afield with our friends Ed and Cathy, we borrowed Gavin long enough to give his parents time to key out a plant or poke about while we enjoyed the lad's fascination with a frog or a swallowtail. Something was exchanged, all around. Now, working on the oyster beds of Willapa Bay, Gavin might recall those days outdoors with family friends from time to time.

Contemporary recombinations of old family patterns permit many variations on the standard types of adult role models. In addition to a growing array of avuncular sorts, children nowadays often have access to more than four grandparents, and the child without at least one stepparent is becoming the exception. I had a stepmother when they were rare outside fairy tales. Stressed by the usual fault lines that mixed families often suffer, ours was not an altogether happy blend. But Pat and her family had a cabin in Crested Butte, Colorado, where they routinely took cool vacations from the flatlands. Suddenly I found myself pitched into a big family with its own rituals and was shy and resentful at first. But Pat's dad, a white-haired, genial teacher, made a new grandpa for me, and her several sisters furnished a flock of friendly and encouraging aunts. That flowery mountain paradise happened to be situated near the Rocky Mountain Biological Laboratory. Out fishing with Dad one day, I drifted off with my butterfly net and by chance met university lepidopterists who were to become major mentors for life. In spite of my attitude, I came out much richer in adult guides for having been a stepkid.

Twenty-five years ago, the question of stepparents came to have immediate meaning to me again, as I became one. When Thea and I were married, Tom and Dory came to live with us, giving me a crack at parenting after all. At the wedding, I read a sonnet for my new family. As John Donne insisted, "He is a fool which cannot make one sonnet, and he is mad which makes two." So I wrote one, celebrating this gift that came to me whole cloth deep in middle age. One line read, "Having no children, I'll not be childless."

They already had a good dad, so Tom and Dory did not need another. Since I did not have to try to become their father, I was free to be a different kind of adult in their lives. We hunted tree frogs for their terrarium and poked among ruins of old cannery villages above the Columbia. They too came to National Wildlife Summits with us for several years in several states, once involving an eight-thousand-mile cross-country trek by train. Though they came from a family that was already oriented to the out-of-doors, I was able to furnish some experiences they might not otherwise have enjoyed.

These days, visiting Tom in his Mexican village home or looking over Dory's shoulder as she juggles motherhood and career in Portland, I am guilty of a parent's pride. The sentiment of my sonnet was borne out richly. And now they have brought their own kids into the mix. A recent Fourth of July expedition to Mount St. Helens included Tom and Iliana's children, David and Cristina, just before they moved to Jalisco, and Dory and Jeb's little boy, Francis. At the meadow where we picnicked, I put nets into their hands, and we all chased off after summer ringlets, Francis scrambling gamely through the grass and thistles to keep up with his older cousins. When they all come to our old Swedish homestead together, and we throw Frisbees for our stepdogs and have snowball fights with snowball-bush flowerheads in June or rake up and leap into leaf piles in the fall, I am every bit as thrilled as Thea to be their grandparent. Step-grandchildren don't give a darn about genetics when it comes to love, a lap, and a book—or a butterfly net out-of-doors. It's all just more grandparents to them and more fun. The fact that we without children can yet have grandchildren is a grace note in our lives and, I hope, in the lives of those children abundantly blessed with elders.

The trend toward what used to be called "barren unions" can only accelerate, as acceptance of alternative lifestyles and human population pressures rise. More couples will decide that they prefer the rewards of life without offspring or that they cannot afford to raise children. Others, like Stephanie Mills, will declare their unwillingness to further populate the planet; still others will decline to introduce children to such a world as this, no matter how much they would like to be parents. Yet this must not be seen as an unmitigated tragedy. As the uncles and aunties of the world increase, so meaningful contact grows between children and adults other than their parents, enriching lives all around. We may finally come to see unions that produce no young as anything but barren. For same-sex couples and unmated individuals who may be denied some traditional satisfactions, the rewards from coparenting the young of the species will become more and more profound.

Frustration of the biological imperative to breed need not (and for our ultimate survival, must not) be a baleful thing. We can be progenitors outside the genetic loop, ancestors who have escaped the helix—parents without children. Though we may never join the great biological parade, we walk alongside, at our own pace, responsible yet for young lives beyond our own.

Back to the Big Spring
Where Rivers Come From, Where They Go
(*Rain*, 2012)

As the LNG ordeal dragged on along the Lower Columbia, I wrote this paean to moving waters as featured speaker at "Spirit of the River," a festival of dissent through the arts. How to write about a Missouri spring in service to a Pacific river? Easy! The evaporation cycle. "Spirit" became an annual event out of our sheer necessity to beat back one misbegotten project after another. Reinforced all along by the indefatigable Columbia Riverkeeper, it took us fifteen years of hearing after interminable hearing, lawsuits over permits, successful recalls of officials, and endless hours of loving, caring citizens' lives, but LNG on the Big River is, hey ho, finally dead.

As a little boy, I was fascinated with water—where it came from, where it went. My own personal watercourse was an old irrigation ditch called the High Line Canal, which wrapped all around the backside of Denver. In the spring it came rushing on with muddy water, then went dry again. It would be years before I understood that the canal's water came from the Platte River, and later went back into it; and how before that, it came from the clouds over the Rockies, and went back there again, too.

In the essay "Ring of Rivers" in *Wintergreen*, I described how I came to know about the water cycle: "Video lay far in the inscrutable future when I attended Peoria Elementary School in Aurora, Colorado. Our visual aids consisted of clunky sixteen-millimeter educational films shown on clunkier big projectors. The films invariably broke or jumped the sprocket, or when they didn't, the bulb burned out. Mostly I remember unrelated flickers on a sleepy screen.

"From those pre-media-center days, however, two movies stick in my mind. One of them concerned apples in Wenatchee, and I probably remembered it because of its Washington theme. (*Washington* was a magic word in my household.) Never mind that the story line celebrated that most forgettable of apples, the Red Delicious, I found the movie compelling.

"The other memorable reel dealt with rain, and the recycling and conservation of water in nature. I suspect that it was a Soil Conservation Service propaganda piece. The simple plot had a raindrop, with facial features, fall from the sky onto a forested hill, irrigate the trees, enter a rivulet, thence a stream, eventually a river, and ultimately the sea before rising to a cloud again as mist. Along the way we shared in all the adventures of Willy Waterdrop: the plunge over a waterfall, the close call with a thirsty cow, the run-in with pollution, and the further insult of having to mix with mud running off an eroded slope. Perhaps memory embellishes, but I remember the concept of cycle coming firmly home."

In a later chapter in *Wintergreen*, I wrote about my unbounded passion for shells, especially land snails, in arid, land-locked eastern Colorado. "When my grandfather took my brother, Tom, and me back East in the Packard," I wrote, "and we called in at the Big Spring in Missouri's Ozarks, I had no eyes for the usual souvenirs: for there I found my first land snail, laying its silver streak on the wall of a cave beside the blue pool of the spring. I was transported with excitement, and the creature occupied me for the rest of the long, hot trip, then died." But that first snail wasn't all I remembered from the Big Spring: it was all that water—where did it come from? Where did it go?

Last month I went back there again, and here is what I found:

Two hundred eighty-eight million gallons a day pump out of the rocks below the caves of the Big Spring in a blue-green and white-crowned surge, past walking ferns and cinnamon ferns, past maples and redbud, past cliffs and meadows, past cardinals and otters and land snails, like the one I found here fifty-five years ago, when I came with my grandfather and my brother. Pump out and flow past all manner of Missouri mosses, wetting white limestone gone green, gone honey brown above the caves, misting the old CCC masonry path with fossilized ripples and stone walls, built in the thirties when FDR was "building for human happiness." Flow past wild ginger, into a great broad pool of aquamarine, beneath dependent boughs of American sycamore.

Into the oxbow arm of the Current River flows that water, over bottoms of emerald algae where, on steamy summer days, hot hordes tube and float and paddle, canoe and splash and fish; but not up here by the Big Spring, not today, after the heat wave when a high summer storm broke the swelter so the breeze beside the spring actually feels cool and everyone went home too soon and we have the place to ourselves, as humidity mounts in the canebrake and the woodchucks retire to the selvage, fifty-five years later.

Kingfisher cuts over the water, alights above the surge, reflects its blue, rattles of waters far away. Saddlebag dragonflies mate in hoop, wheel over the pool after the small flies that pester our faces as we watch the waters, thinking back that half century and more. Now take it back just three more half-centuries to when Clark and Lewis were packing up to leave these parts—imagine! I was here one-quarter of the way back to them!—leaving, to try to find the place where I've just come from, and will return tomorrow; to find where these waters give way to the waters of the West.

Eastern tailed blue butterflies probe the sweat on my big toe as I imagine them pushing off in their pirogues to head up the Missouri not far above where this river, the Current, debouches into the Mississippi, but going the other way. And after the white Missouri Breaks, after the Bannocks, the Sioux, the Crow, when they dropped over Lolo Pass to the Lochsa Road, no road then but a rough Indian way down the Clearwater, western tailed blues sucked at their sweaty moccasins, and water snakes and water striders and water lilies flowed past their bows. Firs and cedars drifted past, and salmon and sturgeon, and before they knew it they came to the difficult portage of The Dalles and the nightmare nights at Dismal Nitch, and finally, "o! the bloody joy! Ocian in view."

But what of the waters of the Big Spring they left behind? That flowed the other way, down to the thick and steamy bayous and out to the Gulf of future petro mess? Oh, they didn't stop there! Gathered up by waterspouts off the cays and tortugas, flung against seawall and palm-trunk, hurled in water balloons against their natural flow . . . but what's natural anyway, as Clark and Lewis cook the waters of the sea at Seaside for salt to get them through that winter of rotten elk and sodden salmon, to get them back up the other way, past the portage at The Dalles, up the Lochsa Road that's not yet a road but will one day be crushed beneath behemoths accessory to the rape of the oil sands in Alberta, but is now a slog-and-a-half up the Clearwater to the Lolo, on down to the Bitterroot, then the Breaks, and back to St. Louis, thank the gods, with nobody dead and York still fit for slavery after the vaunted vote. Only five years for all that, just one-eleventh of the time since I was here before. Home in time to report to TJ: "Mission Accomplished."

But it's too late: the waters of the Big Spring have already made their getaway, flung to the western reaches as vapor, over the sea of Steinbeck and Ricketts, over the stiff middle finger of the Baja, only to fall as fog on Ensenada and smog on Encinitas, and still drift north and north and north on each successive wave lapping thataway until, Lo! the waters of the Big Spring arrive at O! the bloody joy! Columbia in view, for by now it is called that, Robert Gray slayer of sea otters having left the name of his ship, if no more otters, no more condors much longer after Clark, no more beaver after Astor. But just wait, they'll all be back: already a sea otter sighted inside Cape Disappointment, can condors be far behind?

Big Spring Water falls in heavy autumn mist on Baker Bay and Warrenton, falls as winter rain and sleet on slug and fern and clam and seal, falls into the mouth of Clark and Lewis River, onto the tongue of Tongue Point, over the bridges of Young's Bay, and across the bigger bridge to everywhere north. Falls on a place called Bradwood Landing, where it thinks it hears a chorus of voices over the waves' lap and the wind's blow, a joyous chant like "We beat the bastards, we beat the bastards, we beat the bastards," but maybe it was just a freighter's engine thrumming.

Thus refreshed, the Big Spring water flows upstream on neap tide past sword fern and deer fern and glistens on basalt gone black and slicks onto mudstone gone brown, disintegrates into flow and then rises on the hot breath of the land. Backwashes up ravine, up valley, up crease and crotch, ravine and arroyo, then dissipates in unexpected morning sun to rise again in mist and blow still farther east, until it blends into cloud lenticular in LooWit's hole, on PatWah's flank, on WyEast's crown. Then falls again as snow in east-bound canyons, on bumpers of campers headed up the 12 all the way to Clarkston, over the Snake to Lewiston, past Nez Perce bones and horses and up the Lochsa Road, a highway at last, eastward to Bitterroot and down the other side. And so it goes, all the way to Joplin and down Old Miss, off a side-shoot boil of the Big Muddy into the mouth of the Current and down a cave into clarifying limestone, and that's how the Big Spring water makes it all the way home, underground through caves and caverns, only to pop back out the eructant yawn where I was there to see it flow so many years ago, and now once again.

And what, you ask, does water see, in such a crazy loop, from East to West and back again, against all rules of watersheds, which don't account for air, for vapor? I'll tell you: It sees a dozen rivers from the Current to the Clearwater, from little to big, from fouled to pure, from dammed to free. It sees longboats and barges and tankers, fish and drifters, pelicans and terns and cormorants and kingfishers, otters and muskrats and beavers and mink, catfish and sturgeon and smolts and carp. It sees village, town, and city, humans and a hundred other creatures, a thousand other species, living together and apart. It feels the lubricity of time, the savagery of space, the brilliance of light and the nullity of night. Water knows the sensibility of the seasons, the solidity of salmon, the heft of wapiti, the winsomeness of wind. There is little that the water of the Big Spring does not see or feel or know in its grand passage.

And this much it knows for sure: the flow and heart of surge and flux of two great arteries, the main veins of the continent after all; both bent to the purposes of the forked creature that calls itself *dom-i-nant*. One great river fouled and flooded and dead at its very mouth, the other, somehow still alive and free at the finish, in spite of all the concrete plugs in its gullet.

And here is what the water says, as it surges from the Big Spring once more, to make this round in all its improbable rigors yet again. Keep the river, it says, keep it, keep it, keep it still. Never let it go the way the other one went. Never let it flag under the foetid flag of greed, never let it slow and dull and slurry into the sewer of disdain. For this is the river that sustains you. This is the river that makes you whole. This is the river of life for all who walk its shores and ply its deeps and breathe its vapors—and don't you forget it! Thus spake the waters of the Big Spring of Missouri to the Columbia River, and to all who share in it and care for it. Or, as T. S. Eliot put it in "Ash Wednesday," "spirit of the river, spirit of the sea, / Suffer us not to be separated." And who am I to argue with Eliot, or with the waters of the Big Spring?

My Heresy

(*Whole Terrain*, 2013)

When Whole Terrain *announced an issue on this topic, I had to choose among a number of my regular operating precepts that fail to match the orthodoxy of my peers. The one I chose may be the simplest of my sacrileges, and one that most would struggle to perform day after day. Because my heresy . . .*

. . . is that of taking radical joy in the physical world around me, even as it crumbles.

I have fought for conservation for fifty years. When I began, along with other young campaigners in high school and college, we really thought our work would make a difference, and that it would all get better by now (as it sometimes, some places, in some ways, actually has). Surely, few of us expected it to get this bad, this fast. My current reading of the state of things is reflected in the title of another essay I recently published: "Evening Falls on the Maladaptive Ape," and my expected outcome, in its cheerful conclusion: "Evolution will mock our tardy rage." I am still a conservation activist, but my highest hopes now center around preserving the best possible gene pool and substrate for the next iteration, after the fall.

Even in our shared disillusionment, most enviros I know remain capable of taking deep pleasure in the world, which was often their spur for getting into conservation in the first place. But I do observe that many—or most—practice their pleasures somewhat guiltily. Because after all, if we let ourselves have real fun during these parlous times, isn't it tantamount to fiddling while Rome burns? Some of Derrick Jensen's essays, for example, however rich in conviction, seem to me to labor under this burden. But I think Nero got a bad rap—at least as regards that particular cliché, which is probably apocryphal and certainly anachronistic, there having been no fiddles in Rome. Nero was not a nice man, it seems certain. But if your empire were going up in flames around you, how better to spend your time than fiddling—or playing the lyre?

Who among us hasn't sneered at the uninformed, having a ball at NASCAR, a rock concert, or a waterpark, with no thought of tomorrow? Who among us has not envied them? But may we not, in Wendell Berry's words, "Be joyful though [we] have considered all the facts"? This is not a new thought (there being few, if any, new thoughts). Take it back to—of all people—George Eliot!—in, of all places—*Middlemarch!*—who said: "The best piety is to enjoy—when you can. You are doing the most then to save the earth's character as an agreeable planet. And—enjoyment radiates. It is of no use to try and take care of all the world; that is being taken care of when you feel delight—in art or anything else."

Such thinking goes still further back, for example to Carl von Linné (aka Carolus Linnaeus). Did you think his boundless passion for taxonomy and nomenclature came solely from OCD? Not so! He truly loved the world, and every plant and animal that grew or crept upon it. "The starting point must be to marvel at all things," he wrote, "even the most commonplace."

And it has come forward to modern times as well, surviving the ravages of the imperial era Linnaeus lived through and the industrial rapine that Eliot knew— even unto today's postindustrial wasteland. For there is no better expression of my particular apostasy than Bruce Springsteen's rendition, from the epic anthem "Badlands" in *Darkness on the Edge of Town*: "It ain't no sin to be glad you're alive."

As we stride those badlands, the fracked-up, hacked-up, up-chucked leavings of the thoroughly modern extractive economy, we take note that the land ain't what it used to be. We weep, and we gnash, and we curse the gluttony of the six billion besides ourselves. It didn't have to be this way, we're quite sure. And, in fact, it didn't; and doesn't. But for now, it is.

And so, we can grope and moan like wraiths in Mordor, and wait for the worst to come.

OR, we can cherish the remnants of a rich and fecund Middle Earth, laugh at the cosmic joke gone bad, and embrace all the best that's left, for all it's worth. And enjoy it while it lasts.

I choose the latter. Because there really is, you know, quite a lot left—for now. Much more, in terms of wildness, sheer beauty, voluptuous encounter and small wonder, than any one of us could begin to experience if we had forevermore and a moratorium on decay. Even when we cannot get away to the remaining wilds and glories, fascination and enchantment lie in wait for us everywhere we are willing to look: in the autumn-swabbed leaves of alien brambles, in the dendritic phantasms of color in an oil spill beside a stinking industrial track. If your standard is "as it was," you might as well pack it in right now. But if you are willing to take deep pleasure in what's left, while never forgetting what's lost, then life is still worth living. It ain't no sin.

It also ain't just about personal enjoyment. I am speaking here of no less than sanity itself, or what used to be called "mental hygiene." How *can* one support all there is to be deplored, and maintain any kind of an upright keel, let alone level, without a palliative passion? This is not new either: Pepys's loving fascination with the minutia of the world of London got him through the horrors of the plague; Whitman weathered the terrors of Civil War field hospitals by attending as well to the flowers of the field. Whether it's the Inquisition or the ruined climate we face, the Holocaust or the tar sands, the tender mercies of innocent nature in whatever reduced condition yet stand by to save lives and minds. I know a young Marine who survived Fallujah intact in psyche as well as body in part by devoting hours to intense study of the butterflies of the barren compound. Writer Ken Lamberton weathered a long and cruel incarceration by doting on the toads, the weeds, and the other bits of life he could find in the prison yard, as told in his book *Wilderness and Razor Wire*. And before him, of course, there was Robert Stroud, the so-called Birdman of Alcatraz, forty-two years in solitary confinement but for his beloved canaries. In short, a love affair with the kindly fruits of the earth can render the intolerable, tolerable; can render an intolerably damaged world even beautiful, for a while. And sometimes a while is all you need to get by.

None of this is to advocate editing out the bad in order to achieve a rosy final cut with only the good bits left. It is, rather, to argue against the opposite temptation. If we are to entertain any hope at all for meaningful reform and improvement, we must remain both politically engaged and in love with the world. To be engaged requires awareness of that which must not be accepted. To do anything about it requires love of that which may yet be saved, or restored. We must dare to cherish the earth in order to keep on doing this hard work. So I see the heresy of fierce joy in the face of brutal ruin as essential to global redemption, as well as personal. If there is any chance at all for either, we must look both ways, without blinking.

How does one do this? Well, it's not hard to find a useful place as an activist. Whether it's being arrested at the capital with Bill McKibben's 350.org climate campaigners, or guarding sea turtle eggs or snowy plovers on a busy beach, one can dive into any issue and find good work to do. For many, it will be the most local, where few others are engaged. But since there is no end to the need, it is all too easy to be overwhelmed, and end up no use to anyone. Like most of my seasoned activist cohort, I have found it essential to pick my battles—especially since I live in a resource-dependent community where it would be all too easy to become not only burned out by taking on every potential struggle, but also alienated from one's neighbors.

So I decided years ago to concentrate my activist efforts on certain long-term goals: the protection of my home valley, the preservation of the last remnants of old-growth forest in the range of hills in which I live, the conservation of monarchs and certain other rare butterfly populations and habitats, and the establishment of one particular federal wilderness area. By concentrating my efforts thus, I feel I've been more effective than if I picked up every gauntlet thrown down by circumstance. Friends and I worked to obtain preserve status for one of the last old-growth stands in our county; it took us twenty years, but we got there. I know other activists who have worked on particular watersheds for decades, and who can look back over much more land and water saved than had they gone off in every direction. I don't know how anyone can take deep pleasure in nature or anything else without fighting back for it when it comes under threat. But no one can fight on every front, to any good effect.

And just as we must focus our time and energy to do any good, we should also hoard some for fun and pleasure, like a miser. I cannot describe this approach any better than Edward Abbey did in an address to environmentalists, published under the title "Joy, Shipmates, Joy!" In part, he enjoined us all to "Be as I am. A reluctant enthusiast and part-time crusader. A half-hearted fanatic. Save the other half of yourselves for pleasure and adventure. It is not enough to fight for the West. It is even more important to enjoy it while you can, while it's still there. So get out there, hunt, fish, mess around with your friends, ramble out yonder and explore the forests, encounter the griz, climb a mountain, bag the peaks, run the rivers, breathe deep of that yet sweet and elusive air. Sit quietly for a while and contemplate the precious stillness of the lovely, mysterious, and awesome space. Enjoy yourselves."

A few summers ago, I climbed Red Cloud Mountain in Colorado's San Juans. Up above thirteen thousand feet, the setting was as wild and intact as anything I'd known in years. A completely unencultured marmot walked across my boots; not-yet-warmed-out pikas peented and geeked from unmined rockslides, where black Magdalena alpine butterflies sailed across cerulean seas of columbines. Another butterfly, the small, federally endangered Uncompahgre fritillary, showed as we hoped it would, up among the snow willow, well above timberline. Its numbers are down, and still dropping, as temperatures rise and snowfall diminishes. That fact did not leave me unmoved. Nor did the ecstatic alpine heights leave me untouched on their own account.

Later that month I spent an afternoon surrounded by enormous fritillaries, the biggest in the world—female great spangleds and blue Dianas—on another summit: Black Mountain, the highest point in Kentucky. Then, dropping over the other side, into Virginia, I drove right into the gaping maw of a mountain removed for coal. The next twenty-four hours among hyper-polluted and human-ravaged Appalachia were enough to depress a saint, and I'm not one. Unwilling not to look it in the black eye and take it for the horror it was, but equally resolved not to give up my fresh sense of ecstatic encounter with Cybele and Diana, I put on my Janus-face and laughed and wept at the same time. There's no choice, as I see it: the earth demands it of us. So that's pretty much how I go through life these days. And when I do, the world looks like this:

And what about the turquoise-mantled giant clam cemented
in the coral reef beneath antipodean skies, the urchins dragging
spines across the limey bottoms, poking holes in waterbags to make
the ocean new for every life on every tide? Or clouds that drop
their shadows on the desert floor, that parking lot for tortoises,
where cactus reaches out for gods it never knew or needed?
Flash-floods scrape away whatever luck the horned toad
ever had. Which isn't much,
it seems, until you think of otter clamped in orca's gape
or flank of desert oryx running red beneath the claws of leopard,
every desiccated leaf and flower folded in upon itself, until
you think of ants and worms and voles and frogs in tractor ruts
or salmon smolts in heron's bill. Until you think of *this* great ape,
the one that stands upright and poses every question ever asked,
in such a world where everything that grows breaks down
and down, and down, then grows,
and grows and grows, and grows again.

Lines excerpted from the poem "Notes From the Edge of the Known World" © Robert Michael Pyle. The entire poem, read by the author with an original guitar composition written and played by Krist Novoselic, may be heard on You Tube at http://www.youtube.com/watch?v=OoPSHtirAbs.

Free Range Kids
Why Unfettered Play Is Essential to Our Species
(*Orion*, 2014)

In the years following publication of Richard Louv's Last Child in the Woods *and his founding of the Children and Nature Network, the general subject of "nature deficit disorder" (as Louv called the new common condition) was widely aired around the world. One conference at which I spoke in Perth, Australia (in lieu of Louv, who had come into enormous demand) was called "Come Outside and Play." Many state and local programs were begun under the moniker "No Child Left Inside." But I felt the topic of children's unrestrained wandering within their own home ranges, and what its loss might mean for the culture, had barely been explored. I wanted to call the essay "The Freedom of the Day," which is what I felt that I and most of those I grew up with had enjoyed as a matter of course; but the editors decided to title it "Free Range Kids," a term I used in the piece and later learned was also the title of a book by Lenore Skenazy. Having recently experienced my grandchildren in thrall to Pokemon Go, I am undecided as to whether this craze is a step forward or backward in the current context. At least it requires kids to pay attention to the particular details of the ersatz organisms, and gets them out of doors and moving their bodies. I wonder if some players sometimes escape the game's gravitational field and make a dash for the real thing?*

When my older brother, Tom, and I awoke to a fine morning, which was more often than not in the long days of the long summers of our Colorado suburban childhood, our first thought was for a clean getaway. If we had our regular jobs more or less under control it was fairly easy to make a break for it on weekdays, when Mom was in charge. Weekends were trickier, with Dad home and armed with a list of chores for us around the house or the yard. Even so, the common condition was for us to split, together or with friends or on our own, for parts unknown—or, rather, well known. Our usual haunt was the High Line Canal, an old irrigation ditch a mile away, the flowing artery of our lives. But there was also the weedy park, the young shopping center beyond and its still-vacant lots,

Bluff Lake, Barr Lake, the edge of the plains, the crosstown mountains, yea even unto the very state lines east and north as our mobility increased from foot to bike to scooter and cycle and finally automobile. Open the door, blink, and we were out of there. Even at night, if the days were too hot. The only limits: dinner, bedtime, the end of summer, and the beginning of school. And even then, home-work adequately in hand, weather short of an actual blizzard, we were most often gone . . . solid gone.

This was not rare. Kids went on the prowl all over the land: rural, suburban, deep-city kids on buses and subways. "Bye, Mom, see you at dinner" was a com-mon salutation in American culture; or "Get out of here, and don't be back till supper." Nor was it new. In *Middlemarch* (1874), George Eliot wrote, "These are the things that make the gamut of joy in landscape," referring to the plants, ani-mals, and the other actual elements of the living land as "the things they toddled among." There was a time when children everywhere ran such a gamut of joy, as they roamed through their local landscapes unhindered.

And another thing? This was not a gendered phenomenon. The Australian poet Judith Wright, in an interview with Rob Glover, said, "We lived a free and easy life. . . . My mother used to just get us out of the house. I remember falling off a horse when I was two. . . . The kind of life I lived was just so confidence-producing." The paradise ended when Wright was sent to boarding school in Armidale. "Oh, I was so miserable," she recalled. "I had been free and now I was in a cage." Wright's degree of freedom was perhaps extreme, but I remember the girls I knew roaming the neighborhood just as the boys did (we always hoped the right ones might roam past our house, as we did past theirs). One pretty blonde I mooned after in junior high led me to a pasture where we climbed the fence, and she jumped horses and rode them, bareback. This led to big trouble with the owner of the horses, who turned out to be my previous girlfriend. The point is, girls too exercised what I've come to call "the freedom of the day."

When speaking to all sorts of literary, conservation, and other kinds of groups, I often work the topic around to this question: "How many of you had a special place that you can blame or bless for caring about the wider world . . . for being here today?" Almost everyone over thirty replies in the affirmative. I go on, "How many of you had the unsupervised freedom to explore that special place?" Again, almost all the hands go up. And it turns out there is a common repertory of what went on during these excursions: exploring terra incognita, damming or diverting water, skipping stones, building forts (called "dens" in the UK and, wonderfully, "cubbies" in Australia), where all manner of imaginative games and fantasies took place. Either evading the boys/girls or engaging with them, peacefully or not. Catching things: crawdads, polliwogs, frogs, fireflies, butterflies, honeybees, crickets and grasshoppers, minnows, or smaller kids. I've been overwhelmed by the universality of these experiences, whether conducted in a back forty or a backyard, a wilderness or a vacant lot (than which nothing is less vacant to a curious kid). The collective blood pressure in the room drops palpably, as I take folks back to "the things they toddled among" in their minds, and almost all of them have stories from their childhood habitat.

But then comes the troubling bit: when I ask how many folks know any children today—their own kids or grandkids, nieces and nephews, children of friends—who still enjoy the freedom of the day as we did, silence reigns. No hands go up, or very few.

Of course, we all know why this is. The bizzyness of kids, the wholesale retreat of habitats from the places people live, the implantation of the electronic umbilicus at birth, and the bogeyman phenomenon, otherwise known as stranger danger: these new norms have crowded out the old way. Now, if any kids still prowl, it is those in deepest ruralia, or children of the most committed parents (or neglectful: in some states, it is illegal to leave children under nine, or twelve, unsupervised by an adult). Even in my deeply rural valley, the school district requires that kids let off the school bus be met by an adult in a car. So the children are driven that last delicious block, or eighth-, or quarter-mile home. How sad that strikes me. Just as lamentable, gender has now emerged in a big way: any free-range kids these days are almost sure to be boys.

Does all this matter? It seems inconceivable to me that such a large social change—from almost every child experiencing such freedom, to almost none, in just one generation—could fail to have powerful implications. I worry about the kids to come. Children accustomed to prowling their home range (somewhat wider than the usual Wi-Fi perimeter, and unroofed), and to meeting the unexpected with imagination and delight and maybe a little frisson of fear, the overcoming of which brings a flood of satisfaction, are children who will not turn catatonic in the face of social, climatic, or ecological upheaval. When disaster strikes, in the form of hurricane, war, or wildfire, it will be the free-range kids who help their families survive, and who will stand the better chance of surviving themselves. Kids who are sedentary slaves to their games and handhelds will, in such times, most likely crumple, along with the gamers and texters and other watchers-not-doers who possess few skills, habits, or impulses remotely applicable to real life cataclysm.

Still, it has to be asked, and it has, whether all this is just nostalgia. Am I just maundering over something already lost and soon forgotten? As a nimble-minded ninety-three-year-old, a pillar of business and philanthropy, asked after a talk I gave at the Denver Botanic Gardens, "How do you know that what children are doing instead these days isn't just as fulfilling as what you did?"

Of course I had to tell him, "I don't."

So I've been thinking a lot about whether the freedom of the day really amounts to anything we'll miss—as individuals, as a society, as a species. If its loss leaves us deprived, then deprived of what? And at what cost to the psyche of the young hominid? What are the hidden implications of the house arrest (as Richard Louv so aptly calls it) of our young? Whither the well-adjusted person, polity, and planet, after the death of free, unmediated play?

For most of the million-year lifetime of our species to date, people grew up with deep experience of their habitats, or they likely didn't grow up at all. Boys learned how to find food; girls learned how to grow it, and how to prepare and store what the boys brought in. They both learned how to recognize which plants and animals were useful, and which were dangerous. Exploration and education amounted to the same thing, and everyone graduated cum laude or else went hungry, got eaten, or exiled. But this changed as we insulated ourselves more and more from the raw needs of nature. Even by Eliot's time, people were becoming estranged from the workings of the world around them. Even "the quickest of us walk about well wadded with stupidity," she complained. For many of today's plugged-in, tuned-out inmates, "well wadded with stupidity" just about says it all.

But I believe that the loss of the freedom of the day may have consequences far beyond mere spoliation of youthful desires and spirits. It was the play-hunting of the young that prepared aboriginal children everywhere to be useful hunters and gatherers—to survive. In prepastoral, preagrarian, and preindustrial societies, childhood skills gained through outdoor trial and error led to socialization, discovery, and innovation, not to mention cooperation. We are the same species, so why would this no longer be true? As poet Judith Wright wrote, "The kind of life I lived was just so confidence-producing." Risk, and how to gauge risk, and what to do about risky situations is a big part of it. If we hadn't been daily denizens of the High Line Canal, would Tom have thought to react to actual, life-threatening danger by stuffing me into the bole of the Hollow Tree when the devastating hailstorm of July 1954 arose, killing half a dozen cattle in the field next to us?

A large body of professional study backs up the connection between youthful curiosity and physical health. Dr. Gabor Maté, author of *Scattered: How Attention*

Deficit Disorder Originates and What You Can Do About It, told Amy Goodman on *Democracy Now!* that a broad spectrum of modern ills can be attributed to isolation from the physical environment, among other stressful events in childhood. Maté asked, "How do children learn? . . . You learn when you're curious." But under current stresses, children "become hardened, so they become cool. Nothing matters. . . . When that happens, curiosity goes, because curiosity is vulnerable." So the loss of outdoor freedom and the curiosity it gives rise and rein to are mutually reinforcing: lose one, lose it all.

It turns out that actual physical changes are already occurring, which may be linked to the behavioral flux I am talking about. In his book *The Nature Principle,* Richard Louv, citing Australian research, described how young people are experiencing an increase in nearsightedness as they spend less time outdoors, where eyes must focus at longer distances. He suggests that good vision, acute hearing, an attuned sense of smell, spatial awareness, and an ability to learn and avoid danger, may all be eroding, along with "the measurement-defying ability to more fully engage in life."

Another example involves neuroplasticity and our modern media. In *The Shallows: What the Internet Is Doing to Our Brains,* Nicholas Carr says that the culture a person is brought up in influences the content and character of that person's memory. "Personal memory," he writes, "shapes and sustains the 'collective memory' that underpins culture. . . . Each of us carries and projects the history of the future. Culture is sustained in our synapses." And those synapses, and other brain topography, are literally changing with the expansion of time devoted to chip-driven devices instead of to books and fields and streams. Plugged-in people are losing the ability to engage longer texts, and to read deeply. "To remain vital," Carr suggests, "culture must be renewed in the minds of the members of every generation." A culture of close connection to the land is not being renewed much today among the collective offspring; rather, it is actively withering.

Even scarier, Dr. Stuart Brown, founder of the National Institute for Play, has demonstrated the importance of play to social success, and its absence as a common factor among homicidal young males. He describes play as "a long evolved behavior important for the well being and survival of animals," and believes "humans are uniquely designed by nature to enjoy and participate in play throughout life." If true (and it is), why should we be surprised that exploratory, free play has ancient evolutionary roots? Or that its absence might exact heavy costs from both our present society and our future condition?

For my part, I walked or biked to every grade, first through twelfth, from the same house (excepting very cold days, when Dad took me, or later when I sometimes drove my own motors). Oh, those walks! Seldom the shortest line between two points, they led to my first fistfights, first kisses, and even my first extinction, when I discovered a special butterfly colony and then watched it wiped out when the Lutherans paved their parking lot. There were always vacant lots to dawdle in and see what was sprouting or flying or creeping. No one worried if a kid was a little late getting home, as it was understood that all the parents kept a loose eye on all the kids. Once I got stuck in the mud at a building site, lost my shoe, and made it home half-barefoot.

Even the daily penance of school, at least the to and fro of it, promoted the freedom of the day.

And then, praise be, the summers! On vacations at my stepfamily's cabin in Crested Butte, leaving my father fishing, I'd wander the East River meadows and meanders all the way to Gothic, randomly meeting scientists from the Rocky Mountain Biological Laboratory who would change my life forever. Other days it was over the town's coal-slag heaps, into the neighboring aspen groves, where Atlantis fritillaries flashed over Colorado blue columbines. Back home, bicycling with big brother Tommy all across East Denver to Grammy's house or beyond; one time even to Stapleton airport, where Tom, by the gods, actually talked us into a short flight in a Piper Cub.

Of course we got into a little trouble: walking the neighborhood, every street, day and night, having the police descend on me more than once because of moth collecting at people's porch lights; hanging in downtown Aurora with Tom every Saturday after the matinee at the Fox, attracting the attention of the sheriff, who finally nabbed us for a scary lecture after we made "Give to the March of Dimes" handbills on our little printing press and handed them out on a busy corner (I *think* we intended to turn in any money we collected). We tried endless door-to-door sales of seeds, salves, and so on, and picked up lots of stupid short-term jobs, all on our own. Or else, just plain foraged. Literally, *whatever*—just as long as we were home for dinner.

At fourteen, the limits of my home range stretched radically when I got an old Allstate Vespa motor scooter for seventy-five dollars. It took me to the top of Mount Evans above fourteen thousand feet, out to Castlewood Dam on the plains, all the way to the Wyoming line . . . anywhere I could reach in a day or two. And then, when I turned sixteen and bought a 1950 Ford for one hundred dollars, even farther reaches fell to my whim. It is amazing that any of us even survived those seatbeltless years, with carsful of kids cruising at eighty a sleepy hundred miles home from away games, or back down the Front Range from make-out picnics up in the autumn aspens. But then came college, and marriage, and responsibility, and the freedom of the day fled like a fritillary on a stiff wind.

So what did it give me? Decisions; adaptations; discoveries; explorations. The ability to devise plans, and plan Bs. Mistakes, minor injuries, killing creatures, saving creatures, close calls, outcomes. *Consequences.* Above all, the freedom of the day had consequences. They might have been small, but they stuck. And when I came, in the fullness of time, to write books of the road and of discovery and of the blessed glory of happenstance, I knew just where they came from. When I've had to make decisions in my life that affect myself and other people, not that I've always or even often made the right ones, I was not a stranger to the question: Is this right, or should I do that? What could happen if I do the third thing? Is there a fourth? Turn a kid loose, and that is a kid who will have a chance of dancing with vicissitude, and living through it.

True, kids on adventure (especially boys with BB guns) could often be cruel, but that was part of the lesson: palping the edges of empathy, and what it meant to inflict pain. Kids did damage, and came out the larger for it, more aware of the whole neighborhood of life.

It matters to me still, this particular kind of liberty. If I don't experience it every day, at least I remember it. I lie in bed in the morning, before rising, and think about a day on the ditch when I was ten, and what it was like to have the vast, unprogrammed day stretch out before me. How I once possessed free agency, and that I am who I am on that account. And sometimes even now, a day comes when nothing impends, and I can take the canoe out or head for the hills or hit the road and go wherever whim and wonder lead . . . and something of it all comes back.

I'm not alone in this. Many adults remember their liberated youths, and many kids want to experience a world off the game board, beyond the hearing range of parents, and most definitely outside their supervision. We all know there's something better, and long for it. We know there are critical lessons our children are missing, lessons that neither schools nor screens can teach them. So if humankind fails to make it (or make it well) through the era of climate contortion, it will be willfully so. When we can perfectly well read the writing on the wall, yet forge ahead and bash our heads into the wall regardless, the results should not surprise us at all. We know better, yet we carry on. Well, that's just human nature, you'll say: drinking, smoking, gambling, gorging, screwing around, driving too fast—and so it is. But most of these maladaptive acts operate at the individual level. What about when an entire society self-selects for ignorance, for isolation, for alienation? Wads itself well with stupidity, you might say?

For one thing, I foresee evolutionary alterations in the descendents of those who have lost their childhood freedom. Of course, their disenfranchised condition will travel the DNA with lots of other behavioral changes: more and more time spent mated to a monitor or welded to a handheld; fewer and fewer moments, let alone hours, spent out and about; increased gaming- or watching- or networking-driven solitude. Mutations will occur and be selected for. Through nature and nurture acting together, altered traits will pass down. If this is really an evolutionary question, as I believe it is, what sort of animal might our species become?

I picture people much like us on first inspection. But look more closely, first at the hands: the thumbs are overdeveloped, not spatulate like the hitchhiking heroine of Tom Robbins's *Even Cowgirls Get the Blues*, but gracile, long, and even more prehensile than ours. They are attached to atrophied arms, and they, to a narrow trunk with sloped shoulders and a permanent downward cant to the head. Now regard the eyes, and surmise the vision of this creature: the irises do not contract like ours, but remain dilated. Hence, these animals wear shades almost all the time when they go outdoors, which is, however, seldom. The nose is contracted; the olfactory powers, could they be measured, almost absent. The genitalia are reduced, suited for quick, momentary matings, like those of deer, computer-mediated and absent the tedium of archaic courtship. And check out those butts! Broad, deep, and built for comfort in a chair. The appending legs are almost vestigial, for there is little need for locomotion. For this is an organism suited to a stasis: one defined by allegiance to digital routine and endless arrays of cerebral diversion outside any known sense of *outside*. For such narrow purposes, this new-model body is elegantly adapted. But let anything change in its environment, like a hurricane pulling the plug on our electronic aids, and these people are toast. On a recent visit to New England, I asked the saturnine agent at Avis for a local map, and to show me the way out. She said she'd never used a map in her life, and didn't know how to read one. "I just use GPS," she said, proving my point exactly. Even if our bodies themselves don't change, our metamorphosis is already under way.

Is it a given, then, that such a state of deep alienation from nature will come to pass? Not necessarily. The Children & Nature Network, Green Hearts, and suchlike initiatives are working hard to head it off. C&NN, for example, has initiated family nature clubs—well over a hundred of them at this writing, many with memberships of hundreds of families each, one with over seven hundred families. Richard Louv, a C&NN cofounder, reports that, perhaps ironically, independent play takes place more often when the number of families participating is larger. "When one family goes on a hike with the kids," he told me, "the kids tend to clutch and whine. But when several families go for that hike, the kids are off running, playing hide and seek, doing what kids do."

The fact that the things kids do are still being done gives me hope. One night at a mall in suburban Vancouver, Washington, I watched boys skipping quarters on a water feature, just as they would skip stones on a pond or a creek, if given the chance. On a recent Colorado visit, I met Clyde and Ricardo, two ex-ghetto kids at play beside the High Line, doing much the same stuff along the same ditch that Tom and I haunted fifty years ago. I've watched the kids in my own rural neighborhood escape the school-bus-to-car-to-home lockdown by skedaddling back outside as soon as their mom or dad ducks indoors. On every fine day, all summer long, I delight to the shrieks and laughter of the valley children ottering about in the swimming hole below the covered bridge, unaccompanied by adults. And on a recent visit to Yosemite National Park, I spied on two boys in my tent-cabin village as they entertained themselves for most of a morning with a single stick of ponderosa pine that they had cut, whittled, and tested for strength. "This wood is *really hard*," said one to the other, as he whacked his stick on a granite rock as hard as he could. Best of all were my own grandkids, here for an Easter visit. The egg hunt and donkey rides were outdoors of course, and popular. But when the downtime arrived and the devices came out, I thought that was that . . . until they all came to me, and David, the oldest of the gang of four, asked, "Grandpa, will you go for a walk in the woods with us? We want to explore." They weren't asking for my supervision. They were inviting me to wander out of doors with them, and see what we might find. They wanted to have an adventure!

Children still long to experience the freedom of the day: I am convinced that the inclination survives, even if they aren't given license to follow it. They want to confront the world on their own terms. They want to discover what "wild" means, and to find it for themselves. They want to play *off-leash*. Locked into Legos and mortared in Minecraft, they might need a nudge to get them out there. They might need their parents, or whoever is in charge, to encourage them, to trust them, and maybe to keep a loose eye on them from afar. And then, stand back! In the end, I put my faith in the kids themselves, and in my belief that, no matter what, they won't let go of the world around us.

Of Owls and Angels

(Foreword for *The House of Owls* by Tony Angell, Yale University Press, 2015)

This past summer, on the campus of Whatcom Community College in Bellingham, Washington, I spotted a monumental sculpture of three owls elegantly liberated from a block of white granite. I knew from a distance they must have been carved by Tony Angell, and indeed they were: "A Parliament of Owls." Tony is a dear friend from conservation and natural history circles going way back, an artist, activist, and writer I admire immensely. How honored I was to be asked to write the foreword for his latest and most personal opus. Aside from the honorific, the best part of writing a piece like this, or "Reflections in a Golden Eye," is the invitation to comb one's memory for a lifetime of encounters with the creatures in question; and then to try to weave them together in a prose piece that illumines and respects not only the topic but the author or authors of the book one is introducing. It is a difficult but indulgent and delightful task.

Owls. The very word has excited me since I was a lad. Unlike the author of the extraordinary book you hold in your hands, I never caught, raised, or lived with owls. I encountered Hooty the Owl in Thornton Burgess's *Bedtime Stories*, I loved *The Owl and the Pussycat*, and scoured the Aurora Public Library's shelves for owls books, just as I did for otters, seashells, and butterflies. Later I read accounts of people who lived with owls, ending up many years later with Jonathan Maslow's *Owl Papers*, Max Terman's *Messages from an Owl*, and Bernd Heinrich's *One Man's Owl*. And when I read the Harry Potter books, I thought by far the best thing in them was Harry's owl Hedwig, and all the other mail-courier owls. It's only too bad that as a kid conservationist, as I fancied myself, I was way too early for Carl Hiasson's *Hoot*.

As much as I loved reading about owls as a boy, I was even more eager to encounter them in flesh and feather. There wasn't much chance in my postwar Colorado subdivision. But it wasn't long until I escaped the ordered grid and barren young yards, wandering off to the High Line Canal, an old irrigation ditch on the edge of the actual countryside. There, one charmed day, I watched as a great horned owl burst from an old magpie nest in a cottonwood—and all of a sudden, owls had become *real*.

Since that thrilling day, I can remember the first sighting of every species of owl I've come to know in the wild: the first northern spotted owl, on its nest on a low big tree bough in Sequoia National Park. The first hawk owl, crowning a black spruce in the boundless taiga along the Alaska Highway. The first saw-whet, fishing the shoreline of a little lake near Olympia. The first great gray, early in the morning, in the Blue Mountains of northeastern Oregon, even bigger than I'd dreamed. The first *pueo*, gliding toward me like a plane with a face through mist on the shoulder of Mauna Kea. And certainly the first snowy, which until then had been a merely mythic bird: never there for me where everyone said it had been only the day before, or the hour. And then there it was at last, squinting against cutting, windborne snow on a frozen beach north of New Haven, Connecticut.

Actually, it was during those three years in New Haven that owls came to have one of their deeper significances for me. The owls of which I speak neither flew nor hooted. They were ornamental owls—stone, terra cotta, wood, copper, and so on—decorating the campus of Yale University as a frequently repeating symbol of wisdom, learning, and all of the scholarly and courageous attributes of their familiar, Pallas Athena. When I arrived at Yale in the fall of 1974 for postgraduate studies, I got off to a rather slow start thanks to my own intimidation and a little uncertainty as to my thesis plans. Once I began to notice the frequency of the owl motif in the college-gothic architecture of the university and its various colleges, each one a campus within the larger campus, I began collecting them. At first this was chiefly a displacement activity, giving a little structure to counterbalance (or distract me from) my lack of confidence in being there. It wasn't long before the intimidation faded and my dissertation research gelled, so the reason for the displacement activity was gone. But by then I was so much enjoying the hunt that I continued owl-spotting for the whole three years.

By the time I marched in Yale's 275th graduation exercise, I had tallied around seventy-five "species" of owls among its hallowed halls and graven walls; such as the great copper owl weathervane atop Sterling Library, the roundels of owlish gargoyles encircling the Law School's crocketed towers, and various carved owlets on door panels, reredos, and moldings. In the absence of actual owls they served well as a distraction from the heavy academic work. (Many years later, during a joint reading at Redlands College in southern California, my fellow writers and I looked up from our texts repeatedly to watch both barn and great horned owls cruising past the open doors. Had Yale been like that, perhaps I never would have finished my studies!) The elegant blend of art and natural history represented by this indulgent pursuit remains for me nearly as memorable as Professor Remington's inspired lectures on evolution, watching Meryl Streep's student performances in several Drama School productions, and that first real-life snowy, out on the frigid shore of Long Island Sound.

In the forty years since, how very many owls have graced my days and nights! Downy baby great horneds and barns in the basalt rimrock of eastern Washington. Banshee-voiced tawnies in the Somerset countryside. A bouncing, big-eyed burrowing owl peeking over a road-crest at dawn, where I'd been sleeping on the opposite verge, during a very slow hitchhike across the West. Short-eareds cruising the Skagit Flats in company with northern harriers and red-tailed hawks and tens of thousands of snow geese. Particular pygmies and screeches in particular tree-holes, faithfully present year after year. The BC barred owl whose shrill "who cooks for *y'allll*?" convinced a credulous young enthusiast that he had finally recorded Bigfoot. The still-life of a great horned owl, hunched in the crotch of a willow in a Wyoming winter landscape, that I mistook for a bobcat; and the one that cleaned out our hollow tree of its flying squirrels—one broad gray tail on the lawn every morning until they were gone—and then moved on. The barn owl that stooped at my pussycat, and the one I helped restore to its parents and siblings inside the gable of a very high barn, after rehab. The long-eareds, like small totems, lining the limbs of pines in a thick windbreak in the Columbia Basin, watched with Roger Tory Peterson.

Come to think of it, I believe Tony Angell was along on that trip too. I'd met Tony in the sixties in Seattle, one of a number of keen and talented naturalists who made the city so exciting and inspiring for a college kid like me. Our friendship went from there, and will soon span half a century. A few years into it, when I worked for The Nature Conservancy, Tony was chair of the Washington chapter. By this time, it was already apparent that he was one of the premier sculptors, pen-and-ink artists, and writers anywhere, working with birds and mammals. Tony's love of corvids and of owls and other raptors led to a long series of marvelous books. Maybe it was inevitable that he would one day write a book in which he laid out his lifelong passion for owls and what they have taught him. When I learned that just such a book was on its way, I rejoiced. Here, I thought, will be the book to cap all the owl books I've loved before. And so it is.

The House of Owls is, simply, a delight for an strigiphile like me. But it will also delight any birder or naturalist, all those who care about the living world about them and its more remarkable manifestations, and, I dare say, that still-extant class, the Curious General Reader. The author and editors made the canny choice to divide the book into four main sections. "About Owls" gives one the basic facts to understand how owls work, and how they fit into the broader context of life. "The House of Owls" relates the personal saga of a period when Tony and his family lived intimately with one dynasty of screech owls with whom they shared their home habitat. The third section, "Owls and Human Culture," covers just that, and a rich field it is. And then the fourth chapter, which is really the second half of the book, consists of detailed verbal portraits of all nineteen species of North American owls. The genius of this presentation lies not only in its comprehensiveness, and how we come away seeing the birds from all sides; but also in its shifting point of view. Chapters 1 and 3 are largely factual and objective. "The House of Owls," while adding fact, is a deeply personal narrative that carries us not only further into the subject, but also further into the author than any of his earlier books have done. And the final "Owl Biographies" accomplish both, in a masterful blend: each species is introduced through Tony's personal experience with it, and then its image is rounded out with fully researched, up-to-date information on its distinctive traits and lifeways. These accounts are nothing short of fascinating. The brilliant mix of personal and factual renders the whole compulsively readable.

There is one more category of readers for whom *The House of Owls* gives cause for huzzahs, and I count myself among them: Tony Angell fans. A handsome, warm, and imposing man of good cheer and rare intelligence, Tony made a big impression on me those several decades ago that has only grown since. I've eagerly anticipated each of his books, and never been disappointed—except in one selfish respect: I've always wanted even more of the man himself—his personal take, his lyric reflections on his subject—than the strictures of the books have allowed. Now, in *The House of Owls*, this is what we get, yet with no loss to the factual basis of the text. The art and the science are mutually reinforcing, as Nabokov (another fine artist and scientist in the same person) expressed when he asked: "Does there not exist a high ridge where the mountainside of scientific knowledge meets the opposite slope of artistic imagination?" That's just where we find ourselves, in *The House of Owls*, and kudos to Yale University Press for letting it be so.

All this talk of artistic imagination brings us at last to that aspect of Tony's work and this book that may be dearest to him, if not even yet mentioned. That is, his graphic art. Tony is highly regarded as one of the foremost sculptors of birds and mammals, in stone, bronze, and other media. I've long thrilled to his otters, alcids, and other animals that one comes upon in public places around the Pacific Northwest and beyond. But he is also immensely skilled in two dimensions. Many of his adherents acquire his books as much or more for the drawings they include as for their scientific and literary content. *The House of Owls* furnishes a beautiful blend of both. Interleaved among these illuminating pages you will find a round hundred of exquisite drawings of owls in every posture, act, and attitude you might imagine. As Tony says, these drawings "are certainly personal interpretations . . . based on my direct and intimate observations." Clearly he values Nabokov's high ridge and is aiming right at it, for he intends the book to "provide a bridge between the observer and his or her subject, as it puts the emphasis as much on how one feels about the owls as it does on how they appear." And he hopes through this approach to inspire readers so that "the observer of owls will become the student and steward of them as well." I believe they will, and I am certain that every lover of Tony Angell's art will exult in this new gallery. No other birds, by a long shot, have such expressive faces, and Tony captures these in his drawings with uncanny felicity and grace so as to show their true charisma, emotion, and range of personality.

I've always been a lover of owls. Now, a very long time and many miles away from Hooty the Owl, I feel at last as though I have a place to go to fully indulge this passion. Of course, the best place is *out there*, in the night, among the owls themselves. But when I can't do that—or maybe afterward, by the fire—when I hanker to learn more about the birds, relive them through splendid portraits of words and ink, maybe plan the next outing, all this in the good company of my old friend Tony—I shall betake myself to *The House of Owls*, and walk in.

The Earth Whispers and Croons

(Foreword for *Earth and Eros*, White Cloud Press, 2015)

I have always felt a deliciously oedipal tug from, and toward, Mother Earth. Introducing the beautiful book Earth and Eros, *edited by Lorraine Anderson, gave me the perfect chance to examine and explore my lifelong crush on the world.*

One time, for me, it was a Roman snail on the South Downs of Sussex. The apple-sized mollusk spread the slick flesh of its foot over my middle finger as if I were its parthenogenetic partner. Labial, febrile, that slippery lick of my flesh gave me tingles, until a sharp jab let me know that the escargot had actually fired its love dart right into my skin.

Another time, it was among the monarchs in Michoacán, at ten thousand feet. After a great, freezing storm, millions lay dead in windrows and drifts beneath the oyamel firs where the survivors still hung. Sick in my chest from city smog, in my heart from all those dead, I lay back into that cinnamon sediment, and felt myself getting well. Turning over, I embraced the blanket of butterflies like a featherbed, arms, thighs, face, all feathered in wings, stroked by scales.

There was the night of warm waters, salt Gulf waters that I couldn't tell from skin, when the *Noctiluca* bloomed. All over, around, above me their green sparks sparked, between my legs, between my toes, through my hair, the chartreuse shimmers flickered and leaped. Walking through them was a shimmy in emerald sequins.

And the day of the desert sycamores, up a wet chute coming out of the Chiricahuas. I had no choice but to crawl out on that broad branch of the green-barked sycamore. It was not my decision to fondle its round knobs, to cleave to its sinuous limbs, to caress its mossy clefts.

I won't say they weren't sexy, that tree, that shimmy, that lay-me-down in butterflies, that snail. And the times with a lover! Coupling in dry leaves or awkward sand, on ash tree bough, in rough surf. Pressing flowers with our bodies on a coastal heath in Dorset—pink heather, early purple orchids, bog asphodel—but through grace, not gorse.

There is nothing symbolic about any of this. Any more than D. H. Lawrence's lessons of catkins and figs—their long danglers, their purple slits—are merely metaphors. They are their own real things. And Earth IS Eros. Anyone who supposes otherwise, or who still labors under the tired notion that nature and people are twain, need only read on. The poems and prose in this beguiling (and let's face it, very sexy) book will lead you into pathways of sensual connection you may have suppressed, or forgotten, or once celebrated and long to celebrate again.

Lorraine Anderson has artfully selected writing both spiritual and physical, there being no clear difference between the two, as far as I can see; pieces of deep thoughtfulness, and others heedless of much in the way of thought, in favor of passion; poems plain and rhapsodic. Honey-pie-in-the-sky, feet in the sticky mud, bone to flesh to water to rock. The extraordinarily varied authors represented here are each of them clearly in love with the world and all that makes it up. Backed up by Bruce Hodge's blood-quickening images, they will leave you in no doubt that this same world has as much to give your body and heart as you are willing and open to receive.

For why, after all, are salacious jokes and sexual language referred to as being "earthy?" Because there is no randier, lustier lover than the Earth, is why. What better time than now for such a book, when this lover is in distress, and we are stoking her up beyond the boiling point? These days, when pollination is the hottest thing in conservation, shouldn't we recognize the essential sameness between our own desire and every other attraction: electron to proton, duck to drake, badger to humping badger, leaf to mould? As Pattiann Rogers says in "The Power of Toads," "Raindrops-finding-earth and coitus could very well / Be known here as one."

So be it. We lovers of literature and the land, and of one another, may rejoice in the knowledge that we are not alone in bringing our passion to the wind, the trees, the soil. As this book whispers and croons, the passion was already there to meet us.

Headbone and Hormone
Adventures in the Arithmetic of Life
(adapted from Foreword, *Numbers and Nerves*, Oregon State University Press, 2015)

Being asked to write this piece was a real surprise and challenge for me. As I wrote in the introduction, I have always been stronger with words than with numbers. Math was almost my undoing in school, and the second piece in this book was written partly in protest of the quantification of nature and how I felt I was being channeled to take part in that. Finally coming to appreciate mathematics as fundamental to understanding nature was a giant leap for me. In that sense, this essay closes the circle, and provides a perfect note on which to finish.

You have in your hands a book that glides gracefully between two standpoints, the logical and the emotional, illuminating as it does the broad and murky territory in between. Scott and Paul Slovic, in designating the ends of this particular teeter-totter as "numbers and nerves," lay out an elegant template for mapping the poles of our proclivities. We know from the start that we are creatures of compassion and feeling, but also animals of analysis and measurement. Which way of seeing and expressing the world actually achieves our desires, meets our needs, and satisfies our lives to a greater extent? Which makes more things happen? Which can better heal the wounded world?

Maybe both. As Scott and Paul tell us in their introduction, "Despite the compelling power of quantification, despite our sense of the usefulness of numbers, there persists an underlying skepticism toward numbers as a medium of communication and as a gauge of reality." This is certainly so, for as they continue, "There is a space in all people, even in the scientists and economists whose daily currency is the worldview we call 'quantification,' that 'cries out for words,' and for images and stories, for the discourse of emotion." And yet we need our numbers too: acres cut, barrels spilled, degrees risen, hectares flooded . . . people killed. How, then, to navigate between these two ways of relating to the facts of life?

My friend Neil Johannsen served as director of Alaska State Parks for fourteen years, during which he grew the system from one to four million acres. When I asked him how he did it, with a sometimes hostile public, hundreds of employees, and four different governors of two political parties, he answered with pithy concision.

"Bob," said Neil, "it takes the right combination of headbone and hormone."

As author Terre Satterfield told me (and elaborates later in this book), "To my mind, the conversation between the two is far too quiet and poorly integrated . . . each has a lot to contribute to the other." In the pages that follow, you will find a remarkable community of writers brought together to carry that conversation much further, perhaps, than ever before.

For my part, the earliest murmurs of this dialogue came long ago, from the butterflies. Butterflies had hold of my heart from an early age. I fell for their colors, shapes, and changes, their secrets, their beguiling ways. And not long into my love affair with butterflies and their haunts, I began to see that there were different ways of taking in and speaking of the objects of my delight.

My gospel, *Colorado Butterflies*, by F. Martin Brown, furnished a heady mixture of colorful description, exciting storytelling, and taxonomic detail. There was room, it seemed, for both the imagination and factual precision to come into play. At twelve, as one of the younger members of the Lepidopterists' Society, I read its journal with more avidity than comprehension. I was somewhat befuddled, for example, by a spirited exchange between F. M. Brown himself and Vladimir Nabokov, about the importance of statistics in evaluating the patterns of ringlet butterflies. Nabokov, known for his butterfly work at Harvard even before the recently published *Lolita*, argued that keen aesthetic impressions could discern important evolutionary patterns, while Brown insisted on sophisticated statistics to prove their validity. I came away with the strong sense that maybe both approaches were equally important.

Yet I was far from being able to *do* both. In my sixteenth summer I received a small grant from the Colorado-Wyoming Academy of Science to study variation in wood nymph butterflies (relatives of those same ringlets) along my beloved High Line Canal and in other Colorado locations. Their variability proved radical, matching several named subspecies. But I also found that fully a quarter of the dramatically eye-spotted satyrs had bird strikes on or near their ocelli, which demonstrated how natural selection acts to make bigger, brighter, expendable bulls-eyes on butterflies' wings. (*The Origin of Species* had been my hip-pocket companion for years.) I had a powerful data sample from my field work, but I was utterly innocent of the statistical tools necessary to test and express my results in any scientifically meaningful way.

This lapse was driven home when I offered my own first contribution to the august journal. On a field trip with my mother, not long after high school graduation, I witnessed "an extraordinary swarm of butterflies in Colorado"—which became the title of my article. The spectacle really was astonishing: a vast assembly of several species of blues in a milkweed gully near the Black Canyon of the Gunnison. The arroyo was a'shimmer with a living blanket of butterflies. I could go on like that all day about them—and did, in my manuscript, calling them "an azure fog." But how to count them? I couldn't just net a clump of the insects, tally, and extrapolate out over the whole area, as is done with wintering monarchs, for these were mostly moving targets. Even though the adroit editor of the *Journal of the Lepidopterists' Society*, Professor Jerry A. Powell of UC Berkeley, helped me achieve slightly more precise language, the best I could manage was this: "Our consensus could not be finalized to a greater degree of precision than 'many thousands,' although my own estimate proclaimed 'At least ten thousand, and perhaps a hundred!'" To this day, Jerry teases me about my combo of Muirian words and muddy numbers: "An azure fog . . . at least ten thousand, and perhaps a hundred!"

Clearly, if I was going to progress as a lepidopterist (and a conservationist: for by this time, rare butterfly conservation had become my main interest), I was going to have to become something of a mathematician as well—just as lepidopterists must needs be botanists too. But there was a problem: I was no mathematician.

Numbers and I had actually started out on pretty good terms. I enjoyed the subject at school, as long as it was actually called "Numbers"—I think that was about through third grade. I was still okay with "Arithmetic," but things got dodgier when the title became "Mathematics." Until then, I had managed As and Bs, and did all right on the numerical part of the Iowa Basics. But things went bad on the fourth of October, 1957, soon after I turned nine. That was the day the Soviets successfully launched *Sputnik I*, the first artificial satellite to orbit the earth, kicking off the space race in one fell swoop, and dooming me in math while it was at it.

Let me say first that I actually like numbers. I like their forms, their names, the colors and moods and personalities they suggest (for they do), and especially their symmetry—how they fit together in sequences, progressions, palindromes.

Now, I am no numerologist who ascribes meaning or divination to the figures themselves; nor any kind of determinist at all. But that makes it all the more wonderful when numbers appear in delightful sequences merely through random chance and the sheer *number* of possibilities (Jung's "physics of fate," or what I call the glory of happenstance). So, for example, I love to watch the numbers go 'round on my thirty-year-old automobile's odometer, and leave the trip-meter set in sync with the main meter to maximize the numbers. We all love to see a big one turn over, and the joke is how dad watches right up to 99,999 . . . and then gets diverted by a cow or something, and everyone misses it rolling over. 100K is the highest round tally that most drivers will be lucky enough to see. We passed 400K last year, and now we are approaching a really big one: 444,444.4/444.4. Thea thinks I'm a little nuts about this, but it's harmless enough.

Dates can be fun, too. The Mayan calendar notwithstanding, wouldn't 2/22/22 be a grand date, should we be so lucky as to get there? But the best one was surely my American-Mexican grandson David's eleventh birthday—which fell on 11/11/11! The heavens didn't part and he did not ascend as king of the Mayans to lead us all into a new calendrical cycle; but he did have a heck of a birthday party, even if he fell asleep well before the eleventh hour.

You could be forgiven for assuming that such a person as I, who likes to count flocks and herds, likes making lists, and is punctilious about reconciling his checkbook to the penny by hand, was a natural at math. You would be wrong. You would be forgetting *Sputnik*.

The event was exciting for us all, but it created a great strategic scare for the United States, since we suddenly appeared to be well behind the Russians in science. Hence the counter-launch, all over the country, of accelerated math and science classes in the public schools, in a frantic effort to catch up. Nothing wrong with that, as such; but the standards for admission were far too low, in my opinion: if you could count your toes with your fingers, they slung you into the advanced math stream—where some of us drowned.

I made it through elementary arithmetic all right, and also Algebra I in seventh grade. But that wasn't very hard, and besides, I had Mr. Brannan, a genial wit and neighbor who had also taught both my older sister and brother. "Oh no, not another Pyle!" he joked, but treated me kindly. For much of the year he turned us loose on the stock market as an extended exercise, each with $10,000 in play money to invest. Unlike my wheeling-dealing friends, I found a stock I liked the first day on the NYSE: a company called Pyle National, no lie (they manufactured railroad components; under a different name, they still make fancy plugs). I spent all ten grand on Pyle National stock, and just sat on it all semester. I did as well as most in terms of "profit." That was to be my last venture into investment, quitting while I was ahead.

But if my stock margin performed just fine, my grades soon took a dive. My mis-selection began to show. While I'd been used to adequate or better marks in the unsorted math classes, and would have excelled if left alone in the bone-head stream where I belonged, I was close to a dunce in the advanced section. I resented becoming a dunderhead among my peers almost overnight, more and more so as I progressed (crawled might be a better word) through the junior high grades and into high school. Algebra II went poorly, as I struggled for a C; and geometry still worse, even with my track coach as teacher and tutoring from my geometry-teacher Aunt Helen.

I adapted as best I could, swapping math busy-work for English with my math-whiz friend Jack, so we'd both have more time to go out chasing butter-flies, then girls. It wasn't cheating; just division of labor. But by the time I stag-gered into trigonometry and math analysis in my junior year, it was obvious that I would fail. And that would deal college—and scholarships—a fell blow. So, with enough math credits under my belt to graduate, I dropped trig after the first week and signed up instead for aerospace and driver's ed. These proved to be two of my favorite classes, and why not? Romps with affable teachers, largely off-campus, easy A's. (I've always suspected driver's ed was a sight more useful, too: I still believe it, after fifty years of a hell of a lot of driving, and no math anal-ysis whatever.) And when I matriculated college, I was delighted to find that I tested out of the basic math requirement, and was thereby exempted from further classes. I felt gloriously released, and reveled in my freedom-from-numbers, until I flunked physical chemistry—twice—and lost my scholarship. Since I aspired toward oceanography or zoology, and those subjects involved both chemistry and higher math, it seemed my quantitative gap might not prove as adaptive for my ambitions as the wood nymphs' eyespots for their survival.

Those wood nymphs' flight is all flip-flop, flip-flop, through the grasses that fodder their young. I did the same, slipping and dodging through the academic maze, getting credit for birdwatching and bad fiction, and graduating with a late-sixties-make-up-your-own-degree in natural history, conservation, and writing. Copped a forestry master's in nature interpretation, and would have been fine if I'd remained a ranger. But science still called, in service of butterfly conservation. The crunch—the numbers crunch—finally came when I signed up for a PhD. My friends going for a Master of Forest Science had to have had calculus; but as a doctoral student, no one even asked me. Still, it seemed that my willful innumeracy had finally met the wall.

Now, this book is not *about* innumeracy. As several of the essays to follow will show, numerical numbness can afflict the sensibilities of us all, whether we embrace math or not. The most advanced mathematician might be just as put off by the mere quantities of crises, and just as moved by their emotional counterpart, as the most rarefied artistic intellect. Yet numbers matter. Understanding the eyespots of brown butterflies might seem an arcane and inessential whim. But the survival of ecological conditions that allow those butterflies to live and evolve is clearly related to our survival too. If we were to conserve those conditions, along with much that we love of the world as it is, I saw that we would need to engage with both quantities and qualities. Yet in my own instance, my *Sputnik*-inspired blind spot was blocking such a synthesis.

My dissertation problem not only proved this to me, but also showed me the way around it. The intention was to use Washington butterfly distribution to reveal gaps in the state's nature reserve system. Through studies in England, I had seen the power of applied biogeography for conservation. In my first book, I proposed the existence of "butterfly provinces," or regions of natural distribution, but these were erected strictly by gut feelings about the insects and their whereabouts. The challenge now became, how to prove that these patterns held water?

By paying attention in every conference and seminar I attended, every paper I read, I learned through osmosis how figures came to the necessary service of science . . . and how to use them. The field work went well, and I was able to demonstrate that my butterfly provinces had numerical reality—to calculate their acreage and distinctness, using a formula and resemblance trellis drawn from mammalogy. In the end, the butterflies revealed dramatic inequalities in conservation coverage between distinctive regions that had been lumped by managers—gaps that have since been filled with new reserves and wilderness areas, thanks in part to the butterflies and the numbers. My hunches had proved mostly correct; but hunches seldom affect policy.

And so, mirabile dictu!, I came out able to perform field science after all. Yet, along the way, though I shed both my antipathy for math and my resistance to analytical techniques, I also learned that the poet in me was stronger than the scientist. My inclination lay more toward the descriptive and personal response to things. And so I still do some science, and when I do, I use numbers. But much more, I write; and I am not afraid to mingle a lyrical or emotional response with empirical detail. In fact, almost all of the conservation campaigns and issues with which I have been involved have drawn deeply from both sides. My book *Wintergreen* gives chapter and verse of certain less-than-sustainable logging practices in my hills of home, including acres of stumpage, board feet of timber cut, and number of jobs lost and families fractured along with the woods. Weyerhaeuser was unable to discredit my criticism, because I took care to get the facts and numbers right. But it may have been the book's lyrical qualities that affected readers more.

Likewise, in *Chasing Monarchs*, I described both numerically and emotionally the astonishing overwintering colonies of the migratory butterflies in Mexico and California, a threatened phenomenon. It is one thing to speak of twenty hectares of clusters involving millions of monarchs; quite another to read Homero Aridjis's richly poetical and visceral reactions to the spectacle, elsewhere in this book. And as for the Xerces Society for Invertebrate Conservation, which makes more impact: to talk about the biggest job in the world, trying to save ten or twenty million species; or for former Xerces president E. O. Wilson to utter the simple but elegant profundity that insects are "the little things that run the world"?

If there is almost a chuckle in that elemental (and critically important) truth, it is no accident. *Numbers and Nerves* is full of stories of overwhelming importance to us all: hard lessons of human and more-than-human behavior that are seldom funny and often to weep for. Yet when the tale-teller can find a shred, a mote, a moment of human wit or natural humor in the midst of harsh realities, so much the better for the listener—who may be all the more moved thereby. I have always tried to relate what I have to say in narrative, to find the stories in the page-pictures; and sometimes, the humor. *Mariposa Road* is really a catalog of the current plights of our butterflies (and, by extension, of life) thanks to the compromised state of the American landscape. But the litany of loss is leavened, and maybe better assimilated, when interrupted by a Louisiana sheriff's deputy who slowly examines my Xerces Society calling card and asks me, "So, you belong to this *Exorcist Society*?"

So it seems we need to invoke all of our powers on behalf of these parlous times. That suits me fine, for I like to stride that "high ridge" that Nabokov believed to exist between "the mountainside of scientific knowledge and the opposite slope of artistic imagination." And Nabokov is just the one to bring up here, for though he is known chiefly as a superb literary artist with little quantitative education, he performed durable science based on what was then known among butterfly folk as "a good eye"—a trait that often counted for more than mere math. Just how good an eye he had was demonstrated recently by sophisticated DNA work—coordinated at Harvard, right where Nabokov counted scales and dissected genitalia of blues—that has shown his systematic ideas and conclusions to have been remarkably correct, given his simple tools and training. Nor are these just bits and bobs of butterfly esoterica: they involve species at risk for which it is vital to know both who and what they are. Such as the famous Karner blue, which became the cause célèbre for a whole biome, decades after Nabokov discerned it as a separate species of delicate needs. Life's very survival may depend upon both the poet-naturalist's "good eye" *and* the hard scientist's numbers. Nabokov liked to confound doubters by speaking of "the precision of poetry, the art of science." Wouldn't we always like to have each on hand?

Mind you, the balance can swing too far, either way. I have lately listened to earnest graduate students, ignorant of both the lifeways and the poetry of their butterfly subjects, not so much massaging their figures as Rolfing them, in order to squeeze significance out of weak data. On the other side, far too many pastoralists and poets think they can save a place or a population or a people solely through an outpouring of art and heart. Is not the desired state surely to live, speak, debate, and act out of the richness of both heart and head, as the whole people we are?

Yes, it does take both headbone and hormone, if we are going to perceive and respond to the world aright. As I finally understood for myself, *Sputnik* notwithstanding, we need all the math we can marshal for our case, which is the case of the earth and its living things, including ourselves. And we also need all the song, dance, poetry, and emotion we can muster, when we go forth to make that all-important case.

Numbers and nerves, headbone and hormone, abacus and emotion: they all *count,* after all. Let the conversation begin.

Acknowledgments

I would like to thank all the publishers of the original pieces included in this collection, as acknowledged for each with the titles. In all cases I retained full rights to reprint the material. Special thanks to Polly Dyer, Les Line, Paul Trachtman, Aina Niemela, Ellen Chu, Brian Doyle, Jennifer Sahn, Skip Berger, Chip Blake, Steve Forrester, Matthew Shepherd, Barbara Dean, Michael Branch, Dinah Urell, Deanne Urmy, Charles Goodrich, Kathleen Dean Moore, Tom Fleischner, Lorraine Anderson, Scott Slovic, and all the other editors who gave pages to these essays over the years. The project could not have come together without David White's laborious and adept digitization of the many disparate texts from decades of printing technologies. I am warmly grateful to the Three Graces of Oregon State University Press, Mary Braun, Micki Reaman, and Marty Brown, for helping me envision, encompass, realize, and share this big slice of my life. To those dear ones on whom I have utterly depended throughout these fifty years of scribbling, my loving gratitude. Finally, I thank Florence Sage for helping me in many ways to see the thing through.

ROBERT MICHAEL PYLE is a biologist, writer, and Guggenheim Fellow with a PhD in Ecology and Environmental Studies from Yale University. His twenty books include *Wintergreen* (John Burroughs Medal), *The Thunder Tree, Sky Time in Gray's River* (National Outdoor Book Award), two poetry collections, and a flight of butterfly books. He founded the Xerces Society for Invertebrate Conservation and has been named an Honorary Fellow of the Royal Entomological Society. He lives in rural southwest Washington.